Monumental Times

Monumental Times

Pasts, Presents, and Futures in the Prehistoric
Construction Projects of Northern and Western Europe

Richard Bradley

 **OXBOW** | books
Oxford & Philadelphia

Published in the United Kingdom in 2024 by
OXBOW BOOKS
The Old Music Hall, 106-108 Cowley Road, Oxford, OX4 1JE

and in the United States by
OXBOW BOOKS
1950 Lawrence Road, Havertown, PA 19083

Paperback Edition: ISBN 979-8-88857-038-8
Digital Edition: ISBN 979-8-88857-039-5 (ePub)

A CIP record for this book is available from the British Library

Library of Congress Control Number: 2023945754

Printed in the United Kingdom by CMP Digital Print Solutions
Typeset in India by DiTech Publishing Services

For a complete list of Oxbow titles, please contact:

UNITED KINGDOM
Oxbow Books
Telephone (0)1226 734350
Email: oxbow@oxbowbooks.com
www.oxbowbooks.com

UNITED STATES OF AMERICA
Oxbow Books
Telephone (610) 853-9131, Fax (610) 853-9146
Email: queries@casemateacademic.com
www.casemateacademic.com/oxbow

Oxbow Books is part of the Casemate Group

Front cover: Two chambered tombs at Camster, northern Scotland

Contents

'Time which antiquates antiquities, and hath an art to make dust of all things, hath yet spared these minor monuments.'
Sir Thomas Browne, *Urn Burial* (1658)

Preface and acknowledgments

In 2022, I was invited to contribute to a conference of the European Megalithic Studies Group. The speakers were asked to choose their own subjects. I considered several options and had even written an abstract before circumstances prevented me from attending. Despite this setback, possible topics kept coming to mind. Some of them feature here. Others explore related themes, but they do not consider Neolithic sites and are not restricted to the prehistoric period.

It was while I was writing the first chapters that I realised that the volume was becoming a sequel to a series of lectures I gave in Edinburgh in 1992. They were published as *Altering the Earth* and discussed *The Origins of Monuments in Britain and Continental Europe* (Bradley 1993). The new project is concerned with monuments and time, but the focus on ancient architecture is the same. It allows me to revisit the original topics and provides an ideal opportunity for rethinking them. As far as possible, it draws on different examples and on newer information. The format is like that of the earlier book. All the chapters are about the same length – the equivalent of an hour's lecture – and each can be read in a single sitting. Though they are conceived as self-contained essays, taken together they present a cumulative argument. They are aimed at anyone with an informed interest in archaeology.

Much of the book was written while I was kept at home by the pandemic and its sequel. The project would have been impossible without Katherine's help and support. The text has been copy-edited by Courtney Nimura, and, as so often, I have Aaron Watson to thank for the high quality of his drawings and photographs.

The 1992 lectures were the prelude to a series of excavations in Scotland. Gordon Noble visited one of them and became an instant convert. Since that time he has made important contributions to the archaeology of northern Britain. His research spans both the prehistoric and medieval periods and shows how scholars of both phases can draw on similar ideas. I once taught Gordon in Reading; as the bibliography shows, I have learned much from him since. Now a professor at Aberdeen University, he is the dedicatee of this book.

List of figures

Introduction

Chapter 1

Pasts, presents, and futures: Bredarör and the Boyne Valley

Wonder like ours

In 1817, the editor of a weekly newspaper organised an informal contest between two poets (www.economist.com/christmas-special/2013/12/18/king-of-kings; www.poetryfoundation.org/articles/69503/percy-bysshe-shelley-ozimandias). He challenged them to write about an ancient statue described by the historian Diodorus Siculus. One of the participants, Percy Bysshe Shelley, was already famous. The other was his friend and financial advisor Horace Smith. Both were given fifteen minutes in which to compose a sonnet.

The results were very different from one another. As a political radical, Shelley reflected on the transience of earthly power:

> Two vast trunkless legs of stone
> Stand in the desert. Near them, in the sand,
> Half-sunk, a shattered visage lies ...
> On the pedestal these words appear:
> 'My name is Ozymandias, King of Kings.
> Look on my works ye mighty and despair'.
> Nothing beside remains. Round the decay
> Of that colossal wreck, boundless and bare,
> The lone and level sands stretch far away.

Smith, on the other hand, considered how future generations would encounter such remains. He imagined a capital city of which little trace survived. The presence of a solitary ruin would have posed an intellectual challenge:

> Some hunter may express
> Wonder like ours, where thro' the wilderness

> Where London stood, holding the wolf in chase,
> He meets some fragment huge, and stops to guess
> What powerful but unrecorded race
> Once dwelt in that annihilated place.

One poet used the remains to comment on the futility of building monuments to influence the future, while the other considered the difficulty of understanding the past. Shelley's sonnet, 'Ozymandias', is perhaps his best-known poem, but Smith's is remembered for its extraordinary title: 'On a stupendous leg of granite standing by itself'.

Why is it so difficult to study monuments? Is it because they cut across our everyday experience of time? They are easier to describe than they are to investigate (Harris 2021, 154–95). The dictionary definition refers to memorials or tombs, and the term itself comes from the Latin verb *monere* – to remind. Other elements are equally important. Monuments can be conceived on an ambitious scale and their construction often requires a substantial labour force. They are considered in a cross-cultural analysis by Michael Kolb (2021) which emphasises three features: the massive scale on which they are built; the ways in which they influence the actions of people who visit them; and the distinctive time scale of their construction and use. A monument belongs to both the present and the past. As the title of my book suggests, this last feature is considered here.

They play an important role from the moment they are created, but, like the two poems, approaches to their archaeology lead in opposite directions. Structures might be directed to a future over which their builders can exercise no control. They can be adapted, destroyed, or left to decay as their significance is lost. Another perspective is to view them as relics of a forgotten past that survive into the present because their fabric remains intact. They are recognised for their durability, but their purpose is unknown. They pose a particular problem since many of those in north-west Europe date from a time when settlements left little trace. That was true between the middle of the Neolithic period and the middle of the Bronze Age.

Time is of the essence.

Many times

Archaeologists work at the intersection of many different times. A famous site on the coast of south-east Sweden illustrates this point.

Bredarör

At Kivik, Gustaf Hallström constructed a Mycenaean tomb beside the Baltic Sea (Fig. 1.1; Randsborg 1993; Randsborg & Merkyte 2011; Goldhahn 2013). In its present form Bredarör is a modern cairn built of cobbles taken from a ruined monument. The structure erected in 1931 bore a striking resemblance to the Treasury of Atreus, the legendary tomb of Agamemnon which had been excavated a decade before (Wace 1940). The entrance of Bredarör was a copy of the Lion Gateway which led into the citadel at

Fig. 1.1. The 20th century entrance to the reconstructed cairn of Bredarör. Photograph: Fantomen (CCBY 3.0).

Mycenae. The Scandinavian cairn was also described as a 'King's Grave', but there was little to indicate who was buried there. Apart from the tooth of an adult, the remains recovered by Hallström's excavation were those of five young people (Goldhahn 2013).

His reconstruction was just one episode in the history of a complex construction, and the references to Mycenaean architecture were influenced by ideas about the relationship between northern and southern Europe during the Bronze Age. For a long time, they had played a part in establishing a chronology (B. Gräslund 1987). The cairn was damaged almost two hundred years before the investigation took place, but in its centre were the remains of a decorated cist. The few pieces of metalwork that survived pointed to a date in the 13th century BC, and details of the decorated panels suggested contacts with distant regions: 'The overall impression is that of a decorated grave chamber (or a palace) ... It is difficult to escape the notion that the person responsible for the Kivik cist ... had seen Mediterranean land with his own eyes' (Randsborg & Merkyte 2011, 175).

Amber can be found on beaches close to Kivik and is represented by artefacts found in Greece (Kaul 2017). The decorated cist dates from a period when there were rich burials elsewhere in Scandinavia, but Hallström's reconstruction of the cairn referred to the Aegean world. Such connections had played an important role in northern

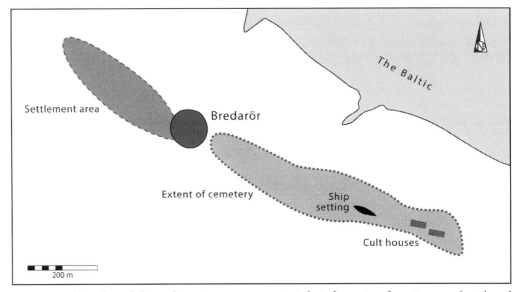

Fig. 1.2. Outline plan of the prehistoric structures at Kivik. Information from Larsson (1993) and Randsborg (1993).

European culture since the 17th century AD when scholars first drew analogies between the Mediterranean and Baltic Seas (Herva & Lahelma 2020, 89–92).

The erection of the cairn was only one episode in a longer sequence. It was preceded by another use of the site and was followed by the creation of additional monuments nearby. It occupied the same position as an older settlement and was succeeded by an extensive group of Late Bronze Age features: a cemetery made up of smaller cairns, two 'cult houses', and a stone ship setting (Fig. 1.2; Larsson 1993). The burial chamber at Bredarör was in use over a protracted period, as radiocarbon dates on the few bones that survive span six centuries from 1400 to 800 BC (Goldhahn 2013). The latest might have been contemporary with structures in the vicinity.

The principal monument seems to be related to other places and times. The construction of a cist was unusual as burials of comparable date were associated with wooden coffins. The chamber may have had more than one compartment and its proportions resemble those of older gallery graves in the same part of Sweden (Fig. 1.3; Blank *et al.* 2020). New research shows that they include human remains that date between 1500 and 1200 BC, but it is not clear that it was when they were constructed; they belong to a Late Neolithic style of building and may have been reused. The decorated cist at Bredarör has a similar plan, but it was not part of a megalithic tomb. Its form may have referred to an established architectural tradition, but its decoration was new.

Its layout reflects its position by the Baltic. Randsborg's analysis focused on the organisation of the images within the structure itself. Here he identified two important themes. One was a striking contrast between the land and sea. The other highlighted

Bredarör   Gallery graves

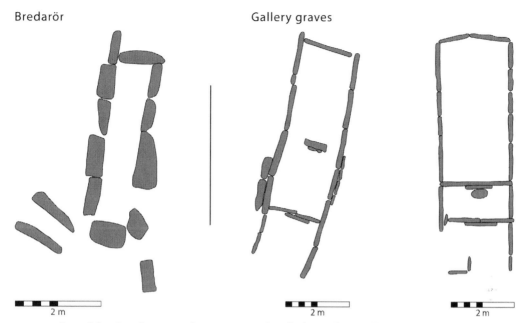

Fig. 1.3. Plan of the chamber at Bredarör compared with those of two gallery graves in the same part of Sweden. Information from Randsborg (1993) and Blank et al. (2020).

the importance of the sun. If certain of the pictures seemed unfamiliar – even exotic – they were consistent with what was already known about Bronze Age beliefs in northern Europe (Randsborg 1993).

The same relationships were reflected in the local landscape:

> The cist ... is orientated virtually north-south, with the northern end and eastern long side towards the sea. The western long side and southern end are towards a backdrop of hills ... crowned by a massive rock rising about 100 metres out of the Baltic (Randsborg & Merkyte 2011, 106).

The form of the monument was related to other features, but not all were built constructions. The well-preserved ship setting followed the general direction of the setting sun; it also depicted a vessel travelling towards Bredarör. The great cairn was not far from the water's edge and was constructed of boulders taken from the beach. It shared the same form and dimensions as a feature of the local topography: 'a large natural 'cairn-shaped' outcrop of quartzite with a diameter of ... 60 metres ... [It] carries powerful scars of quarrying of boulders and slabs' (Randsborg & Merkyte 2011, 177). Five of these pieces were used in the ship setting.

The Boyne Valley
The same points are illustrated on a larger scale. In Ireland, they are epitomised by the chambered tombs of Newgrange, Knowth, and Dowth. Here the archaeological sequence was more extended.

Fig. 1.4. Part of the reconstructed Neolithic cemetery at Knowth. Photograph: Jean Housen (CCBY 3.0).

Three major tombs overlook the River Boyne (Eogan 1986). They may not have been constructed simultaneously and each was modified or even rebuilt during the Neolithic period (Eogan 1984; Eogan & Roche 1997; Eogan & Cleary 2017; Eogan & Shee Twohig 2022). Newgrange and Knowth have seen large-scale excavation, while the third site is less well known. Two have been restored to present them to the public, so that, as Kolb (2021) says, they are simultaneously both prehistoric and contemporary buildings (Fig. 1.4).

The principal tomb at Knowth remains largely unaltered, but the smaller passage graves around it have been reconstructed. By contrast, Newgrange underwent a drastic transformation during the 1970s and in its present form the façade of the monument looks like that of a shopping centre (M. O'Kelly 1982; Hensey 2015). There must have been a setting of quartz boulders towards the entrance, but it was not necessarily the sheer wall that visitors encounter today (Cooney 2006; Hensey & Shee Twohig 2017). It contained cobbles from a wider region, including the east coast of Ireland (Mitchell 1992).

Other periods played a part at all three places: their distinctive form is not only a mixture of Neolithic and 20th-century elements. They also attracted attention during the medieval period. One of the earliest literary sources, *Seanchas na Relec* (the History of the Cemeteries), described the passage graves as royal tombs. They were where the kings of Tara were buried. Newgrange was 'not merely a mausoleum, but an abode of some sort into which people could enter and out of which they could emerge' (M. O'Kelly 1982, 46). Because of these associations the mounds were originally attributed to the 1st millennium AD.

Their chronology became clear in the light of modern excavation, and it is accepted that they were first used between about 3300 and 2900 BC (Eogan & Cleary 2017, 331–79). There were other times at which these structures played a significant role. Newgrange and Knowth featured during the Bell Beaker phase as well as in the Iron Age. Together with Dowth, they gained a new importance during the early medieval period.

Every monument had a separate sequence. The most extended was at Knowth where even the Neolithic features are difficult to interpret. The earliest were wooden houses and a palisaded enclosure (Eogan 1984; Eogan & Roche 1997). After an interval, circular dwellings took their place, and then the first megalithic tombs were erected on the site. Their layout is distinctive as they are arranged in a ring around a central mound which was eventually enlarged (Fig. 1.5; Eogan & Cleary 2017; Eogan & Shee Twohig 2022). Some of the building material was embellished with megalithic art, and excavation found that decorated panels had been reused in later structures. Just as successive buildings were dismantled and replaced, individual stones were worked on more than one occasion and motifs were removed (Robin 2009). A similar process happened at Newgrange where pieces with pecked designs were recycled from older monuments. Less is known about the other great tomb at Dowth, but George Eogan (2009) suggested that it was modified in the same way. One chamber was aligned on the midwinter sunset.

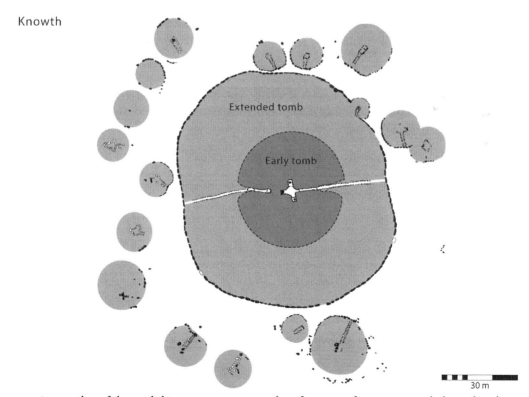

Fig. 1.5. *Plan of the Neolithic cemetery at Knowth. Information from Eogan and Cleary (2017).*

Outside the largest tombs there were smaller structures: isolated monoliths, hearths, and settings of posts. They were associated with Late Neolithic ceramics and the remains of feasts (M. O'Kelly *et al.* 1983). It seems as if the focus of activities changed from the interiors of these passage graves to the areas around them. That process continued into the Beaker phase before it came to an end. The same period saw other developments. There was early metalworking, and the area between Newgrange and the river was occupied by a series of earthworks whose positions acknowledged those of older megaliths – in fact several enclosed these structures, and one shared the same alignment as the principal passage grave (Davis & Rassmann 2021). A multiple pit or post circle was created beside its mound, and a ring of standing stones surrounded the great chambered tomb (M. O'Kelly 1982; M. O'Kelly *et al.* 1983; Sweetman 1985).

After that phase, use of these sites ended or was greatly curtailed and did not resume until the Iron Age. Then between about 40 BC and AD 200 the main tomb at Knowth was surrounded by burials containing rings, beads, dice, and gaming pieces like those found in barrows of the same date (Eogan 2012, 13–44). Similar artefacts have been recorded at Newgrange. In the 3rd and 4th centuries AD metalwork including coins and ornaments of precious materials was deposited in front of that monument (Carson & C. O'Kelly 1977). They are usually interpreted as offerings, and it may have become a cult centre (M. & M. Gibbons 2016).

Although Newgrange was celebrated in Irish literature, it is Knowth and Dowth that provide archaeological evidence of early medieval activity. Dowth was obviously accessible in the Middle Ages as a souterrain was added to the existing structure (M. & C. O'Kelly 1982). The chambers at Knowth were also visited and include inscriptions in ogham and insular script of the 8th and 9th centuries AD (Byrne *et al.* 2008, 89–119). More significant changes affected the principal passage grave. There were further burials outside it, and the ancient earthwork was reshaped by two concentric ditches to create a distinctive stepped mound (Fig. 1.6). Earthworks of this kind were associated with the ceremonies at which new rulers were inaugurated (FitzPatrick 2004; Gleeson 2020). Now the ancient tomb became a royal capital, and eventually an unusually rich settlement was established on its summit (Eogan 2012).

Calibrating monumental architectures

Traces of such structures are observed in the present but are attributed to different periods in the past. This is particularly relevant to the successive features at Knowth which formed during the Neolithic, Copper Age, Iron Age, and medieval phases. All were represented together in the modern excavation. The monuments visited by the public are architectural compositions that bring together elements which may never have been combined so explicitly before. That is still more obvious at Kivik where the remains of a Bronze Age grave exist in an uneasy relationship with a modern Mycenaean tomb.

Of course, many ancient features are preserved in the structures exhibited today, but others have to be concealed in the interest of framing a narrative. Thus, the presentation

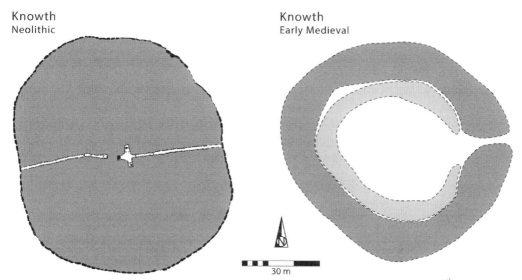

Fig. 1.6. Outline plans of the principal passage tomb at Knowth in its Neolithic form, and its reconstruction as an early medieval earthwork. Information from Eogan and Cleary (2017) and Gleeson (2020).

of Knowth displays the main passage tomb, but the medieval ditches cut into the mound that covered it were refilled once they had been investigated. It resulted in greater clarity but obscured the point that such elements were originally juxtaposed. Excavation was more than a method of bringing them to light – it was also a technique for telling them apart and placing them in order. That is not always possible. It is why there are differences of opinion concerning the development of Newgrange (Stout & Stout 2008).

Visitors to the Boyne tombs encounter them as 20th-century structures which attempt to combine the traces of ancient buildings with contemporary ideas about the past. They aim to preserve their features for future visitors and researchers. It is hard to say whether Newgrange and Knowth looked alike during the Neolithic period. The modern versions of both monuments try to recreate their appearance, but they are very different from one another. The reconstruction of Bredarör was influenced by other considerations. It emphasised the close relationship postulated between the Aegean and the Nordic Bronze Age. Both examples emphasise the importance of *multi-temporality* (Olivier 2011; Lucas 2021; Lucas & Olivier 2022).

Inevitably other questions arise. How continuous were the sequences documented by fieldwork? Were there any direct connections between successive structures? And what kind of narrative best describes these relationships? As the introduction made clear, they might have been directed towards an unpredictable future. At the same time once these buildings had been constructed, they must have been understood retrospectively. Their meanings and significance could change and there might be little or no continuity between successive pasts (Harris 2021, 209–15).

Another observation is important here. The archaeological record is commonly thought of in terms of superimposed strata: a conception influenced by the relationship between excavation and geology during the 19th century (Lucas 2001). Monuments offer a different perspective, for many of them are not concealed or covered over. They survive from one age to another, and it is their appearance in the present that has to be explained. Structures built at completely different times may be found together, and it is necessary to investigate the interplay between them. Their histories might be continuous or discontinuous. Thus, the Late Bronze Age ship setting at Kivik was connected to the Early Bronze Age cairn of Bredarör, but three thousand years after the main passage tomb at Knowth was built it was ringed by Iron Age burials. Comparison with other sites suggests that their positions would have been indicated by low mounds, as they were around a similar monument at Kiltierney (McHugh & B. Scott 2014, 126). Both might have remained visible for a long time afterwards, but how would later generations understand the relationship between them?

Sequences like these are generally seen in hindsight, as though they led to a definitive outcome that the people who erected the earliest structures would have been unable to envisage or accomplish. That is obvious from the categories that researchers use today. The Neolithic period in Britain features a group of enclosures known as 'formative henges' (J. Harding 2003; Burrow 2010). The term does not shed any light on why they were built. They are only interesting as stages in the evolution of a better-known type of monument. The description is confusing, and in any case 'henge' is a name that became fossilised in the language of archaeology before much was known about earthworks of this kind. Another influential example was in Scottish archaeology where some simple stone chambers associated with long cairns were described as 'protomegaliths' (J. Scott 1969).

The same problem can be recognised in other parts of Europe, for it seems as if certain buildings matter because of subsequent developments: developments that the people who erected them never intended, and of which they would have been unaware. Danish archaeology illustrates this way of thinking:

> The forerunners of the *real dolmens* are the dolmen cists in the long barrows ... At the beginning the cists were exposed, but later ... they were covered by large amounts of mound fill. The earliest *real dolmens* followed this tradition (P. Eriksen & N. Andersen 2016, 87; my emphasis).

The authors provide a convincing analysis of how such structures changed, but their choice of language is revealing. It suggests that the people who built the monuments shared the long-term aim of constructing an authentic kind of megalith. A similar concept featured in German archaeology where one kind of stone chamber was described by the term *Urdolmen*, which translates as the precursor of a dolmen (Schuldt & Gehl 1972).

Different wavelengths

The French scholar Fernand Braudel (1969) organised his account of Mediterranean history around three separate time scales: geographical or environmental time (the *longue durée*), the intermediate scale of economics, societies, and politics (the *moyenne durée*), and the short-term history of events (*histoire événementielle*). His ideas have influenced thinking in archaeology (Bintliff 1991; Lucas 2021), but, rather than apply these concepts directly to the study of ancient buildings, I shall follow his suggestion that the past can be analysed according to different wavelengths. The examples already considered provide evidence of various time scales in the past.

Extended time: the influence of 'natural' features
The first group includes elements of the 'natural' world, although the use of this category raises problems which will be considered later. Geological formations played an important part in the genesis of ancient monuments. Such factors must have been acknowledged long before any structures were built (Bradley 2000b; Boivin & Owoc 2004; Tilley 2004; Harmananşa 2014). Local topography exerted a particular influence. The great tombs of Newgrange, Knowth, and Dowth were situated on raised ground overlooking the River Boyne. In the same way, the cairn at Bredarör was erected beside a rock formation of almost the same size which provided material for a later construction.

They were not the only factors in organising them. Two of the Irish tombs were laid out so that their chambers were illuminated by the sun on the shortest day of the year (Prendergast *et al.* 2017). The directions of the solstices must have been recognised long before the tombs were erected. The relationship between such buildings, the River Boyne, and the sea was emphasised by deposits of beach cobbles outside the passage graves. Something similar may have occurred at Bredarör where the great cairn was constructed of boulders from the shoreline.

There were other influences at Kivik. If a prominent outcrop inspired the form and position of the Bronze Age monument, the relationship between the principal cairn and the Baltic Sea was emphasised by the nearby ship setting. The vessel was travelling along the coast and was also directed towards Bredarör and the setting sun. These features connected the grave to the water. As Randsborg (1993) recognised, the same elements are illustrated by the images inside the cist. They must have been important before the cairn was built.

Longer sequences
All these monuments were used again, but it happened after a lengthy interval. There were secondary burials around the main passage grave at Knowth where excavation found a series of graves. There might have been similar graves at Newgrange before the area in front of its entrance was chosen for deposits of valuables imported from the Roman world (Carson & C. O'Kelly 1977). There is nothing to suggest that the Neolithic chambers and passages were accessible. Now the covering mounds became the most important element, and it was no longer possible to reconstruct the original roles of these places. Their significance had changed.

It happened again during the early medieval period when literary sources shed some light on how the Irish sites were understood (M. O'Kelly 1982). The archaeological evidence is equally revealing as it was then that the principal structure at Knowth was transformed. It was reshaped by two deep ditches that turned the ancient earthwork into a stepped mound (Gleeson 2020). There is nothing to suggest that anyone knew quite how the Neolithic building was used, but by this stage its chambers had been reopened, so that people had the option of relating their own activities to two separate pasts: a very remote past in which the tomb was first conceived, and a less distant phase when Knowth became an inhumation cemetery. It is revealing that there were early medieval burials in the same area as the Iron Age graves, but they did not extend inside the original monument. Use of the site was discontinuous, and episodes of intensive activity were separated by long intervals.

Shorter sequences

The Boyne Valley tombs also referred to a more recent past. Knowth had a significant history, for it was a living site long before any megaliths were built there. A similar sequence was documented at Bredarör where the Early Bronze Age cairn was built over the position of an older settlement. Its chronology is poorly understood, but enough is known to show that the location was already important. Extraordinary buildings were established in places with a past that might have been significant.

Even more striking is the evidence that new monuments were erected in relation to others more recently established. Existing elements were continually reworked. The simplest sequence was probably at Bredarör where the ship setting, two cult houses and a cemetery were close to the existing cairn (Larsson 1993). Although their initial construction took place at different times, the ship setting must have been related to the principal cairn. Dates on the bones excavated by Hallström show that its central cist remained accessible for a long time. Towards the end of the sequence these structures may have coexisted (Goldhahn 2013).

In some respects, the Boyne Valley illustrates a similar sequence. Here there were two main elements. The principal tombs remained important for many years after they were built, and a timber circle was erected outside the main tomb at Knowth (Eogan & Roche 1997). There may have been similar features at Newgrange (M. O'Kelly *et al.* 1983; Sweetman 1985). It was probably during the same period that circular enclosures were established between the passage grave and the river (Davis & Rassmann 2021). Although this distinctive landscape must have changed its character, there is no obvious sign of discontinuity.

Occasionally these developments can be traced in greater detail. It is obvious that Irish passage tombs were repeatedly adapted and rebuilt. The main structure at Newgrange included decorated stones from structures that no longer survive, and something similar happened at Knowth where the main tomb was extended and enlarged (Eogan & Shee Twohig 2022). Standing stones or entire buildings were relocated and their components were transported from one place to another. No one can reconstruct the 'lost' monuments from the surviving fragments, but they were decorated in the same style as intact tombs in the vicinity and may have taken a similar form.

Comparisons

Bredarör, Newgrange, and Knowth were used for different lengths of time and the sequences recognised there took distinctive forms. At Kivik, the construction or use of individual monuments may have happened continuously during the Bronze Age, and here the entire sequence extended over at least six hundred years. The form of the burial cist might have been inspired by that of existing gallery graves. After 800 BC its active role was over until it was disturbed by quarrying in 1748 and rebuilt in the 20th century.

The older monuments of the Boyne Valley illustrate the same kind of sequence, although the dating of some of the structures is not secure. But subsequent phases represented a new departure. The Iron Age cemetery at Knowth developed at a time when the passage grave was largely derelict, and the same applies to Newgrange where the ancient mound might have been modified (Ó Néill 2013). The interval between these developments was about two thousand years, yet the abandoned tomb was still a conspicuous landmark. Another interval passed between the deposition of valuables in front of the kerb and the reopening of the chambers at Knowth and Dowth during the early medieval period. In this case the chronological gap was rather shorter and two of them were partly rebuilt. Eventually Knowth became a fortified settlement as well as a royal capital (Eogan 2012). The developments took place over a similar duration to those in early prehistory, but, apart from the presence of the mounds, there were no direct connections between them.

Cross currents in contemporary archaeology

Braudel's three-fold division of history is only a starting point for a more complex analysis. If there are different wavelengths in the histories of early monuments, there are sources of interference, too. New developments raise problems concerning the passage of time. This section introduces some topics whose implications are becoming apparent only now.

The first is the development of an archaeology influenced by thinking in anthropology and philosophy. It rejects the distinction between nature and culture that underpinned most 20th-century research and treats other forms of life on equal terms with the humans who have always been the focus of attention (Harris & Cipolla 2017; Crellin *et al.* 2020). It draws on studies of well documented societies in which places and things can be living beings. The 'new animism' (Bird-David 1999; Fowler 2021) has already influenced writing about prehistory. In Europe, this approach has been most successful in Fennoscandia where these sources can be combined (Herva & Lahelma 2020) but, in the absence of ethnographic evidence, written accounts, or folklore, this method may not have enough information to support a convincing analysis. Then rhetoric takes over and a cloud descends.

How does this development affect the questions considered here? It may be misleading to maintain a rigid distinction between elements that were human creations, the materials of which they were built, and the physical features with which they were associated. In the same way, it could be wrong to distinguish between the activities that people carried out there and other processes that were drawn into those events; the obvious example is the movement of the sun across the sky. 'Natural' places can, and should, be studied in similar terms to prehistoric architecture, but their histories would have been far longer. Chronologies based exclusively on human constructions may be entirely misleading. The point will be considered again in Chapter Two.

During the 20th century most studies made an implicit assumption. They supposed that monument complexes developed at an even rate as new features were added. Architectural forms were remarkably long-lived, and individual structures might have been used for extended periods. This approach was plausible when their chronologies were fixed by the presence of diagnostic artefacts. Radiocarbon dates made an important contribution, but in recent years their accuracy has improved with new techniques for analysing small, unmixed samples. Now the use of statistical methods for studying the results provides much greater precision (Bayliss 2015). Some of the findings have been unexpected. The application of Bayesian methods has identified cases in which monument building happened at particular points in what had seemed a lengthy sequence. Several of the developments identified in past research proved to be surprisingly abrupt. Chambered tombs provide a well-documented example (Scarre 2010).

Another complication results from developments in archaeological science. Until recently most researchers assumed that successive structures in a single group were built by the same population. For that reason, Copper Age activity around the Boyne passage tombs did not raise any problem, nor did the evidence for early metalworking at Newgrange. The presence of Neolithic and later artefacts in the settlement at Kivik was evidence of cultural continuity, and so was the selection of the same site for the Early Bronze Age cairn. The extraction of DNA from ancient human bone raises difficulties for this approach (Brandt *et al.* 2013; Haak *et al.* 2015; Cassidy *et al.* 2016; Reich 2018; Whittle *et al.* 2023). It suggests that the first metallurgists in Sweden and Ireland were immigrants – the smooth transitions postulated by prehistorians may have been more abrupt. This has disturbing implications for any notion of long-term continuity. The time scales illustrated by monumental architecture need to be reconsidered.

I began with a very conventional definition of monuments. It seems as if they were built to enshrine a particular view of the world. They were often conceived on a massive scale and were intended to influence the course of history. The discussion has found problems with this formulation, and there are others to consider. Why were special structures so often built in the same locations – what was the relationship between them? Is it helpful to think in terms of social memory (Van Dyke & Alcock 2003)? What were monumental times, and how can they be studied more effectively? All these questions need an answer.

A synopsis

The book is in two parts. Following this introduction, Chapter Two considers whether foragers had different perceptions of time from early farmers and how this could be related to the first appearance of monuments. Ethnographic evidence shows that among hunter gatherers unmodified places can play similar roles to architectural features and that mobile communities show a keen awareness of their pasts. These observations find support in the archaeology of the Mesolithic period, but there is less to indicate the same concern with the future. Despite these characteristics, there was little continuity between the use of special places by people who lived on wild resources, and the creation of early monuments during the Neolithic period. In most parts of the study area that possibility is excluded by radiocarbon dating and the evidence of ancient DNA. The chapter concludes by discussing other reasons for the contrast.

Chapter Three considers the ways in which Neolithic communities in Britain, Ireland. and the near-Continent developed a conception of the long term in which the future would be at least as important as the past. One way of illustrating this point is through the choice of building materials for their projects. This account places a special emphasis on the contrast between domestic dwellings, which were generally built of wood, and mortuary monuments of the same date that were frequently made of stone. It also discusses exceptional cases in which timber or stone were used together. The choice of these materials suggests how long they were expected to last. The discussion draws on the results of excavations in northern Germany, Wales, Ireland, and north-west France.

Chapter Four takes this approach further by contrasting two groups of structures with very different histories. Again, it considers the same study area. The first Neolithic mortuary monuments were not designed for a long period of use, and in some cases their erection was among the final acts to take place on a particular site. It might have been intended to bring their histories to an end. Structures may have looked like one another but they were the outcome of different processes in the past. Although there were many exceptions, they include long barrows, stone circles, and henges. By contrast, the erection of other buildings according to a widely shared template was simply the starting point for developments that would extend into the future. In this case local sequences diverged. Typical examples include the construction and reconstruction of causewayed enclosures in the Neolithic period, and the growth of stone alignments in Brittany.

Chapter Five considers the relationship between processes in the 'natural world' and the creation and use of monuments. It focuses on the controversial topic of 'megalithic astronomy'. How were prehistoric structures related to the time scales set by the daily and seasonal movement of the sun? And what was the difference between those with exact alignments on celestial bodies, and others that emphasised more general (but still significant) directions? In Britain and Ireland this account identifies an important change from tombs and other buildings aligned on the rising sun to those inclined towards the sunset. There was a new emphasis on midwinter. It can be interpreted with the help of Irish folklore and, in northern Europe, the Poetic Edda.

The second part begins a discussion of how these structures were reused in subsequent phases. During the earlier prehistoric period, many abandoned monuments were brought back into commission. They were extended or rebuilt and often provided a focus for further burials or deposits of artefacts. At the same time entirely new examples of the same kind were built around them. Others were erected in the vicinity but took different forms. The growth of these complexes is illustrated by the establishment of linear barrow cemeteries in Britain and the Netherlands. The reuse of megalithic tombs during the Bell Beaker phase is considered too, and the discussion extends to examples in Ireland and north-west France. These developments have been discussed in terms of social memory, but new research raises the problem that some of them may have been associated with migrants rather than the descendants of the original builders.

Chapter Seven shares that emphasis on monument complexes, but in this instance their phases were separated by longer periods of time. Now they were ancient constructions that left lasting traces behind when they were abandoned. They stood for a past that was actually beyond recall, but one that could still be reclaimed and reinterpreted. It was an important process at times of political change, and this account focuses on the appropriation of ancient features at early medieval royal centres. It shows how the presence of prehistoric remains influenced the creation of new structures in Denmark, Sweden, and Scotland. At the same time attitudes to ancient features changed with the adoption of Christianity. Churches took their place, and in Britain sites associated with the distant past lost their original significance. Now they were considered threatening and a source of evil. One way in which they were used was for the execution of criminals.

Chapter Eight brings in another source of information. It draws on literary accounts of significant places which shed some light on how their histories were understood. How was the past remembered? The discussion considers the ways in which oral sources were composed. It compares the changing make up of monument complexes with the heroic narratives in which their importance was celebrated. The discussion focuses on literary and archaeological evidence from early medieval Britain (royal genealogies and the epic poem *Beowulf*), Ireland (the Ulster Cycle), and Classical Greece (*the Iliad* and *the Odyssey*).

Finally, Chapter Nine summarises the observations made in earlier sections, drawing on another extended sequence like that in the Boyne Valley. This was the Upper Kennet complex in southern England which featured three separate periods in which monuments were erected or reused. Its Neolithic archaeology is well known to one group of specialists, who study a series of impressive structures from West Kennet long barrow to Avebury and Silbury Hill, but it is also a focus for authorities on the Roman period because a small town – quite possibly a sanctuary – developed at the foot of that mound. The same complex saw another phase of activity in the late 1st millennium AD when its earthwork was modified, and a Viking warrior might have been buried there. The discussion of these elements draws on all the themes considered in the book and provides a summary of the argument.

PART ONE
Key considerations

Chapter 2

Hunter gatherer times

The tyranny of typing

It is impossible to write about deep prehistory without engaging in a certain amount of abstraction. No individual testimony survives and the only 'statements' we can identify are examples of public architecture, artworks or formal deposits of objects, human remains, and animal bones. Their special character may be apparent, but their meanings are never explicit. Faced with these limitations, archaeologists must develop general models of ancient economies and social systems. But these are ideal types that overlook many variations.

The same applies to the *type sites* around which accounts of the past are organised. The concept raises difficulties. What is it that makes these examples 'typical'? Will their special status change as new finds are made? In practice, most of them were defined at an early stage of research and provide a point of comparison with subsequent discoveries. They may have been excavated, analysed, and published to a high standard and their physical remains may have been well preserved, yet primacy in the history of fieldwork should not give them exceptional status among interpretations of the past. Like the ideal social forms that were proposed by anthropologists, their evidence may be misleading, and research can become increasingly distant from the realities we are studying.

The problem is most severe with the remoter parts of prehistory. This account begins in the early postglacial period which supplies the ideal example of these difficulties. It shows the confusion that arises when a type site turns out to have an exceptional character and is interpreted in terms of models that may not be appropriate.

The influence of Star Carr

That site is Star Carr in north-east England which was excavated by Grahame Clark and made famous by the publication of a monograph seventy years ago (Clark 1954).

It plays an inescapable part in any account of postglacial Europe and has been quoted and reinterpreted ever since the results of his fieldwork entered the public domain. That is not surprising as this was an exceptionally accomplished project. Its impact is due to its unusual quality and to Clark's influence as a teacher. The problem arises because new questions have been asked since his project took place. In some cases, they cannot be answered on the basis of the published record. The wooden platform identified by Clark has been the subject of debate (Milner *et al.* 2018). Was it a deliberate structure or was it formed of driftwood? Was it inhabited, or were the associated artefacts simply refuse discarded from a settlement on dry land? Were certain items found along the water's edge – in particular, masks made from red deer skulls – deposited there as offerings?

All these questions followed naturally from Clark's own presentation of Star Carr, but in recent years there has been the recognition that few of its most distinctive features have been found in other places. Some do occur singly, but the combination of elements seems to be unique. At the same time general models of Mesolithic occupation in Britain and northern Europe (these regions had not been separated when the site was inhabited) are based on its exceptional record. It raises a problem – either Star Carr provides supporting evidence for a general model, or its status as a type site must be questioned.

Some of its main characteristics were underemphasised until recently, and it took a new programme of fieldwork to redress the balance (Milner *et al.* 2018). It identified the remains of wooden houses on dry land beyond the limits of Clark's excavation and showed that the occupied area was larger than he had supposed (Fig. 2.1). It suggested

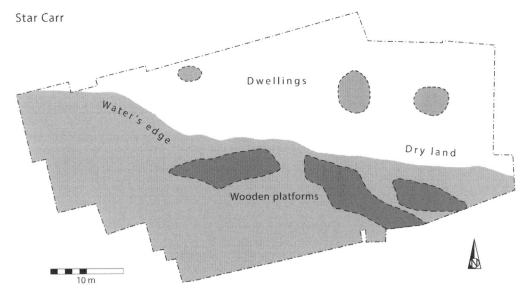

Fig. 2.1. *Plan of the excavated area at Star Carr, showing positions of the dwellings on dry land and the wooden platforms at the water's edge. Information from Milner* et al. *(2018).*

that the successive platforms along the lake edge were more sophisticated structures than was apparent before; in the new report they are described as 'architecture'. Some objects might have been deposited during rituals. The same places were used, although not continuously, for about 800 years.

Every field project is influenced by current ideas, and interpretations of Star Carr were no exception. It was first investigated at a time when the archaeology of hunter gatherers was dominated by practical considerations. There was an emphasis on ecology, mobility, seasonality, and the efficient exploitation of resources. All these elements came to dominate the work inspired by Clark's research. Although it was informed by ethnographic observations, the main emphasis was on the food supply. Animal bones, plant remains, and soils played a key role in these studies. Such approaches were summarised by two edited volumes published in the 1970s. Their very titles are revealing: *Papers in Economic Prehistory*, and *Palaeoeconomy* (Higgs 1972 & 1975).

Other publications suggested the potential of a different approach, and eventually led to a new programme of fieldwork at Star Carr. In 1980 the anthropologist Tim Ingold, who was already familiar with the work of Clark's Cambridge colleagues, published a book on *Hunters, Pastoralists and Ranchers* which provided the social perspective on the inhabitants of northern Europe that had been under-emphasised before (Ingold 1980). Five years later, James Brown and Douglas Price followed a similar course in their book *Prehistoric Hunter-gatherers: The emergence of cultural complexity*. Now there was a growing interest in community organisation, exchange systems, status, and mortuary rites (Brown & Price 1985). Monuments played a part in this thinking. Clark's interpretation of Star Carr had drawn selectively on ethnographic sources, but it was dominated by subsistence. New excavation at the site drew on similar sources but introduced additional elements. It placed more emphasis on the roles of public gatherings, ritual, and animism.

Models and stereotypes

Hunter gatherers and farmers

For a long time, prehistorians treated hunter gatherers and farmers as ideal types, and even today this kind of thinking can influence accounts of Mesolithic and Neolithic archaeology. One of the most influential studies was by a specialist on African societies, Claude Meillassoux (1972). He recognised a crucial distinction. Food production among hunter gatherers was a straightforward process, undertaken by an informal work group. Territories were not defined explicitly, and no one depended on the work of previous generations. Social and economic transactions were simple, and, in his words, they represented 'a type of instantaneous production whose output [was] immediately available' (Meillassoux 1972, 99).

Cultivators worked to a different tempo. They farmed specific areas of land which might have been cleared over several years. And they made careful plans for the future. Some of the produce was stored after the harvest, as there had to be enough for them to plant new crops. As a result, food production extended across the generations and drew on a different conception of time. That was why farmers showed more concern with ancestors and the past. His approach attracted European prehistorians because it seemed to explain why ancestors assumed greater importance during the Neolithic period (Jeunesse 2021). The most striking contrast, however, was not considered by Meillassoux and those who adopted his ideas. Many of the first farmers in Europe built monuments in which to house their dead, but comparable evidence is rare from the previous period.

Although such models were consistent with characteristics of the archaeological record, they operated at a very general level and described several pertinent features but ignored others. It is a moot point how many hunter gatherers in the study area conformed to this stereotype. Not all of them need have followed a mobile way of life, and some of their settlements might have been occupied for most, or all, of the year (Brown & Price 1985). In certain cases, they do seem to have stored critical resources, drawing on them for special occasions such as feasts. There were also regions in which the dead were especially significant and where they were buried in cemeteries. But the fact remains that groups of foragers rarely engaged in monument building. Was that because they had a different conception of time, as Meillassoux suggested?

Farmers and monument construction

Sequences were important. In 1988, Julian Thomas identified some problems in the Neolithic archaeology of Britain and Ireland and compared it with developments in southern Scandinavia, as they were known at the time. Although this was supposedly the period of the earliest farmers, it provided surprisingly little evidence of sedentary settlement. Nor were there many signs of cultivation. Monuments appeared from the beginning of this phase, but it was difficult to identify any houses. The remains of domesticated animals were common, but that did not apply to cereals. The first crops must have been introduced from other parts of Europe. The same applied to sheep and goats, but it was not clear whether cattle and pigs could have been domesticated locally. Although wild animals did not play much part after the transition, wild plants were used during the Late Mesolithic and Early Neolithic phases.

New kinds of material culture were adopted roughly simultaneously on both sides of the North Sea (Thomas 1988). It was obvious that they drew inspiration from neighbouring regions of the Continent, but it was uncertain how or why they were adopted. For a long time, Neolithic artefacts, especially stone tools, reached indigenous communities in southern Scandinavia. Were there similar connections across the English Channel? Were new ideas widely shared? The clearest indication of such links was the construction of monuments of kinds that were already established on the mainland: long mounds and long cairns associated with human remains, and earthwork enclosures defined by discontinuous ditches. Thomas argued that in both regions local hunter gatherers adopted Neolithic lifeways from their neighbours. That was why the process had a limited impact, and why a mobile pattern of settlement endured.

It remained to consider the relationship between monument building and farming. Here some well-known characteristics of Neolithic architecture seemed to play a part. The presence of the first monuments changed the configuration of the landscape and might have altered the occupants' conceptions of time. Did this development make farming more acceptable? The relationships claimed by earlier writers could even be reversed (Bradley 1993, 16–21 & 1998, 20–35). Imposing earthworks and cairns were not the expression of an agricultural surplus or a form of conspicuous consumption, as they had suggested. Rather, the presence of those structures helped to establish the time scale on which a new kind of food production would become both thinkable and possible.

Today this sequence must be rejected in the light of scientific evidence. Nor is it so attractive in the light of developments in anthropology and Mesolithic studies.

New departures

Meillassoux's ideas were published fifty years ago, but his way of thinking remains influential even now. Here it is helpful to draw on the results of more recent accounts of hunter gatherer ethnography and archaeology.

Ethnographic studies

A collection of papers published in 2016 encapsulates some of the principal themes in modern research on hunter gatherers. *Marking the Land* provides a series of case studies, extending from densely forested environments to the open conditions of the Arctic tundra. Other chapters consider the occupation of arid landscapes and deserts. The papers extend across North and South America and include other contributions on Africa, Australia, and Malaysia (Lovis & Whallon 2016). Europe is not represented, but the geographical gap was filled by Peter Jordan's edited volume *Landscape and Culture in Northern Eurasia* published five years earlier (Jordan 2011). The link between these books is even closer since a chapter in the 2011 collection has the same title, 'Marking the land.'

The features considered in these books are not only landmarks in the conventional sense of prominent but unmodified features. The authors study the importance of topographical markers for people travelling across unpopulated territory. More subtle signs play a critical role in wayfinding and are especially important for hunters with their experience of tracking.

Some clues refer to paths that had been used by people in the past and can include trees, mounds, cairns, petroglyphs, rock paintings, settings of boulders, and arrangements of animal bones (Fig. 2.2). Nearly all these places are given names that pass down the generations. In addition, there are changes of vegetation caused by earlier episodes of settlement. In many instances the trails lead towards sources of

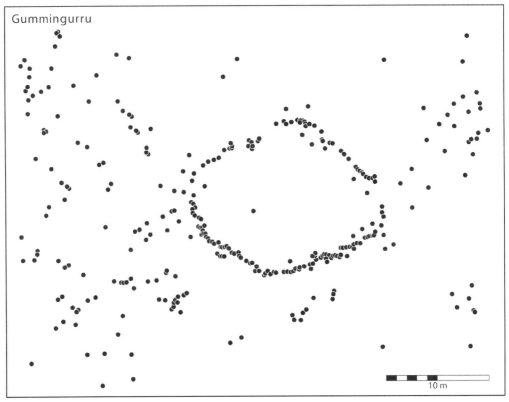

Fig. 2.2. An indigenous stone setting at Gummingurru, Australia. Information from Ross et al. (2013).

fresh water or concentrations of edible plants. The same locations may support an exceptional density of game.

As well as marking the routes between different places, some of these features provide clues to a longer history. Like archaeologists, the mobile groups documented in these accounts can recognise traces of past occupation. They can identify the positions of abandoned shelters, the remains of hearths, the temporary clearings where people lived, and the discarded artefacts and food remains that were left behind. They treat them with respect. These locations are more than productive habitats and play a part in oral histories that extend over the generations – quite how far back they reach is difficult to tell. These considerations are particularly important when such places include graves.

These sites provide vital links to the past but more prominent features can attract greater attention; otherwise, the entire landscape may be sacred. The idea is particularly important in the light of animistic beliefs that trees, stones, and water are alive. Important places are given names. Their significance goes back to the origins of the world and that is why they are celebrated at special events. For example, prominent rock formations can be treated as petrified people or other beings and may even be identified as ancestors. People travel long distances to commemorate their origins. Such locations provide a connection with the distant past.

For the editors of *Marking the Land* there remains a link with the distribution and exploitation of resources. When dispersed communities come together at public events they bring their knowledge of a wider environment, and information passes between the different participants. It might concern the availability of plants and animals in specific regions, and the best times and locations at which to exploit them. It also provides an opportunity for sharing knowledge about the routes between distant areas and the easiest ways of going there. The sacred character of ceremonial sites does not prevent them from fulfilling practical roles (Layton 1986).

In their introduction to *Marking the Land* William Lovis and Robert Whallon go further and compare the functions of these places with those played by formal monuments:

> When one talks of alteration of space generally, or of hunter gatherer alteration of space, the notion is one of creating a marked and / or intentionally built environment .... Such alterations may include more durable outcomes .... This 'built environment' may at times reach an extreme that some have termed 'monumentality' (Lovis & Whallon 2016, 2).

It is obvious that there is a continuum between a network of informal signs extending across the landscape, and the presence of more durable structures. It is equally clear that unmodified places – however conspicuous their appearance – can play similar roles to monuments which by their nature must be deliberate constructions. The rarity of architecture among hunter gatherers gives a misleading impression. These observations shed some light on attitudes to the past.

Mesolithic studies

The results of field archaeology make an important contribution to these discussions. They often share the same point of departure. An important theme in studies of Mesolithic Europe is the special significance of the shoreline, and this is particularly true in two regions: southern Scandinavia and north-west France. Less is known about the coastal archaeologies of Britain and Ireland.

There are problems in addressing this topic. The most serious is caused by rising sea levels during the postglacial period. It means that many occupation sites will have been lost to rising water, especially when this process was most severe in the Early Mesolithic period (Astrup 2018; Bailey *et al.* 2020). In some regions only the later settlements remain intact, although there is more information from areas of isostatic uplift. There are further problems in establishing the relationship between coastal communities and those living further inland. To some extent they can be resolved by studying the stable isotopes preserved by human and animal remains (Outram & Bogaard 2019, 50–74), but another difficulty arises because of the marine reservoir that affects radiocarbon dates from the shoreline.

There are striking contrasts between the evidence from three areas studied in later chapters. Coastal sites survive in Scandinavia (particularly Denmark) and north-west France. They have a direct bearing on the circumstances in which early monuments appeared. In Britain much more is known from inland areas.

Coastal settlements in southern Scandinavia and north-west France
Although shell middens are widely distributed, those in Denmark and Brittany are particularly revealing. Although they share features in common, there are important contrasts between them. The examples in north-west France were in a region that was rapidly inundated by the sea (Scarre 2011). They may be all that survive of a wider pattern, but the Danish examples are preserved where the land has risen (S.H. Andersen 2004). That may be one reason why they are more extensive than their French counterparts.

Those in northern Europe show considerable variety. Some are very extensive, and others are considerably smaller. They can overlie older living sites and in certain cases the middens were only one component of a larger complex; in other instances, activity was restricted to the mounds themselves. Sites were occupied, not necessarily continuously, for up to 1000 years (S.H. Andersen 2004). There is little to suggest that inland resources were used equally intensively, and here Mesolithic material is sparse (Gron & Sørensen 2018). That contrasts with the situation from the beginning of the Neolithic period when settlements were established at new locations in the hinterland. On the other hand, the contents of the middens document a more subtle change (Sørensen & Karg 2014). During the Late Mesolithic period they provide a little evidence for the introduction of domesticated livestock and cereals as well as Neolithic artefacts, and the process continued on an increasing scale after southern Scandinavia was settled by farmers. A key site is Bjørnsholm where a shell midden was occupied discontinuously across the period boundary. It remained in use when one of the first long barrows was built beside it (Fig. 2.3; S.H. Andersen & Johansen 1990; S.H. Andersen 1991).

The Breton evidence is most familiar from Téviec and Hoedic, two cemeteries associated with Mesolithic shell middens, although similar sites have been investigated more recently (Scarre 2011). Radiocarbon dating is difficult because of the marine reservoir, but in this case the sites may have been used for 500 years (Schulz Paulsson 2017, 31–2). Isotopic analysis suggests that some of the people buried in these places had lived on coastal resources, while others came from inland areas (Schulting & Richards 2001). In contrast to the evidence from southern Scandinavia, field survey has located numerous Mesolithic sites in the hinterland (Gouletquer *et al.* 1996).

It is the unusual form of the burials that makes them relevant to the origins of architecture. At Hoedic they were covered by the deposit of shells, and the graves were lined and covered by slabs of quarried stone. Still more important, the position of one of them was marked by a small menhir. The locations of similar graves at

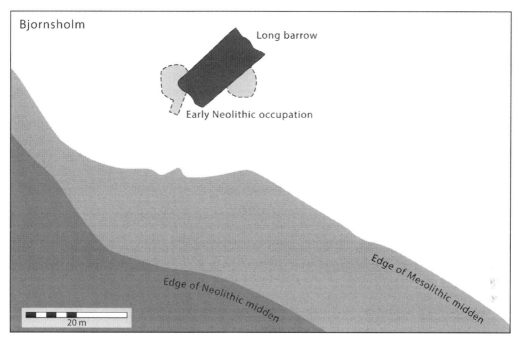

Fig. 2.3. The shell midden and other features at Bjørnsholm. Information from S.H. Andersen and Johansen (1990) and S.H. Andersen (1991).

Téviec were indicated by cairns. For some authors they are the earliest sign of monument building, but the evidence is ambiguous. A stronger case depends on the recognition of an alignment of standing stones – one of them embellished with human features – close to the cemetery on Hoedic (Large & Mens 2008). Its precise date is uncertain, but it may have been constructed at the very beginning of the Neolithic period (Scarre 2011). If so, these features – the graves and the row of standing stones – may represent the earliest stage, or stages, in the development of megalithic architecture. According to Bettina Schulz Paulsson (2017) this is the region with the first stone tombs in Europe.

Inland settlements in Britain
In Britain there is less sign of intensive settlement along the coast, although a considerable amount of evidence must have been lost to the sea. An exception is in the west of Scotland where conspicuous shell middens still survive. Like those in Denmark, they are associated with human burials and remained in use into the Neolithic period (Mithen 2022). As was the case in Brittany, these sites may have been related to activities across a wider area.

Field survey in Britain has identified numerous findspots further inland (Conneller 2022). There seems to have been a striking contrast between the sheer number of Mesolithic artefacts recovered by this method and those of later date.

That is true even where there are other indications of Neolithic activity, for instance pits containing pottery. There are several reasons for the contrast. One is purely practical – Mesolithic artefacts included composite tools with detachable elements which were easy to replace piecemeal; that would increase the total number of finds. Again, surface collections can span a longer period than those from excavated contexts. But neither argument accounts for such a striking pattern. The evidence is not consistent with a simple change from mobile land use during the Mesolithic to sedentary occupation during the following period. It is easier to recognise early 'sites' in the field than it is to find Neolithic examples. The oldest artefacts commonly occur in concentrations, while the later material is scattered over a wider area (assemblages associated with earthwork monuments are the main exception). The number of Mesolithic items is quite unusual, and excavation has recorded limited concentrations that include as many as 300,000 items; at Stainton West, an estuarine site in Cumbria, excavation recovered a similar quantity of artefacts dating from the 5th millennium BC (Brown 2021). Concentrations of finds on inland sites may have accumulated over a long period but they were densely distributed. Such figures can be compared with the number from the Neolithic enclosure at Etton in East Anglia which was almost completely excavated. It was as extensive as most of the Mesolithic sites, yet the ditches, pits, and internal area produced fewer than 7500 worked flints (Pryor 1998). On the other hand, a similar earthwork at Great Wilbraham in the same region was more productive (Evans *et al.* 2006). So were two unusual groups of surface finds in the Fenland (Edmonds *et al.* 1999).

The same observations apply to individual features in these locations. For the most part they were inconspicuous, but there are obvious exceptions. Among the elements that suggest more sustained periods of activity are a few Mesolithic pit houses (Waddington 2007; Mithen & Wicks 2018). These structures were dug into the subsoil and could have been reconstructed several times. They were employed, perhaps discontinuously, over substantial periods; estimates based on radiocarbon extend between 80 and 350 years. They can be associated with large quantities of artefacts.

In the past such features were confused with the holes left by fallen trees (Evans *et al.* 1999). Some of these features might have been modified by human activity, making the conventional distinction between 'cultural' and 'natural' elements problematical. It is easy to assume that they provided shelter from the elements, and there are cases in which they were associated with post holes, stake holes, and hearths. But that does not explain why so many artefacts should be found there; for example, there were over 10,000 items in one such feature at Farnham; other tree throws on the same site contained between 3500 and 9000 pieces of worked flint (Clark & Rankine 1939). They may have been a source of raw material but during the Neolithic period similar hollows were used for formal deposits of objects (Lamdin-Whymark 2008). Comparison with ethnographic sources suggests that individual trees could have been significant.

Referencing the past or anticipating the future?

It would be easy to explain such findings as the result of intermittent settlement in particularly productive locations, but this provides only part of the explanation. It hardly accounts for the superimposition of successive living sites where more space was available. The occupants must have recognised the traces of earlier activity. It could have altered the character of the local environment, and later inhabitants would have had no difficulty identifying discarded artefacts since they used the same raw materials and the same technology for working them. For that reason, they must have been aware of a distant past and might have wanted to relate it to their own activities. People preferred to occupy places that had been inhabited before. In the absence of oral testimony of the kind documented by ethnographers, this relationship seems to be significant. A similar preference was identified by the authors of *Marking the Land* (Lovis & Whallon 2016).

The practices considered so far were directed towards the past, but certain structures do suggest an interest in the future. There were a few built constructions. The timber platforms at Star Carr provide the obvious examples, but they were not unique. One of the achievements of Irish archaeology is the identification of less substantial features along the banks of lakes. They have seldom been investigated and it is not clear how long they remained intact (Warren 2022, 150).

Shell middens occupy an ambiguous position. They could be conspicuous landmarks and accumulated in places where marine resources were consumed on a large scale. They are among the most substantial Mesolithic features in north-west France, Denmark, and the Hebrides, but less prominent examples have been found elsewhere. They are unusual because they preserve structural evidence, and some sites are associated with human remains. These mounds were the result of periods of occupation in the past and people might have expected that these features would continue to accumulate in the future.

Lastly, recent excavations have identified settings of pits or post holes dating from the Mesolithic period. The best known is in the same location as the later monument of Stonehenge where a row of these features was aligned on the position of a tree (Cleal *et al.* 1995, 43–7; Parker Pearson *et al.* 2022, 19–23). Isolated examples have been recognised elsewhere in southern England (Allen & Gardiner 2002), but three Scottish sites are more informative. The best-known example, at Crathes, consists of a line of 15 pits (Fig. 2.4; Murray *et al.* 2009). There was another row of Mesolithic pits at Welhill (Brophy & Wright 2021), and there may have been something similar at Miltimber where there is less to suggest a single layout (Dingwall *et al.* 2019, 32–46). Radiocarbon dates suggest that new elements were added piecemeal over a long period of time.

There are two ways of looking at this evidence. One possibility is that these projects were directed towards the future. At intervals new elements were added to the basic design. This interpretation raises problems. When the latest pits were excavated, their predecessors would have been reduced to inconspicuous hollows in the ground. It is difficult to envisage the unfolding of a plan that took so many years

Crathes
Mesolithic pits

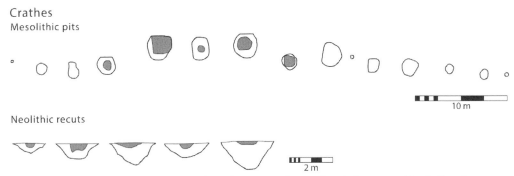

10 m

Neolithic recuts

2 m

Fig. 2.4. The line of Mesolithic pits at Crathes, showing evidence of Neolithic recuts (shaded). Information from Murray et al. (2009).

to accomplish and left so little behind. An alternative is to see the addition of new pits to long-established alignments as yet another acknowledgement of the past. It would happen again when these features were reopened during the Early Neolithic period.

Approximations and exaggerations

Clearly, these observations are not consistent with the ideal scheme proposed by Meillassoux fifty years ago. Nor are the results of excavations conducted since *Rethinking the Neolithic* was published. How do the original ideas fare today? What light can more recent studies shed on ideas of continuity between the Mesolithic and Neolithic periods? And what are their implications for monument building?

One of the new developments is a better appreciation of chronology. The previous section drew attention to some striking features of the Mesolithic period: the prolonged but discontinuous occupation of the same areas of land; the extraordinary quantity of artefacts found in excavated concentrations; and evidence for the building of structures such as platforms and pit houses. There were also cemeteries, alignments, and shell middens. While all these features might seem to anticipate characteristics of Neolithic archaeology, their chronology is not consistent with this idea. Shell middens are almost the only features that extend across the period boundary (Gron & Sørensen 2018; Mithen 2022). The same is true of a few human burials, but the best-known graves of hunter gatherers in southern Scandinavia are too early to suggest much continuity with subsequent developments (Grünberg et al. 2016). In fact, older Mesolithic cemeteries in Europe tend to be larger than later ones, and burials of that date are much less common than Neolithic examples (Jeunesse 2021).

The most striking developments had already happened by the 7th millennium BC when the pattern of settlement was affected by developments in the natural environment. Rising sea separated Britain from the Continent, and this was a period of climate change (Astrup 2018; Bailey et al. 2020). There were other changes towards the end of the Mesolithic period. Radiocarbon dates suggest that the British population was falling several centuries before the adoption of agriculture (Conneller 2022, 356–419). It weakens the case for cultural continuity, but the evidence is very different in other regions. In Brittany the marine reservoir affects samples from coastal sites. It leaves a degree of ambiguity that has yet to be resolved.

There are other problems in combining Meillassoux's approach with information from the Mesolithic period. Archaeological and ethnographic sources suggest that similar gatherings of people happened both at unmodified places and monuments. Their beliefs were important whether or not they were emphasised by building projects and enshrined in architectural form. At the same time, hunter gatherers in the regions studied here obviously shared a conception of time that extended far beyond Meillassoux's concept of 'instantaneous production'. But there could be an important distinction between their ideas of temporality and those expressed by Neolithic constructions. Most of the archaeological evidence illustrates Mesolithic attitudes to *the past*. There is less to indicate the same concern with *the future*. Excavated evidence from Neolithic and later structures suggests that monuments had a different significance.

New radiocarbon dates shed light on the relationship between farming and monumental architecture. The clearest evidence comes from the direct dating of cereals and domestic animal bones. At the same time fishing lost most of its previous importance (L. Cramp *et al.* 2014). The extent of land clearance is documented by fossil insects and pollen (Whitehouse 2006; Fyfe *et al.* 2013; Woodbridge *et al.* 2014). These methods provide evidence of farming from the onset of the Neolithic in Britain, Ireland, and southern Scandinavia where it was contemporary with the use of material culture of Continental inspiration (Sheridan 2010; Sørensen & Karg 2014; Sheridan & Whittle 2023). Around the Irish Sea robust wooden houses are recorded from this early phase (Smyth 2014; Whitehouse *et al.* 2014; McClatchie *et al.* 2016). It seems as if long-established interpretations of the Neolithic period have been vindicated three decades after they were questioned. The chronology of stone and earthwork constructions can also be reconsidered. Comparatively few were built during this initial phase; for the most part they were a later development, and they were built on a larger scale when the first phase of clearance and cultivation was over. By that time domestic architecture left less trace (except in northern Europe), and there may have been a greater emphasis on stock raising and a mobile pattern of settlement. The close relationship between these elements was recognised by Julian Thomas (1988). What is new is the recognition that they were not a feature of the *earliest* Neolithic period. They were a subsequent development.

The recovery of DNA from human bone has made a greater contribution (Brace *et al.* 2019; Brace & Booth 2023; Sheridan & Whittle 2023). It is constrained by the survival of human remains, meaning that there is little evidence from north-west France, but in other parts of the study area there are signs of a dramatic change. To varying extents the genetic signature of indigenous hunter gatherers is reduced or disappears and there are indications of a new population related to farmers in more distant parts of Europe. Where sufficient information is available it is the dominant strand. This supports the traditional idea that new areas were settled from overseas.

There are good reasons for adopting a fresh approach. The features of the Mesolithic period that suggest a concern with the long-term date from the *earlier* part of this period, and most of them predate the changes that happened between 7000 and 6000 BC. They may provide evidence of similar attitudes to those of monument builders, but in the north and west they disappeared long before the adoption of agriculture. When Neolithic architecture was first established it was associated with settled farming and the new structures were built by immigrants. There is little to support a notion of gradual acculturation. What was once an attractive hypothesis can no longer be sustained. The abundance and scale of Mesolithic activity are no longer in doubt, but they make the virtual absence of monuments especially puzzling.

Origins

Studies of the first monuments can be teleological. The point is made by David Graeber and David Wengrow (2021) in their book *The Dawn of Everything*. It offers a critique of the use of ideal types by anthropologists and archaeologists who are influenced by notions of social evolution that go back to the beginnings of both disciplines. It is not surprising that one of their targets is the idea that hunter gatherers did not, or could not, build monuments; in the conventional view, that was the prerogative of societies who practised agriculture. Their argument works well in Jomon Japan (Mizoguchi 2013), and in the New World where an obvious exception to this generalisation is the earthwork complex at Poverty Point (Hargrave *et al.* 2021). The site was an important ceremonial centre used by mobile people. Was the same true of examples in prehistoric Europe?

In one case their argument is flawed. There is no justification for saying that Stonehenge was built by people who lived on hazelnuts during a period in which agriculture had failed (cf. Stevens & Fuller 2012). The communities who used the site may have followed a mobile lifestyle, but they raised domestic animals and did make some use of cereals. They should not be confused with hunter gatherers. Another example quoted by Graeber and Wengrow is more informative, although it is outside the area studied in detail here. They discuss the great stone structures at Göbekli Tepe in Anatolia. Among the elements they might have considered are the first megaliths – menhirs, tombs, and alignments – in Brittany (Schulz Paulsson 2017), and the stone houses, burials, and sculptures at Lepenski Vir on the Danube (Brami *et al.* 2022). They have something in common, for while they could have been built by people who exploited wild resources, these communities might have been in contact with others who practised agriculture. Although Göbekli Tepe is associated with the remains of game animals, the stone tools from the site provide evidence for the intensive processing of cereals (Dietrich 2021). In time it would lead to the development of domesticated varieties. The form of the stone buildings was influenced by specialised architecture in places where that process occurred. A new study of the human remains from Lepenski Vir based on DNA shows that some of the occupants of the settlement came from farming communities (Brami *et al.* 2022).

The Breton evidence is particularly relevant. The local sequence is difficult to assess as bone seldom survives except in coastal middens. As a result, there are not enough radiocarbon dates. These cemeteries included massive cists, and the southern Morbihan must have been one region in which Late Mesolithic communities encountered farmers settling the region from the east. The first monumental architecture seems to have developed during this phase (Scarre 2011, 57–95). That is not unlike the situation at Göbekli Tepe where similar relationships were expressed on a larger scale. In both cases stone buildings may not have originated before the earliest contacts between populations that followed different ways of life. Whoever undertook the actual work of construction, the idea of doing so did not arise spontaneously.

One way of achieving a wider perspective is to consider the worldwide distribution of megalithic architecture. Here a vital resource is a new collection of 72 papers with the title *Megaliths of the World* (Laporte & Large 2022). Its scope is as wide as the title suggests, and the volume contains regional studies which draw on archaeological and ethnographic sources as well as more reflective essays. The emphasis on stone buildings has advantages and disadvantages. Their distribution is obviously limited to regions with suitable building material. On the other hand, such structures have a greater chance of surviving and being identified than other types of monuments. In 85% of the regions reviewed in the book, megaliths of one kind or another were associated with people who exploited domesticates: cultivators or pastoralists. They might be either mobile or sedentary – the key issue is that they *owned* the resources on which they lived. Of the remaining groups featured in these papers, another 5% occupied regions in which hunter gatherers and farmers of some kind coexisted. They included three of the examples already quoted here. The Breton evidence, for instance, conforms to a wider pattern.

In two minds?

These comparisons suggest a different approach to the question. If the first monuments in north-west France originated during a period of interaction between local hunter gatherers and people who practised farming, what accounts for the contrast between their attitudes to the built environment? Why had the indigenous communities not erected impressive buildings before, and why did the settlers take a different attitude to such projects?

The first question is difficult to answer as it draws on the character of hunter gatherers as an ideal social type – exactly the procedure that this chapter has questioned. It depends on whether certain beliefs were as common during the prehistoric period as they are in the ethnographic present. The best archaeological evidence concerns the treatment of wild animals. At excavated sites in Britain and Scandinavia their remains could be reconstituted after the meat had been consumed, and they were buried in formal deposits. In the same way their components could be used as raw material for making special objects. Chantal Conneller (2004 & 2022) suggest that these features illustrate the importance of animism; similar practices are documented in the anthropology of northern Europe. Is it possible that the entire landscape was sacred? It had to be treated with respect and could not undergo radical alteration. Might that be one reason why Mesolithic people left few structures behind and why they did not build lasting monuments in the study area? The differences between ways of obtaining food were less significant than those between different worldviews.

It is easier to argue that the farmers who impinged on their way of life engaged in different practices from hunter gatherers. It is true that farming transformed the local environment, but another feature may have been just as important. With the growth of settled communities in central and eastern Europe the building of substantial settlements and houses provided the focus for settled life (Whittle 2018). They were *the outcome of collective labour*, and to some extent social relations depended on the sharing of important tasks. That was particularly true with the construction of longhouses (Hofmann 2013). Even when the settlement pattern changed, these practices remained important. Although it found expression in different architectural forms, such as mounds and enclosures, the basic principle was unchanged.

The onset of the Neolithic did not initiate a complete break between mobile and sedentary ways of life, but it was when people who had deliberately eschewed large building projects encountered strangers for whom such undertakings played a fundamental role. As local and immigrant populations merged, so did their views of a wider world.

It influenced the conceptions of time considered in Chapter Three.

Chapter 3

Material differences

Houses of the dead?

The title of this section is taken from an edited volume which considers the relationship between domestic dwellings, burial mounds, and cairns in Neolithic Europe (A. Barclay *et al.* 2020). It is one of the most recent contributions to a discussion that has engaged archaeologists since Gordon Childe wrote on the subject in 1949. Like other contributors to the debate, the authors did not reach any clear conclusion; there were too many regional and chronological differences to support one interpretation. Since the connection between longhouses and other monuments was first proposed, most accounts have focused on the ground plans, orientations, and chronologies of these structures, but there is little to indicate a single overarching pattern. The same applies to the parallel hypothesis that the forms of circular passage graves in Atlantic Europe echoed those of roundhouses (Laporte & Tinévez 2004). Both traditions include sites at which dwellings and tombs coexisted, but they represent the exception rather than the norm. In this respect there is little new to say.

One point has been overlooked in many of these discussions. A more striking comparison concerns the choice of building materials. With very few exceptions, Neolithic houses in northern and western Europe were built of wood, and in many regions this remained the case into later periods. Monuments associated with the dead included some timber buildings, but they were more often constructed of stone. In other cases, they were conspicuous earthworks. Unless they were deliberately destroyed, they could be expected to last a long time. In fact, there was a contrast which is seldom considered. Domestic dwellings had a finite lifespan, and their fabric might not remain intact for many generations. On the other hand, barrows and cairns – especially those described as chambered tombs – were so durable that their remains survive today. This chapter considers some of the differences between them.

The discussion begins with a sample of excavated sites in Britain, Ireland, and the near-Continent. They include comparatively unusual cases in which the remains of domestic buildings were directly associated with megaliths or menhirs but illustrate a broader pattern that extended throughout the regions studied here.

Hoedic, *Le Haut Mée, and Les Fouillages*

Chapter Two considered the evidence from north-west France, one of the regions where Late Mesolithic hunter gatherers encountered immigrant farmers. It was where some of the earliest monuments were built. Standing stones were of particular significance and were represented in the cemetery of Hoedic and the nearby alignment where one of the components was shaped to resemble the human form (Large & Mens 2008; Scarre 2011, 64–7).

There was a still more striking juxtaposition at Le Haut Mée in Brittany, for here excavation found the site of a trapezoidal building (Cassen *et al.* 1998). This example dated from an important transition, as it came at the end of a long history of monumental dwellings and was among the first Neolithic buildings in that part of France. Radiocarbon dates for the site fall between 5000 and 4700 BC and overlap with estimates for Late Mesolithic shell middens on the coast.

Around the house was a series of elongated pits. They were organised in pairs, one of them filled with loess and the other with rubble. They are difficult to interpret, but in one feature of this kind was a partly worked stone of similar proportions to another menhir. Like other examples in north-west France, it had been shaped to represent the human body.

The site has features in common with Les Fouillages on the Channel Island of Guernsey, where excavation found a megalithic tomb built over the position of an older settlement (Kinnes 1982). Again, it dated from the beginning of the Neolithic sequence. Its plan resembles that of the building at Le Haut Mée and the dates of both structures overlap (Fig. 3.1). One feature is particularly relevant here. According to

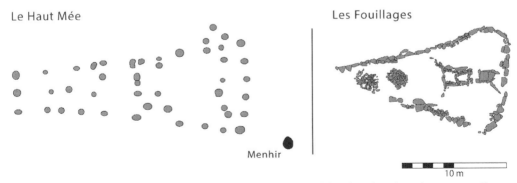

Le Haut Mée

Les Fouillages

Menhir

10 m

Fig. 3.1. Outline plans of the Neolithic house at Le Haut Mée and the chambered tomb at Les Fouillages. Information from Cassen et al. *(1998) and Kinnes (1982).*

the excavator, 'at the east end of the cairn stood a shouldered menhir or marker slab, perhaps chosen for its generalised anthropomorphic resemblance' (Kinnes 1982, 26). It was surely the equivalent of the worked stone beside the wooden house on the mainland. Others accompanied barrows in Brittany (Scarre 2011, 88–95), and Le Haut Mée and Les Fouillages illustrate an early stage in the interplay between materials. Stone was used for tombs and sculptures, but domestic dwellings were built of wood.

Parc Gybi

At Parc Gybi in north-west Wales a substantial Neolithic house was occupied between 3700 and 3625 BC (Kenney 2021, 33–54). Excavation found slighter traces of occupation in the surrounding area, but in this case the most striking feature is that the building shared the same axis as a megalithic tomb nearly 100 m away (Fig. 3.2; C. Smith & F. Lynch 1987, 1–88). The only radiocarbon date from the cairn gives a *terminus post quem* of 4000–3700 BC, but more evidence is provided by diagnostic pottery.

The cairn went through three periods of construction. The earliest component was a circular passage grave. It was replaced by two successive long cairns, and it was these structures that had the same alignment as the house. According to the excavator, the simplest hypothesis is that the domestic building was orientated on the first chambered tomb. They were paired more explicitly during a subsequent phase. Not only were they aligned on one another, in its final form the megalithic monument was almost the same length as the domestic building. They might have been conceived as mirror images.

The differences between them may be as significant as the similarities. Although they shared a common alignment, it was only in its later stages that the Trefignath cairn had an elongated ground plan like the dwelling; initially its entrance had faced in a different direction. The original construction was extended on two occasions. The cairn must have remained open for a long time since its latest component contained sherds of Middle or Late Neolithic pottery.

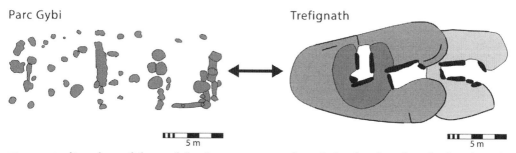

Fig. 3.2. Outline plans of the Neolithic house at Parc Gybi and the chambered tomb of Trefignath. Both monuments shared the same alignment. Information from Kenney (2021) and C. Smith and F. Lynch (1987).

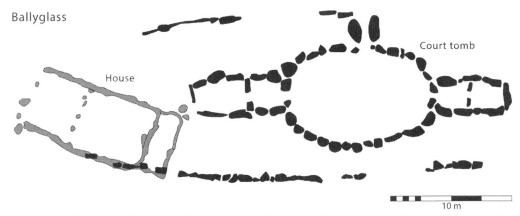

Fig. 3.3. *Outline plans of the Neolithic house at Ballyglass and the chambered tomb that succeeded it. Information from O'Nualláin (1972) and Smyth (2020).*

Ballyglass

At Ballyglass in the west of Ireland traces of domestic dwellings were identified during the excavation of two megalithic tombs, but in each case their positions did not overlap completely. The best preserved was 13 m long and 6 m wide and was demonstrably older than one of the monuments (Fig. 3.3; O'Nualláin 1972). It was associated with radiocarbon dates between 3950 and 3650 BC and may have been set on fire when it went out of use. The cairn was carefully sited so that part of its kerb followed the same course as the outer wall of the dwelling (Smyth 2020). The orientations of the successive structures differed by about ten degrees, but one chamber of the later tomb respected the position of the house; their relationship is particularly striking as they were only 2 m apart.

A nearby monument of almost the same kind – a court tomb – was associated with three more dwellings, but it is difficult to establish the chronological relationship between them (O'Nualláin 1988). Their remains were ephemeral, but they contained a similar range of artefacts. In plan at least two of the buildings respected parts of the cairn, but here the sequence is less important than the choice of materials. There was the same contrast between timber domestic architecture and a stone construction.

Rastorf

At Rastorf in northern Germany a mound with a stone chamber was built over the position of another Neolithic house, which is dated between 3500 and 3300 BC. The building was constructed of timber and was 6 m wide and 18 m long (Steffens 2009). Outside it there were pits and hearths. The author of the definitive report considered that it was occupied for two or three generations, but there were no indications that the structure had ever been repaired. After it was abandoned the position of the building was ploughed, and then a stone and earthwork monument – one of a number in the vicinity – was constructed over it. A second mound of similar form was built alongside.

Rastorf

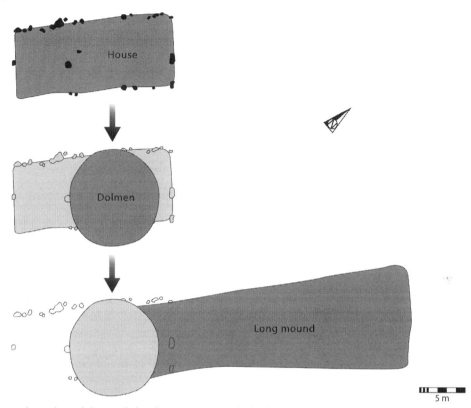

Fig. 3.4. Outline plan of the Neolithic house at Rastorf which was overlain by a circular monument later extended to form a long barrow. Information from Steffens (2009).

The principal structure underwent several modifications and was gradually enlarged, but its layout obviously commemorated the earlier house. There were two important developments. First, a circular mound covered the principal room of the dwelling (Fig. 3.4). At its centre was a megalithic chamber of the kind described as a dolmen. During a second phase the earthwork was extended by constructing a slightly trapezoidal mound nearly 40 m long which followed the axis of the original house. These were not the only changes to its form, and the excavation report postulates as many as seven phases of remodelling. That contrasts with the simple history of the dwelling.

Parallel developments

These examples span nearly two thousand years, but with an emphasis on the 4th millennium BC. They transcend the detailed classification of megalithic tombs and include examples originally described as closed chambers, dolmens, gallery graves, and passage graves. In the same way, the domestic buildings extend from the trapezoidal house at La Haut Mée, which was 20 m long, to smaller rectangular or oval dwellings at Ballyglass.

One characteristic links the sites considered here. Whatever the stratigraphic and structural relationship between individual houses and monuments, the domestic buildings were built of wood whilst the chambered tombs and allied structures made more use of stone. The distinction did not depend on local conventions or the supply of raw material, for it was a general feature across the study area. This contrast is only emphasised by the first appearance of menhirs and megalithic alignments in north-west France.

The structural histories of houses

Two patterns seem to be particularly common.

From their first appearance in western and northern Europe Neolithic houses shared some striking characteristics. Almost all were built of wood, meaning that they are usually represented by a setting of post holes; traces of their floors seldom survive, although some evidence has been recovered by phosphate analysis. That was true of many different structures, from the massive Linearbandkeramik (LBK) longhouses with which the Neolithic sequence began, to later and less robust examples. In principle it should be difficult to recognise their outlines amidst a wider distribution of excavated features, but this is seldom the case. The oldest dwellings were often flanked by borrow pits that provided material for the walls, but they became less common with time and eventually disappeared (Coudart 1998). Although their presence made them easier to identify, later settings of posts also stand out. Although there were a few exceptions after the LBK, domestic dwellings were usually replaced in new locations and their positions did not overlap (Bradley 2020b).

Secondly, individual buildings were inhabited for unusually short periods of time. There are few indications that they were repaired or reconstructed on a significant scale. Although there are signs of piecemeal extensions to the longhouses of the LBK, there is little to suggest that domestic dwellings had a lengthy history (Coudart 1998). There are signs that they were abandoned while they were structurally sound. A few were destroyed by fire, and in other cases their wooden framework might have been recovered, but normally they were left to decay. Although the clearest evidence comes from this early phase, after the LBK the same considerations influenced the treatment of domestic buildings.

Perhaps the histories of these dwellings reflected the histories of the people who lived there, rather than the condition of the houses themselves. It is possible that LBK buildings were abandoned when one of the occupants died or as a new generation followed its predecessor. In some cases, the sites of older dwellings might have been marked by mounds of daub and thatch left as they collapsed, or by the hollows marking the positions of borrow pits (Bradley 1998, 44–8). New houses were often located in between the positions of abandoned dwellings. In such cases both 'living' and 'dead' houses would share the same spacing and orientation across the settled area. Taken together, they adhered to a single layout that connected past structures with those that took their place (Bradley 2020b). Although there was greater flexibility, similar conventions were followed during subsequent phases. Outside western Europe practice was more varied.

The structural histories of tombs

By their nature stone tombs were more durable than wooden dwellings. The same was true of mounds and cairns. On the other hand, access to the chambers and passages associated with them would have been easy to control. It was common to block their entrances with orthostats, walls, or rubble, although there were cases in which the interior was reopened later. Unburnt bodies were introduced at intervals. Then bones that had lost their flesh might be rearranged, and relics could be taken away to circulate among the living. The same applied to cremations. Some monuments were used for long periods of time, and others much more briefly, but unlike the timber houses, their fabric remained intact, allowing them to be revisited or brought back into commission. It would have been more difficult in the case of abandoned settlements.

That is one significant contrast with domestic architecture, but another is equally obvious. Few domestic buildings were reconstructed or rebuilt on a significant scale. In most cases they were inhabited for a limited period before they were replaced. It is rarely true of the tombs. Even a fairly simple example like that at Trefignath was modified more than once; its counterpart at Rastorf was extended or enlarged on no fewer than six occasions. This practice was by no means unusual. Such developments might have happened according to different time scales, from the relatively short sequences associated with dolmens or small passage graves to the histories of the largest chambered tombs. What had begun as a series of separate structures might be incorporated in a single monument, as happened at the north German site of Flintbek where seven episodes of construction took place over a period of a hundred years. Four dolmens were incorporated in a single long barrow; in turn the mound itself was erected over two phases (Mischka 2011).

Other barrows could be completely rebuilt. That was what happened with the Carnac tumuli of north-west France where mounds or cairns that were originally associated with closed chambers were encapsulated in larger passage graves. A good example of this process is documented at the Tumulus de Saint-Michel (Scarre 2011, 103–8). Other instances include the most conspicuous passage graves in the Boyne Valley which featured in Chapter One. The principal mound at Newgrange covered the remains of an older earthwork (A. Lynch *et al.* 2014), and its counterpart at Knowth showed an even more complicated sequence. It was massively enlarged, and its structure incorporated the remains of another megalith whose original position is unknown (Eogan & Cleary 2017).

Informative anomalies

So far this account has described individual sites. There are other cases in which entire groups of houses or monuments were related to one another over longer periods of time – their distinctive forms were copied, but only after an interval. Again, the choice of building material was significant.

Stalled cairns and stone houses in Orkney

Among the closest links between Neolithic houses and megalithic tombs are those between stalled cairns in Orkney and domestic buildings of the type recorded at Stonehall and the Knap of Howar. Their plans were surprisingly similar (Richards & Jones 2016, 225–30). Both were rectangular or oval and were entered through the end wall. The interior was organised as a series of separate compartments on either side of a central passage (Fig. 3.5). There could be more subdivisions within the chambered tombs, but that was not always the case and there was considerable variation. It is thought that the forms of these buildings were closely related.

They are very different from the pairs of structures considered so far because both the tombs and houses were built of stone. Until recently, there seemed to be

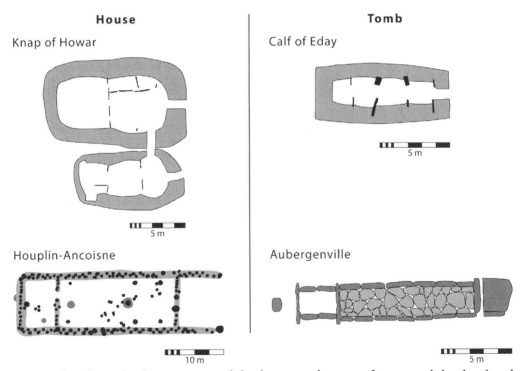

Fig. 3.5. The relationship between two Neolithic houses at the Knap of Howar and the chambered tomb of Calf of Eday. The illustration also compares the plans of a large timber building at Houplin-Ancoisne and the small allée couverte at Aubergenville. Information from Richards and Jones (2016), Joseph et al. (2011) and Masset and Soulier (1995).

an explanation for this contrast. Today Orkney has few trees, and it was assumed that the use of timber in prehistory depended on a supply of driftwood washed up on the shore. The fine quality of the local flagstone made it an alternative building material, and the fabric of the surviving monuments shows how effectively it was employed.

New research provides another perspective (Bayliss *et al.* 2017). Excavation has shown that the first Neolithic houses in Orkney were constructed of timber, and pollen analysis reveals that oak and pine were present in significant amounts when the archipelago was first settled by farmers (Bunting *et al.* 2022). These species became less common once land use intensified around 3400 BC. At the same time the chronology of local buildings has been refined using Bayesian statistics which demonstrate that wooden houses were in use between 3560 and 3360 BC and coexisted with the first chambered cairns from about 3500 BC. It follows that even in Orkney timber dwellings and stone tombs were employed together at the start of the Neolithic period. It was as the supply of suitable wood decreased that structures of both kinds were built of stone. That accounts for the increasingly close relationship between stalled cairns and houses.

Allées couvertes in Atlantic France

Allées couvertes are a distinctive class of Late Neolithic tomb, defined by a stone antechamber and a larger rectangular chamber. Some examples are embellished with depictions of axes and human figures. These sites are widely distributed, but many are on acid soils, meaning that little is known about their original contents. Where bone does survive, however, they include the remains of unburnt bodies that seem to have been packed into separate compartments (Masset & Soulier 1995).

Structures with a similar ground plan were built of wood and have a wide distribution in France. They have been investigated by excavation and aerial photography and are sometimes described as longhouses (Joseph *et al.* 2011; Nicolas *et al.* 2019). They are not like those of the LBK as they were built in a different way and were often divided into separate rooms (Fig. 3.5). In any case they are very much later in date. The smallest examples seem to have been domestic dwellings, but larger and more monumental versions of the same design could have been public buildings. In every case they were of wood.

It is tempting to suggest that their roles varied according to the materials used to build them: the tombs were of stone, but the houses and related structures were constructed of timber. That might well be true, but it is increasingly obvious that they were not contemporary with one another (although some allées couvertes show signs of secondary reuse). The megaliths date from the late 4th millennium BC (Scarre 2011), but most of the timber buildings they resemble are assigned to the period between 2900 and 2500 BC (Nicolas *et al.* 2019). If there were explicit links between them, as most authorities suggest, the forms of these houses referred to the appearance of older tombs. As Chris Scarre says, 'the third millennium 'great houses' of northern and western France were not models for the tombs but modelled upon them' (2011, 265). Although the selection of building materials conformed to a wider scheme, the chronological sequence was unusual.

Lillemer and mud brick houses in Atlantic France

A third anomaly results from excavation at Lillemer in north-west France. The main feature of this site was a substantial Neolithic enclosure built around a rocky hill. This site was unusual because its entrance included a setting of orthostats which shared architectural elements with local chambered tombs. According to the excavators, 'one gate [of the enclosure] .... can be considered as megalithic' (Laporte *et al.* 2015, 804).

Preserved beneath the bank of the enclosure were the remains of mud brick houses. Luc Laporte and his colleagues emphasise the striking contrasts between these short-lived buildings and the conspicuous enclosure that took their place. They compare this sequence with the construction of stone monuments to the dead over the positions of older dwellings. They also emphasise the implications of their discovery for the wider pattern of settlement:

> [It] clearly differs from the model of a domestic structure... [applied to] most Neolithic villages known in western Europe ... Could the [identification of] mud architecture ... trigger a revision of our understanding of the degree of mobility associated with Neolithic groups? (Laporte *et al.* 2015, 815).

As they say, there is similar evidence from more temperate regions, but in the study area this is a new discovery. In the same way the defences of the excavated enclosure of Champ Durand in the west of France made extravagant use of drystone walls, but the only evidence of internal features is provided by pieces of clay daub (Joussaume 2012).

Vertical and horizontal expressions of time (Fig. 3.6)

Laporte and his co-authors compare the use of mud or cob construction near the Channel coast with better known evidence from eastern and central Europe. It is also documented in the Iberian Peninsula, the Mediterranean and in other parts of France. The contrast with more durable architecture at a site like Lillemer is important, but the use of this material has a wider significance.

In eastern Europe and beyond, many structures built of mud and earth were superimposed on one another, leading to the formation of a conspicuous mound or *tell* (Blanco-González & Kienlin 2020). In the past this observation has been interpreted in practical terms. Perhaps these features resulted from the decay of domestic buildings over long periods of time. As older dwellings went out of use, they would have been easy to replace. But there are objections to this scheme. The first is the recognition that these tells did not necessarily represent the whole of the settled area – there are sites where the accumulation of demolished or abandoned buildings occupied only part of a larger complex which included areas of 'open' settlement (for a good

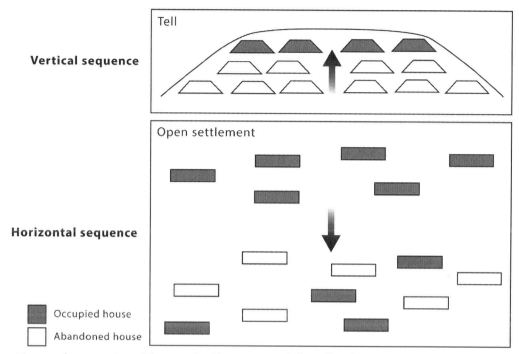

Fig. 3.6. The succession of domestic buildings in a Neolithic tell and in a settlement of longhouses.

example see Racky & Anders 2008). The superimposition of successive buildings was not a universal practice and might have been a deliberate choice.

At the same time more attention has been paid to the processes accompanying the destruction of domestic dwellings and their replacement in the same positions. It is no longer enough to suggest that closely packed houses were vulnerable to accidental fires and to suppose that it was why so many of them burnt down. The process was not restricted to tells and has been recognised at open settlements across large parts of south-eastern Europe. It seems more reasonable to suggest that when their use came to an end they were destroyed during a specific ritual (Chapman 1999). The case is particularly plausible in the light of experiments which show how much effort would be needed to gather sufficient fuel. Much of the resulting debris was recycled in constructing the next generation of dwellings and it was sometimes mixed with deposits of infant bones. Not all these episodes can have been the result of misadventure, and many of them may have been governed by social conventions.

In some cases, the strongest argument against a mundane explanation is the precise superimposition of successive buildings. It involved more than practical considerations since it extended to the locations of wall paintings, or the placing of human and animal remains within the layout of the dwelling. So exact was the duplication of such elements in the formation of the settlement mound at Çatalhöyük that Ian Hodder (2012) describes some of the successive structures as 'history houses'.

It suggests a fundamental contrast in the development of Neolithic settlements across different parts of Europe.

Where mud architecture was widely used, people expressed a 'vertical' concept of time, not unlike the stratigraphic sequences documented by generations of archaeologists in the Near East. But as Neolithic farmers came to colonise parts of central Europe the relationship between the present and the past was laid out in 'horizontal' terms – the positions of new buildings were interspersed with the abandoned, but still visible, sites of older ones (Bradley 2020b). The process began during the LBK when longhouses were spaced across the inhabited area in the way described earlier. This process was more difficult to recognise as the absence of deep stratigraphy made it hard to place them in order, but to a large extent that has been achieved by seriation of the associated pottery, scientific dating, and the use of Bayesian statistics (Whittle 2018). Taken together, they suggest that the inhabitants of Neolithic houses shared similar concerns in different parts of Europe. Individual houses were occupied for finite periods of time and were soon replaced in new locations. Some were abandoned before major repairs were needed, and others were destroyed by fire.

Monumentality

How were those practices related to the creation of monuments? In one sense such structures played little part during the earlier stages in which Europe was settled by farmers. In another way, their role was fundamental, but their creation was so completely integrated into domestic life that their wider significance can be overlooked. Yet the tells formed out of the remains of superimposed buildings could be larger than many of the earthwork mounds erected in western and northern Europe during the Neolithic period, and fieldwork has demonstrated that some of them were enclosed by ditches of considerable proportions (Chapman & Gaydarska 2006). They did not belong to a separate sphere of activity described as 'ritual' or 'ceremonial'. Instead, they formed a vital component of domestic life, and at the same time were an expression of history and social identity.

Might the same have been true of the great longhouses of the LBK and their immediate successors? It is telling that they first appeared as settlement expanded beyond the regions with tells. Those buildings were conspicuous features, too. They required a team of people to erect them and consumed a large amount of timber (Startin 1978; Hofmann 2013). They were conceived on a greater scale than most of the farmhouses occupied during later periods, and it was not until the Iron Age that there were many structures of the same proportions in western Europe. It follows that these were far more than shelters from the elements or places in which to keep produce and livestock. The first longhouses were monuments as well as domestic dwellings. Like the tells, they expressed a new commitment to particular places. They were also where daily life took place.

One reason for saying this is that monumental architecture in the conventional sense rarely coexisted with the longhouses of the LBK or its successors. Although there was a little overlap towards the end of these periods, most notably in Poland (Pyzel 2020) and northern France (Chambon 2020), the best evidence for the building of specialised mounds came *after* domestic architecture had changed its character, at a time when settlements no longer took such prominent forms. It was when smaller and slighter houses became the norm that they were increasingly often accompanied by megaliths (Müller 2011 & 2017). If there was any link between the longhouses inhabited in the past and the barrows and cairns whose forms referred back to them, the connection was not between ordinary dwellings and ancestral tombs so much as two kinds of public architecture, separated from one another by an interval of time. Settlements and houses became less ostentatious, and, by comparison, stone structures assumed a dominant role.

Materials and the passage of time: the earlier Neolithic

After the LBK the distinction between timber and stone became increasingly important. So did the construction of enclosures, mounds, and cairns. Domestic buildings and entire settlements played a less obvious role in social life and large numbers of monuments were built in other locations. They were made from the new materials: both earth and stone. But one distinction remained important. The history of an individual house was comparatively short; these buildings did not remain intact for a significant period before they were abandoned. People might have compared the life expectancies of these constructions with those of their inhabitants. Both extended over a finite length of time, and there are ethnographic examples in which houses, like the wood used to build them, are thought to be alive (Carsten & Hugh-Jones 1995).

It is tempting to contrast this with the character of stone which might seem unchanging or inert, but there are risks in making this claim. Ethnographic sources can be helpful, for they show that some societies think of rocks as living beings – examples of this way of thinking were quoted in Chapter Two. It certainly applies to the treatment of menhirs depicting the human body, a few of which were built into megalithic tombs (Robb 2009; Laporte & Bueno Ramírez 2022). Whatever the perception of stone in particular societies, daily experience would show that it is extremely durable. When chambered cairns were built or when large earthworks were constructed, they were likely to outlast any timber building. They would have had an impact in the present, but it was possible to think of them as extending into a future – however that future was imagined. This was an important development. In certain cases, those issues became still more explicit as earthen long barrows dating from early in the Neolithic period were rebuilt with stone chambers, forecourts, or kerbs. It happened on both sides of the North Sea. But the converse did not apply. Stone tombs were never rebuilt in wood – the process of reconstruction went in only one direction.

Materials and the passage of time: the later Neolithic and after

There are indications of an even more general sequence. Between the middle of the Neolithic period and the beginning of the Bronze Age domestic buildings become more difficult for archaeologists to recognise. Of course, there are exceptions – their remains survive in southern Scandinavia and are abundant in Orkney – but over the course of time enclosures, mounds, and cairns played an increasing role in the prehistory of northern and western Europe. Lasting structures of various kinds – from walled enclosures to passage graves; from alignments to rings of monoliths – came to dominate the landscape. The use of chambered tombs had a lengthy history, but in most regions monumental houses with Neolithic antecedents went out of use by the end of the 3rd millennium BC (Bradley 2021). The use of timber became less significant than the extraction and deployment of stone. These materials had different properties.

Settlements built of stone

A new study of the Late Neolithic and Early Bronze Age identifies some widespread patterns. In geographical terms the first stone houses are mainly a feature of the Mediterranean, the Iberian Peninsula, and parts of the Atlantic coast. These buildings were generally oval or circular in plan, and a few were approximately boat shaped. Further inland towards the north and east, domestic dwellings were generally constructed of timber and some of them attained greater proportions. In this case they adhered to a rectilinear ground plan (Lemercier & Strahm 2018; Risch *et al.* 2022). The histories of both architectural traditions could have overlapped with those of the last chambered tombs in parts of the western Mediterranean. Although the field evidence is incomplete, it seems as if the proportion of stone houses increased between the last centuries of the Neolithic period and the beginning of the Bronze Age. During that time a major development was the appearance of Bell Beakers (A. Gibson 2019).

In southern France and the Iberian Peninsula, the building of walled enclosures echoes this basic trend and was under way by 3000 BC. They were usually associated with the adoption of stone houses. Individual examples feature towers, bastions, and impressive gateways, and some of these places provide evidence of craft production (Lilios 2020, 201–10). The distribution of domestic structures could extend well outside the defences, as it did at the Portuguese site of Zambujal (Kunst 2017).

Another informative anomaly

These new developments are typified by the well-known group of megalithic monuments at Los Millares in south-east Spain which combines roundhouses with a cemetery of passage graves (Fig. 3.7). Both were associated with considerable walled enclosures. Their ground plans had important features in common. The dwellings and the chambered tombs were of similar proportions, and both were constructed of stone. A system of outlying forts shared their circular outlines. The entire complex was dated to the Copper Age (Lilios 2020, 204–7).

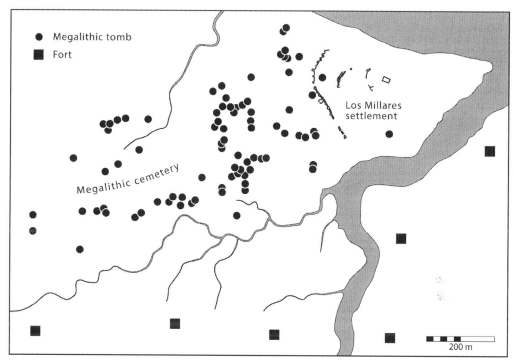

Fig. 3.7. The relationship between Los Millares, nearby stone forts, and megalithic tombs. Information from Aranda Jiménez et al. (2020).

Like the structures in Orkney considered earlier, their chronology has been revised. The results were studied by Bayesian statistics and provided unexpected results (Aranda Jiménez *et al.* 2020). In fact, the distinctive chambered tombs were significantly older than either the enclosures or the houses, both of which belonged to a subsequent phase. The only pairing between these elements was if individual passage graves were reused during a later period. According to the most recent analysis of Los Millares:

> Mortuary practices preceded the first evidence of housing activity by up to 230 years. It seems that the location of the settlement could have been determined by the very special symbolic and sacred significance of the site (Aranda Jiménez *et al.* 2020, 14).

In these cases, roundhouses constructed of stone were not the counterparts of chambered tombs. If anything, it was those passage graves that provided the inspiration for domestic architecture. That was rather like the treatment of allées couvertes in western France.

Subsequent developments

It was in the Bronze Age of the western Mediterranean that stone architecture became a dominant feature. It happened on the mainland of southern Europe and on several islands – the Balearics, Sardinia, and Corsica – which developed their own kinds of monuments. Now most of them were settlements (Kolb 2005). They took a wide range of different forms – *motillas*, *torres*, *talayots*, and *nuraghi* – but during the 2nd millennium BC they had no equivalents anywhere in western or northern Europe.

The interplay between wood and stone remained important in the study area. Perhaps the clearest demonstration comes from Late Neolithic / Copper Age complexes in Britain and Ireland where rings of posts echoing the form of a roundhouse were replaced on certain sites by stone settings. The sequence was not as widespread as commonly supposed, but where it happened it usually took the same course. It seems possible that around 2500 BC the timber monuments at Woodhenge and Durrington Walls were linked to the megalithic structure at Stonehenge. In the light of this discussion, it comes as no surprise that Durrrington was used comparatively briefly – for little over fifty years during the Late Neolithic period – while Stonehenge retained its significance well into the Early Bronze Age (Parker Pearson *et al.* 2023).

As this chapter has shown, the relationships between timber and stone took different forms, but almost all of them have implications for changing attitudes to time.

Chapter 4

Closing and opening

Interior spaces

The previous chapter began with an account of four chambered tombs and their relationship with Neolithic houses. The same monuments introduce another issue. How long did they remain accessible after their construction? The question extends to other prehistoric structures and depends on an important distinction between buildings that *ended* the use of a particular location, and those which *provided the starting point* for future developments.

Chambered tombs illustrate each kind of sequence, and the examples considered earlier illustrate both possibilities. The example at Rastorf contained a stone chamber which would have been inaccessible after it was built (Steffens 2009). That remained the case when the monument was extended. Les Fouillages was built over another settlement, but in this case only one of the chambers was out of reach: 'A subrectangular cairn of tightly-packed boulders ... enclosed a small domed cist with a single capstone ... [It was] covered by the primary mound' (Kinnes 1982, 26).

On the other hand, the same mound had two chambers which could have been used for longer. There were: 'An unroofed double chamber reinforced by drystone walling ... [and] a small slab-built chamber with three capstones ... [They] remained *open and accessible after mound construction*' (Kinnes 1982, 26, my emphasis).

The tombs at Ballyglass were simple structures and shared many elements in common. One of them had a forecourt, leading into an open enclosure and two stone chambers. The other had its entrance in the side wall. It led to a slightly larger court, with pairs of chambers situated at either end. All these features would have remained accessible after the monuments were constructed (O´Nualláin 1972 & 1998).

The chambered tomb at Trefignath illustrates another variation, for the position of the entrance changed twice as it was rebuilt. It was initially a circular cairn with a single chamber reached along a passage leading from the north. In a later phase it was encapsulated in an elongated cairn with a concave forecourt to its east. Now it had a new entrance and a further chamber, but it is not clear whether the interior of the previous structure remained open. Finally, the cairn was extended again. Its forecourt was replaced, and yet another chamber was built (C. Smith & F. Lynch 1987).

That contrast between accessible and inaccessible chambers plays a crucial role in a new study of megalithic architecture. Schulz Paulsson (2017) provides a Bayesian analysis of the dates associated with the first stone tombs in western and southern Europe. (Those in Scandinavia were later constructions and for that reason they play a smaller part in her study; so do their counterparts in Britain and Ireland.) She argues that the oldest examples were in north-west France, but the same concept was adopted in other regions along the Atlantic and Mediterranean seaboards. The process may have been influenced by maritime contacts. They are illustrated by the distribution of axes made of Alpine jadeitite (Pétrequin *et al.* 2012), and that of Spanish variscite jewellery (Herbaud & Quarré 2004).

Her results cut across the fine detail provided by earlier studies which focused on regional styles of architecture and their parallels in other areas. They transcend the established classification of these structures which emphasised the shapes of the mounds or cairns and the organisation of the chambers within them. She identifies a sequence that applies to all the regions with satisfactory dating evidence. Developments were by no means simultaneous, but they followed a similar course for three hundred years or more. There were two basic configurations which echo the examples considered here. They extend across the entire distribution of early chambered cairns. Schulz Paulsson emphasises a key distinction between inaccessible tombs which were constructed at the beginning of each local sequence, and more accessible tombs which were a subsequent development. Her findings have important implications for the use of megalithic architecture.

Closed chambers or cists could be erected on the ground surface or dug into the bedrock. They lacked an entrance and, when they were sealed by a barrow or cairn, they were completely cut off from the living – in effect *they were assigned to the past*. The best examples are found in north-west France where they date from the Early Neolithic period. One was sealed beneath the Tumulus de Saint-Michel at Carnac and others have been investigated more recently (Schulz Paulsson 2017, 36–47).

From the 19th century the distinction between gallery graves and passage graves played an important part in discussions of Neolithic architecture, but both types shared an important feature. Their chambers remained accessible and structurally sound after they were built, and they could have been utilised for a considerable time. Thus, they existed in the present but might also have been *directed towards a future*. This is apparent from the deposits found within them. It was after a significant interval that some of their entrances were blocked.

Closing

If the construction of certain monuments ended the histories of particular sites, that development was not limited to stone tombs. The point has a wider application. It is obvious that it applied to other elements, including some of the most conspicuous features anywhere in the prehistoric landscape. This section continues the account of mortuary monuments, but extends to earthwork enclosures, stone circles, and henges. Nor are these ideas restricted to Neolithic archaeology, as some of the structures date from the Copper Age and Early Bronze Age.

Earthen long barrows in Britain and Denmark

These impressive monuments provide the first example. As Torsten Madsen showed in 1979, they share almost the same structural elements on both sides of the North Sea, and their dates overlap although they are not the same (Rassmann 2011). The Scandinavian examples are usually rectangular or trapezoidal and can be flanked by side ditches. Some are bounded by wooden palisades and have a timber facade at one end. Several mounds were constructed within a series of rectilinear bays, separated from one another by fences; and among the features associated with special artefacts and human remains there are pairs of massive sockets that must have held complete or split tree trunks. Nearly all the features identified by Madsen are shared with British examples, of which the well-preserved site at Haddenham in eastern England provides the best example (Evans & Hodder 2005; Noble 2017). Here human bones were inside a chamber formed from a dismantled oak tree.

It is tempting to compare these wooden elements with their counterparts in megalithic tombs, and at one time that was the usual procedure: the differences between these structures were explained by the availability of building material. Ian Kinnes wrote about their wooden 'chambers' or 'mortuary houses', forecourts, and facades (Kinnes 1992). But there are other ways of thinking about these features. More recent work has shown that all the elements of which long barrows were composed can also be found on their own – that was the case on both sides of the water (Bradley 2019, 56–62). Moreover, the sites adopted by long barrows had already been used in many ways. Before these mounds were built there were rectilinear enclosures, middens, pits, scatters of artefacts, cultivated plots, and even wooden houses (Fig. 4.1), but none of these elements is particularly common and some of them date from significantly earlier phases than the mounds themselves. There was enormous diversity – from places with lengthy histories to the choice of entirely new locations (Bradley 2020a). The only feature that connects them is the presence of a covering barrow (or cairn) that takes the same basic form. In their final incarnation places which had little in common before they were built came to resemble one another and conformed to a single 'type'. After that stage, activity came to an end and similar monuments were constructed somewhere else. They shared their distinctive forms and were the same size. Some of those in southern England resembled one another over a period of at least three hundred years, between about

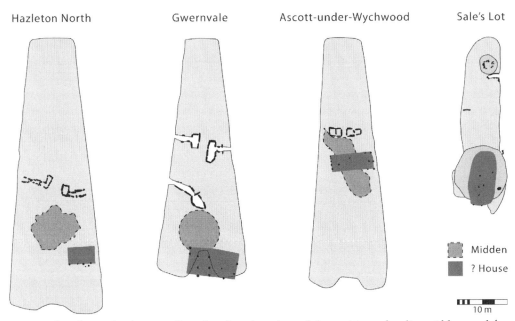

Fig. 4.1. The relationship between four chambered tombs and the positions of earlier middens and / or houses. Information from Britnell and Whittle (2022) and Darvill (1996).

3800 and 3500 BC. Although they had so many features in common, they were built at different times. Detailed studies, employing Bayesian statistics, show that some of these constructions were very short-lived, while others were used for longer periods (Bayliss & Whittle 2007). Estimates from the few sites analysed by this method extend from one human generation in the first long barrow at Wayland's Smithy to seven or eight at Fussell's Lodge. Both were in central-southern England. Excavation has shown that mounds and post settings could be extended or rebuilt, and in one case an oval mound with a wooden mortuary house was replaced by an accessible megalithic tomb.

In Britain and southern Scandinavia this information presents a paradox. Barrows of remarkably similar kinds were built in places whose previous histories had little in common. At the same time, they combined several elements that can be identified in isolation or in other contexts. There is little to suggest that they were built according to a single blueprint. Analyses of how they were constructed suggest that the work involved some improvisation (McFadyen 2007; Richards 2013). Once a monument achieved its final state, it could be abandoned, left to decay, or even set on fire. If these places were reused, as occasionally happened, it took place after an interval. There is nothing to suggest that a single process resulted in the construction of these mounds. The same result was achieved along many different routes. Rather than creating a lasting structure that might have served future generations, the builders *brought the use of these locations to an end.* The construction of the monuments did not open a new chapter in the development of particular places. Instead, their histories were over.

Henges, stone circles, and palisaded enclosures in Britain

Great circular enclosures – henges, stone circles, and palisades – were constructed in Britain between about 3000 BC and the Early Bronze Age a millennium later (Bradley 2019, 115–24). They have been investigated for many years, but it is easier to study them in plan than it is to work out the development of individual sites. Much depends on the availability of samples for dating, and they are more common with timber structures affected by fire than with settings of monoliths where charcoal is rarely found in suitable contexts. There is a further problem that the stone settings produce comparatively few artefacts, apart from those associated with secondary burials. It means that any new information must come from the sequences defined by excavation.

Accounts of these monuments have features in common with traditional interpretations of long barrows. They can group their features together to devise an overall classification (Catherall 1971). But just as the uniform appearance of long barrows concealed the various processes by which they reached their final form, it could be wrong to assume that the perimeters of stone and earthwork enclosures were integrally linked with the features in the interior. For many years there was a tendency – not always stated explicitly – to treat all these elements together and to compare the external banks of henges with those of Roman amphitheatres. Perhaps an audience would watch events happening inside an arena. But it would have done so from a distance since the internal space was bounded by a ditch.

That approach assumed that the perimeters of henges were contemporary with the features within them. New research suggests otherwise (A. Gibson 2010; Bradley 2011). Again, there are signs of considerable diversity. No doubt some henges did enclose places where ceremonies were performed, but it is not certain that this was usual. Instead, fieldwork has identified examples where the earthwork perimeter was a subsequent development. It overlay the positions of older features or impinged on settings of posts or standing stones that were already there. Moreover, there are several cases in which radiocarbon samples obtained beneath the banks of henges are later than those from other components of the same sites. Perhaps some structures were cut off from the surrounding area at a late stage in their histories. It might have happened as they went out of use and could have been intended to protect their special character. Like the long barrows considered in this chapter, the construction of the banks and ditches brought activities there to a close, and the monuments were largely abandoned.

It is more difficult to take the same approach to stone circles where there is less dating evidence, but excavation at sites in northern Britain documents a similar sequence. Structural evidence shows that in some cases the rubble enclosures known as ring cairns were enclosed by circles of monoliths during a subsequent phase (Bradley 2005). It also occurred at chambered tombs. In the case of Clava passage

Fig. 4.2. The north-east passage grave at Balnuaran of Clava. Photograph: Aaron Watson.

graves in northern Scotland it happened when access to their entrances was restricted or closed (Fig. 4.2; Bradley 2000a). Among a neighbouring group of structures, a ring of standing stones surrounded an existing cairn, and a massive recumbent stone blocked access to the site (Bradley 2005). This development brought the sequence to an end and these places were closed, if only for a while. These sites are considered in more detail in Chapter Five.

It is commonly supposed that special monuments were defined by earthworks or rings of standing stones, but fieldwork and aerial survey over the last two decades have identified a series of palisaded enclosures in Britain and Ireland. They were of similar date. In some regions they may have been the local equivalents of henges, and in certain instances, for example at the Scottish site of Forteviot, they contained small examples within their circuit (Brophy & Noble 2020). Elsewhere they could be older than the earthwork, as happened at Durrington Walls (Parker Pearson *et al.* 2023); alternatively, they might have been a later addition, which was the case at Mount Pleasant (Greaney *et al.* 2020). There were sites where the timbers were allowed to rot in the ground, and others where they were burnt. At that point their histories came to an end.

Closing or opening?

Linearbandkeramik (LBK) enclosures

A key site in the identification of LBK settlements is Köln Lindenthal which was excavated before the Second World War (Bernhardt 1986). It became famous because it was one of the first places where the post holes of longhouses were exposed across a large area, although the investigators concluded that these features marked the sites of barns and that the borrow pits beside them were the actual dwellings. The confusion was soon resolved, but it drew attention away from another characteristic of the same site: the presence of two conjoined enclosures defined by ditches and palisades. Other examples have been identified more recently.

It was natural to suppose that each enclosure at Köln Lindenthal bounded a group of buildings, but a reinterpretation of the sequence raises another possibility. It began with the establishment of an open settlement. The earthworks appeared after the first houses on the site had already gone out of use. These enclosures were a late development. In some phases they did surround domestic buildings, but at other times their interiors were empty, and the ditches bounded an open space where the longhouses had been abandoned (Bernhardt 1986; Bradley 1998).

There are various ways of accounting for these developments. There are signs of conflict towards the end of the LBK and the ditches could have provided simple defences (Meyer *et al.* 2018). But there is another possibility. Perhaps the construction of these enclosures marked the end of a period of settlement and could even have commemorated its existence. Similar sequences can be recognised at other LBK sites where an earthwork contained the same area of land as a group of older longhouses. In some cases, apparently empty enclosures were near the positions of former villages. Like the long mounds considered earlier, it suggests that those locations were 'closed'.

Opening

Causewayed enclosures
The building of other enclosures marked a development that was to last a considerable time. After the LBK, ditched enclosures – especially those with segmented or 'causewayed' ditches – became a widespread feature. They are best represented in regions and phases during which settlements were composed of slighter structures; others are represented by scatters of artefacts and pits and lack convincing house plans. To some extent these earthwork enclosures *replaced* the villages inhabited in the past. During early phases groups of longhouses had provided a focus of social life. As settlement became more dispersed and probably more mobile, monuments of this kind may have played a similar role.

The causewayed enclosures were stereotyped and extraordinarily long lived (N. Andersen 1997). Eventually their distribution reached as far north as Scandinavia and as far west as Ireland (Müller 2017; Whittle 2018, 25–34.). There were notable concentrations in northern France and lowland England. Their chronology was extended too and reached from the 5th millennium BC to the 4th. They retained the same basic layout from first to last: most were curvilinear and were defined by discontinuous ditches (Fig. 4.3). Some were accompanied by palisades and others had complex entrances, but over this enormous period the similarities outweighed the differences between them. A common interpretation is that they were built by groups

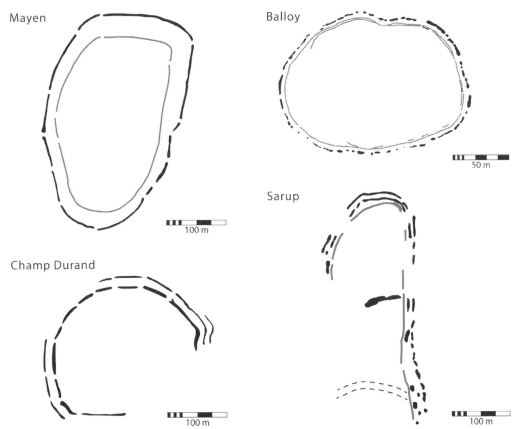

Fig. 4.3. Outline plans of four Continental causewayed enclosures. Information from N. Andersen (1997).

of workers drawn from a wider area whose separate contributions were distinguished in the form of the earthwork.

They conformed to distinct regional groups, each with its own chronology (Müller 2017). Despite the features shared between these structures, those in different areas were built at different times. Thus, the earliest examples were in northern Germany and northern France. The British examples followed, and their counterparts in Denmark and the west of France were among the latest of all. It is not obvious how rapidly such enclosures were adopted, but a programme of radiocarbon dating shows that in England most of them were built during the 37th century BC. Nor is it clear how long they remained important, and that project demonstrated that individual examples in Britain were used for a little as twenty-five years or as long as three centuries (Whittle *et al.* 2011; Whittle *et al.* 2022).

Although most of these monuments adhered to the same stereotyped layout, they soon took on a life of their own and were utilised in many different ways. The structural evidence is extremely varied. Some of the earlier examples on the Continent contained groups of houses, but later earthworks could enclose empty spaces. A few assumed defensible proportions. There is evidence that occasional examples were attacked and that people there were killed (Meyer *et al.* 2018).

Causewayed enclosures were sometimes associated with long barrows and contained other deposits of human bones. They included the bodies of animals, the residues of feasts, and deposits of non-local artefacts which had been taken out of circulation and buried there. Some sites contained very few objects and could have been used for short periods. Others were reconstructed and enlarged as new earthworks were added to the original circuit until they assumed enormous proportions. There was immense variety. Some could be completely isolated, but others were constructed in pairs; the artefacts associated with them show certain contrasts and these places may have had separate histories, as happened at Hambledon Hill (Mercer & Healy 2008, table 11.5). Superficially similar monuments were employed in different ways.

Such developments pose a problem. Almost all the structures conformed to the same distinctive template, yet the regional groups of causewayed enclosures across Europe date from distinct phases, and individual examples were maintained for very different lengths of time. They were also employed in particular ways and on contrasting scales. As a result, there was virtually a continuum from enclosed settlements to hillforts, and from small informal sanctuaries to elaborate ceremonial centres. Yet all of them shared the same outward form.

There is an obvious contrast with the development of long barrows. Again, they were of similar types. They were erected in locations that had gone through different histories, and it was only the erection of a mound that created any kind of uniformity. At that point the use of most sites ended, and they were closed. Causewayed enclosures followed the opposite trajectory. They might have had a common starting point – the excavation of a causewayed ditch around an open space – but from that point onwards their histories diverged. Groups of enclosures might have been built at about the same time, but certain monuments were soon abandoned while others were enlarged. Many hosted occasional gatherings, and they could act as cemeteries, settlements, or even defended strongholds. It remained important that their perimeters should adhere to the distinctive form that was shared across large parts of western and northern Europe. Their configurations kept their significance for hundreds of years. If the building of a long barrow to a widely accepted plan 'closed' the use of a particular locale, the construction of causewayed enclosures 'opened' a new range of possibilities.

Linear structures in Britain and France
Some of the same issues arise with a series of linear monuments: alignments of standing stones in Brittany, and cursuses in Scotland and England.

The Carnac stone alignments
The stone rows in north-west France may have originated at the beginning of the Neolithic period (Fig. 4.4; Cassen 2009). It is difficult to establish their chronological

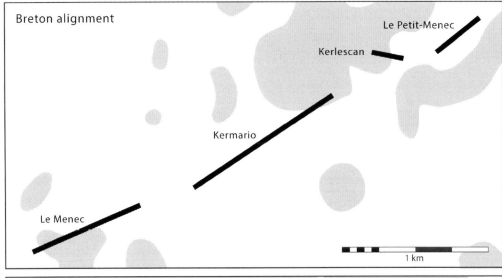

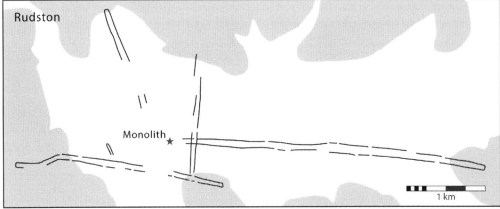

Fig. 4.4. *Two groups of Neolithic linear monuments: stone alignments in the Carnac complex, and cursus monuments around Rudston. Information from Burl (1993) and Loveday (2006).*

contexts with any precision, but in at least two cases their relationship with other monuments is informative (Scarre 2011, 117–30). In the great complex at Carnac, excavation found that the Kermario alignment crossed an existing long barrow. It followed the same orientation and even incorporated a decorated monolith that formed part of the original structure. At the same time its axis echoed that of similar mounds in the vicinity. Two alignments of standing stones – Kerlescan and Ménec West – led to the megalithic enclosures sometimes described as cromlechs; one was approximately square in plan and abutted another long barrow. The rows of standing stones might have guided visitors to their entrances, but the initial construction of these alignments seems to have provided the stimulus for a more sustained period of building. In both cases the oldest files of menhirs were incorporated in a more elaborate design. Eventually they extended over a greater distance, and the original rows of monoliths were supplemented by others (Burl 1993, 131–46). The process seems to have developed a momentum of its own. Short sections of standing stones of similar proportions appear to have been erected together; sometimes they departed from the axis of the monument and impinged on the positions of those that were already there. Perhaps separate groups of people participated in the construction but worked on these sites at different times.

This process must have changed its character as the sheer scale of the enterprise eclipsed the original conception. In the end, individual lines of menhirs extended past the enclosures that had been their original destinations. The basic design was obscured by the growth of the project and the size of the operation.

Timber and earthwork cursus monuments
Similar monuments have not been recognised in Neolithic Britain, but the post and earthwork alignments described by the term *cursus* raise some of the same issues. Like the initial construction of causewayed enclosures, they inaugurated a series of new developments. They took two main forms. There was an important distinction between the earlier examples which were mostly in Scotland, and their successors whose distribution extended to England and Wales (Thomas 2006; Brophy 2016).

They were of two distinctive kinds. Unlike the Breton alignments, these monuments consisted of elongated rectangular enclosures with terminals blocking both ends. Their lengths extended from about 100 m to several km, and they could be constructed singly or as parts of a larger complex in which several of them occurred together. They might run parallel to one another, and individual examples were lengthened in each direction. Occasionally they cut across one another (Loveday 2006). The earlier examples were constructed of wood, although they might also have been defined by rows of pits (Millican 2016). The later cursuses were earthworks. The first were built by about 3700 BC and the last were constructed up to four centuries afterwards.

They are related to other structures. In many cases cursuses are defined by an internal bank and an external ditch, but a few examples enclose an elongated mound extending down the centre. The clearest example is Cleaven Dyke which seems to have begun as a long barrow of the kind considered earlier (G. Barclay & Maxwell 1998). Others are related to similar monuments. Cursuses can be aligned on burial mounds and may even incorporate them in their paths (Barrett *et al.* 1991, 47–51). In most cases their distribution avoided that of causewayed enclosures, but there are two sites in eastern England where they cut across earthworks of this kind (Bradley 2019, 79–80). It would be wrong to extend this sequence too far, for the earliest dated examples in Scotland were contemporary with the building of such enclosures in England and Wales (Thomas 2006). Unlike those sites, cursuses are seldom associated with artefacts, although there have been finds of human remains.

The first cursuses were constructed of wood and were commonly set on fire, although they could be replaced by similar structures on the same sites or by other ones nearby. It was during a secondary phase that individual examples were replaced by earthworks (Thomas 2006). Unlike their wooden precursors, they do not seem to have been levelled and could have remained intact for long periods.

Such earthworks have a wider distribution than their predecessors. In common with the earlier monuments, they can be found in groups, but in this case they include some of the largest constructions of this kind. At Rudston in north-east England there were five examples whose distribution focused on the tallest prehistoric monolith in Britain (Fig. 4.4). Taken together, they ran for ten kilometres. The Dorset Cursus was formed of two such enclosures built end-to-end; their final form achieved the same length (Bradley 2019, 73). Radiocarbon dating shows that it was one of the last to be built. Several earthwork cursuses, for instance the Dorset Cursus and that at Dorchester on Thames, were orientated on the solstices and might have been employed from year to year.

They remained prominent features in the landscape long after they were built and provided a point of origin for larger groups of monuments whose chronology extended into the Late Neolithic, Chalcolithic, and Early Bronze Age periods. They included a few henges and stone circles like those considered earlier. The reuse of these structures will be considered in Chapter Six; at this point it is enough to say that the creation of a cursus complex became the starting point for extended local sequences in the way that had happened with causewayed enclosures. But that did not apply to their timber counterparts whose histories were more like those of earthen long barrows. The contrasts between these developments are considered in the following section.

The life histories of early monuments

Many features, both physical and social, would have influenced the histories of individual sites.

The simplest were practical considerations. How easy was it to build them? How many people were involved, and were they drawn from an extensive area? How long would the construction of a particular monument have taken? How were the labour forces organised on the ground? How were they sustained while the work was taking place, and where did they obtain the raw material? After the task was complete, how long was any structure expected to remain unchanged?

These are among the most difficult questions to answer, and in many cases the crucial information may not survive. There are a few estimates for the labour invested in monument building (Startin & Bradley 1981). They extend from about 10,000 worker hours for a long barrow and 50,000 for an average causewayed enclosure, to 500,000 for the earthworks of the largest henges in southern England. Some made extraordinary demands: half a million worker hours for the enclosure complex on Hambledon Hill (Mercer & Healy 2008, 748–53), and a similar estimate for the Dorset Cursus (Barrett *et al.* 1991, 45–6). It is harder to calculate the sizes of the teams who participated in the work. Perhaps they were organised in small groups. That would explain several puzzling features: the obvious subdivisions in the enclosure ditches; the small internal bays within the fabric of long barrows and long cairns; and the separate sections of standing stones that contributed to the Carnac alignments. There is nothing to indicate how long any of the tasks would have taken, or whether they were accomplished continuously or episodically. It is seldom obvious where the building materials were found. Quarries have been identified close to chambered cairns and other structures, but some of the stone may have been brought over greater distances (Richards 2013). The most compelling evidence comes from Carnac where monoliths were obtained from the bedrock in the same place (Mens 2008); their erection was not especially demanding. The large collections of meat bones found at some of the sites – both enclosures and henges – are usually regarded as evidence of public events, but they could also be the remains of feasts intended to sustain a labour force (Hayden 2014). Isotopic analysis can shed light on where the animals were raised (Craig *et al.* 2015; Madgwick *et al.* 2019).

The decision to build a timber enclosure rather than a bank and ditch has a more obvious implication, since the people who did so must have known that it would have a limited lifespan. That may be why such structures were replaced nearby. It follows that, unlike a conspicuous earthwork, such monuments were not meant to remain intact for very long. That is even more obvious where they were set on fire. Although it can never be established that this was the intended outcome, the same had happened at a number of barrows and houses built during an earlier phase (Noble 2006; Brophy & Millican 2015). While the plans of timber cursuses were related to those of earthworks, their histories must have been quite different. The same applies to the relationship between palisades and henges. When the earthworks were abandoned, they would have retained their original configuration, and their positions could be identified on the ground long afterwards. On the other hand, the locations of palisaded enclosures would eventually be lost. The choice of raw materials provides additional information on ancient notions of a future.

There were important differences between the processes considered here: closing older monuments (or sites) and creating new ones. They have often been confused because in many cases they left similar traces behind. It is only when their histories are investigated in detail that the distinction becomes clear. The best way of making the point is to consider how particular sequences were expected to unfold. For the people who built one kind of structure the future was preordained. They would have known how the history of a specific place would unfold and perhaps the stages that it would follow from its creation to its final dissolution. They would have been aware of the time it took for posts or palisades to decay – how long could the timber settings associated with long barrows retain their structural stability, and what was the maximum lifespan of a cursus built of wood? There were natural processes that would have been familiar from daily life, but there were more dramatic ways of bringing the use of particular locations to an end. The most obvious was fire. It meant that the closing of certain structures could be a spectacular event. Even the histories of stone circles might have followed a prescribed course from their initial construction to the moment when they were closed, and the cessation of activities there might have been almost as dramatic – in north-east Scotland their entrances were closed by manoeuvring enormous stones (Bradley 2005). People would have known that very similar sequences would be played out at comparable sites in the future.

By contrast, the histories of other monuments – which were not necessarily any larger or more impressive – were open-ended. At the outset they were built according to the widely shared templates that allow them to be recognised as diagnostic 'types', but their trajectories diverged over time and space so that individual examples might be used in a variety of ways. Their futures were difficult or impossible for people to envisage, and certain of these structures were remarkably long-lived. Their roles might have changed so completely that their original purpose was obscured. That is why the sequences established by field archaeology can be so revealing.

Chapter 5

Time and the sky

Celestial mechanics

The previous chapter discussed the temporality of prehistoric monuments in different parts of Europe and the ways in which the people who constructed them might have foreseen them developing in the future. Some buildings brought the use of a particular place to a conclusion. Others initiated a history that was unpredictable and open ended. From the outset the currencies of these structures were determined by human agency. Other factors would eventually play a part, but, as Chapter Three has shown, the choice of building material and the effects of natural decay exerted a particular influence.

The people who erected monuments would have been aware of various ways of experiencing time. They involved elements that were outside their control, including the life expectancies of individual people, and the lengths of human generations which could never be estimated accurately. There were cyclical processes too, and they affected the human body. Local environments changed as well. There were seasonal variations of weather, temperature, and light, and in the growth and decay of vegetation. They were not the same between different places, and it would have been impossible to predict them exactly.

At the same time there were visible processes that did follow regular cycles, even if their workings were hard to explain without the methods of modern science. They were most obviously illustrated by the movements of the sun and moon which allowed time to be segmented into consistent units. It could be subdivided into days and nights, months, and years. The contrast between midwinter and midsummer was particularly obvious because the sun changed its course at the solstices. As these elements followed a regular tempo, they must have influenced human notions of time. Recognisable developments could be related to those that were important for farmers, hunters, and fishers, including the growing and ripening of crops, the supply of winter fodder, rising and falling tides, and the availability of wild animals as prey.

Did ancient monuments reflect these concerns? And did these buildings play any practical roles, or were their purposes more arcane? These questions have been considered by field archaeologists for more than a hundred years (Ruggles 1999). Not surprisingly, interpretations have varied, and some of the dominant themes have reflected the professional expertise of the people who first discussed them. That was particularly true of a group of early researchers who investigated the relationship between monuments and the sky. Sir Norman Lockyer was the Astronomer Royal, Henry Boyle Somerville undertook surveys for the British Admiralty, and, more recently, Alexander Thom was a professor of engineering. They were skilled in precise observation and accurate measurement. It is not surprising that they thought that the people who erected chambered tombs, standing stones, and circles of various kinds shared the same concerns (MacKie 1977).

At one time there was a danger of confusing the metrical accuracy of the surveys on which modern studies depend with equally sophisticated observations of the sky during the prehistoric period. This approach was epitomised by Euan MacKie's book *Science and Society in Prehistoric Britain* published in 1977. Inspired by the work of Alexander Thom (1967), he suggested that certain people had special skills in surveying and observations of the heavens. Like Thom's' theories, his interpretation was controversial, but forty years later it was restated, largely unchanged, in MacKie's last, posthumously published book (MacKie 2022). Although he was no longer satisfied with his original conception of 'science', his analyses of a series of ancient sites remained the same.

A common element in many discussions of 'prehistoric astronomy' has been the practical task of identifying and recording the alignments of individual structures. In some cases, it does not present any problem. For example, a chambered tomb with a lengthy passage like that at Maeshowe has an obvious orientation (Downes 2020); so does a monument like Newgrange with its roof box that admits the sunlight (M. O'Kelly 1982). But others are more fragmentary or were less carefully constructed. Michael Hoskin (2001) found this problem in working out the alignments of chambered cairns in southern Europe and provided a frank discussion of the difficulties of studying them – it is possible that some of them were never meant to have exact orientations. Another problem arises in the case of stone rows like those in Scotland, Ireland, and Brittany. Should the putative alignment pass between the centres of the monoliths, or ought it to follow one of their edges? If so, which side of the stone should feature in the analysis? Accounts of these structures can be revealing. The settings may be imprecise, but these studies treat them as if the uprights were like the slender ranging poles used to plan them in the field. Sometimes the precision achieved by modern research is at odds with the vagaries of the original design. In such cases it is vital to distinguish between *exact alignments*, which were real but comparatively rare (Ruggles 1984), and constructions that indicate no more than *a general direction*. They are separate phenomena and should not be confused with one another.

Then there is a second question to consider. Thom, and some of the scholars influenced by his work, considered that monuments could be used to predict celestial events. In that sense they acted like a calendar (Thom 1967, 107–17). But there was a fundamental problem with his approach. It is true that certain structures did conform to precise alignments – the most convincing were those on the sunrise and sunset – but that information must have been known before they could be built. Otherwise, it would have been impossible to design them. It follows that their creation might have *celebrated* celestial events but could never have been a way of establishing when and where they would occur. There is a risk of imposing contemporary procedures on the concerns of people in the past.

Recent fieldwork in Scotland suggests an alternative explanation. Here certain monuments emphasised orientations that had already been recognised and treated as significant. There are two especially clear examples. The greatest concentration of Neolithic stone and earthwork buildings on the Mainland of Orkney was around the natural isthmus at Stenness (Edmonds 2019). It was in line with the setting sun which crossed its path six weeks before and after the solstice. People who had observed this during their daily lives might have emphasised the relationship in architectural form. It could have influenced the layout of the nearby passage grave of Maeshowe (Fig. 5.1; Richards 2013; Downes 2020; D. Scott & McHardy 2020, 66). In the same way, at Croftmoraig a glacial mound with a prominent erratic embedded in its surface commanded a spectacular view of the midsummer sunset behind a local mountain, Schiehallion. In Scottish folklore its peak is the exact centre of the country. During the Early Bronze Age, the mound was reshaped, and this distinctive rock was enclosed by a series of stone and timber settings (Bradley 2016 a & b).

There was a different kind of sequence at Stonehenge where the original monument consisted of a circular bank and ditch with two entrances, one to the northeast and the other to the south. The north-eastern entrance faced in the general direction of the midsummer sunrise, but, if that was the intention, it was misaligned by about five degrees (Pollard & Ruggles 2001). The situation changed when the central setting of sarsens was erected and at this stage that entrance was rebuilt and the other was closed. Only now did the main stone structure adopt a strict orientation on the summer and winter solstices: its well-known axis was established in a secondary phase. Until that stage the course of periglacial gullies visible in the local landscape may have provided the clearest indication of where the sun would appear on the longest day of the year (Parker Pearson *et al.* 2020, 413–14). Developments at the site provide the clearest illustration of the important contrast between *directions* that were significant and more precise *alignments*.

Finally, there is a fundamental difference between buildings that allowed people to view celestial events from a distance, for example by sighting along a stone row, and those that were illuminated by light coming from outside; megalithic tombs

Fig. 5.1. The entrance passage inside the megalithic tomb of Maeshowe. Photograph: Aaron Watson.

provide the obvious example. All too often this distinction has been overlooked, so that observations made by looking down an alignment of monoliths are considered in the same terms as the orientation of a passage grave. At Newgrange the remains of the dead were illuminated by the midwinter sunrise (M. O'Kelly 1982). The sun played an active role in this relationship and there need not have been a living audience.

There is another way of considering this information. Monuments of different kinds have been recorded accurately, whether or not the researchers were concerned with astronomy. In the case of mounds, cairns, and stone circles there is evidence that certain directions were important in the past, and many studies have shown how their layout might have been influenced by the solar cycle. This chapter considers structures whose layout might have been influenced by the rising sun, then it discusses the relationship between the setting sun and another group of buildings. In addition, a few examples were aligned on both events. Such cases are comparatively rare, but the best-known example is Stonehenge (Pollard & Ruggles 2001).

Less is said about the lunar cycle, although it would have been important. It has been considered by researchers like Alexander Thom (1967), Clive Ruggles (1999), Lionel Sims (2006), Douglas Scott, and Stuart McHardy (2020). The following sections discuss only the commonest element in accounts of the prehistoric sky: the changing position of the sun over the course of the year. But there were other processes that are not considered here. They include the monthly changes in the appearance of the moon, and more subtle variations in its passage across the sky over periods of almost two decades. Conspicuous galaxies may have been significant, too. No doubt they were observed, but these features may have not been so closely related to ancient conceptions of time.

The rising sun

Most studies of chambered tombs in Neolithic Europe document a concern with the eastern part of the sky (Scarre 2020). It seems as if the entrances to many of these monuments – whatever their actual forms – were directed towards the sunrise or, more often, the position of the sun in the morning sky. Some obvious exceptions are discussed later.

The relationship between monuments and the rising sun takes many forms, but this point is not always appreciated in accounts of 'prehistoric astronomy'. Long mounds or long cairns were often directed towards the east or southeast. The same can be true of their entrances, but there are cases in which access to the interior was through a portal located in the side of the earthwork rather than its eastern end. That is not the only problem. In cairns of different forms, the internal chambers could extend at right angles to the passage, as commonly happened in north-west France (L'Helgouach 1965) and southern Scandinavia (Midgley 2008), meaning that sunlight would not have reached the parts associated with human remains. Indeed, the forms of certain structures may have been meant to emphasise the distinction between a section towards the entrance illuminated by the sun, and areas that remained in darkness throughout the year (Bradley 1989). It might be here that the dead were buried, in which case they were entirely separate from the world outside the tomb.

Most studies have been concerned with the directions faced by individual monuments, from those with precise solar alignments to others with less exact orientations. The results of individual studies are often combined to provide a general picture of the relationship between different buildings and the position of the sun. In the Iberian Peninsula, western and central France, Britain, and Ireland, they illustrate a concern with the eastern sky (L'Helgouach 1965; Ruggles 1999; Hoskin 2001; D. Scott 2016). The same pattern has been identified in northern and north-eastern Europe, between Poland, Germany, Denmark, and Sweden (González Garcia & Costa Ferrer 2006; Midgley 2008). In most cases it seems likely that sunlight was directed to the dead.

At first sight the results of these studies are compelling because there were so few regions in which western orientations were preferred. The outlines of the chambers and passages survive even where the covering structure has been damaged. That is often the case with circular cairns. But there are problems with analyses that consider the orientation of long mounds. That is because they were often recorded at separate sites distributed across an entire region. Again, the results are amalgamated to

Passy   Fleury-sur-Orne

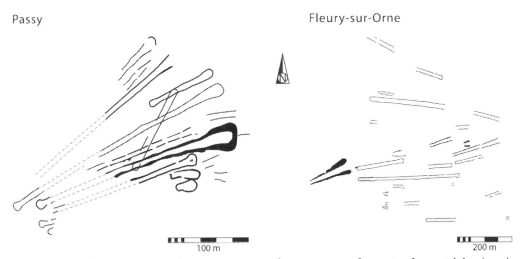

Fig. 5.2. Plans of two monumental cemeteries in northern France. Information from Midgley (2005); Chambon and A. Thomas (2010); Ghesquière et al. (2019); Chambon (2020).

provide a composite picture. But to study the original significance of long barrows it is essential to begin the analysis with individual monuments and with the *oldest* examples. There are differences of opinion among the scholars who research them, but at present it appears that the first monuments of this kind appeared during the mid-5th millennium BC in Poland (Pyzel 2020) and the Paris Basin (Chambon 2020). It is not clear whether the people who constructed these structures were in contact with one another. Their forms may have been suggested by domestic architecture in each of these regions (Fig. 5.2).

Two important points seem clear. They were first built in regions where massive timber longhouses were present or had recently gone out of use. That would account for the striking similarities between the ground plans of both groups of monuments. There is a further observation. The first long mounds *were built in groups*, and so were open enclosures with a similar footprint. For that reason, famous sites like Sarnowo in Poland, or Fleury-sur-Orne in the Paris Basin, are described as 'monumental cemeteries' (Midgley 2005). Their layout recalls the plan of a settlement, but there is an important difference between them. The monuments associated with the dead were directed towards the east, but *they did not conform to a single alignment* even within the same complex: they were organised on either side of that axis, like the ribs of a fan. At Sarnowo, for instance, their orientations extended between E, NE, and ESW. At Passy-sur-Yonne they were between E, NE, and E, and among the 20 structures at Fleury-sur-Orne they ranged from ENE to ESE. Their layout may have emphasised the direction of the rising sun, but it did not achieve the precision required by the astronomical hypothesis; maybe they were built at different times of year. This finding is even more apparent in comparison with the evidence from settlements. Whether or not longhouses had gone out of use by the time long barrows developed, all the domestic buildings conformed to a single alignment which extended from the newest dwellings to the positions of those occupied in the past.

The evidence for a direct relationship between megalithic tombs and the solar cycle is equivocal. The same applies to long mounds without stone chambers. In each instance there could have been a connection between the dead and the rising sun. This would have been most obvious during the summer months when it travelled furthest across the sky. The relationship was seldom exact, but the fortunes of the dead may have been associated with regeneration of the world after the hours of darkness. Only occasionally were individual monuments associated with particular events. They were usually midsummer and midwinter (arguments that involve the equinox are less conclusive). The structures with unambiguous celestial alignments were among the most elaborate buildings and were usually passage graves. They dominate accounts of prehistoric architecture but were exceptional. In Ireland, for instance, they account for only a fifth of the well-preserved structures of this type (Prendergast 2020).

The setting sun

Other monuments were directed towards the setting sun. They are considered in more detail as their significance is seldom appreciated. They are not found in most parts of Europe, but Hoskin (2001) showed that they were a regular feature of chambered tombs in three areas of the Mediterranean: Provence, the eastern part of Languedoc, and the Balearics. Otherwise, south-western alignments were a peculiar feature of Britain and Ireland where they were restricted to later examples than most of those directed to the sunrise. They generally date from the Late Neolithic, Chalcolithic, and Early Bronze Age. Several kinds of prehistoric architecture are considered here: recumbent stone circles in north-east Scotland; Irish wedge tombs; and in western Britain a small group of mounds or cairns with 'blind entrances' or 'false portals'.

Recumbent stone circles in Scotland (Fig. 5.3)

One of the most distinctive styles of prehistoric architecture in Britain is the recumbent stone circle; monuments of this kind have already featured in Chapter Four (Bradley 2005; Welfare 2011). Their distinctive form is comparatively easy to recognise, and they have been treated as an important regional tradition whose distribution is restricted to north-east Scotland. In certain respects that is true, but some of their defining characteristics can be found more widely. They have three main components: a circular cairn; a ring of monoliths graded according to height with the lowest towards the NE and the tallest towards the SW; and an enormous stone (the 'recumbent') lying flat on the ground in between the two tallest uprights (the 'flankers'). Most of these components occur in other regions. In northern Britain they extend to the Clava Cairns of the inner Moray Firth; these are ring cairns (a kind of rubble enclosure), or passage graves enclosed by circles of standing stones. They also

Fig. 5.3. The recumbent stone circle at Tomnaverie. Photograph: Aaron Watson.

feature at monuments whose kerbs are graded by height or mass (Bradley 2000a). A more distant parallel is easily overlooked because it is in southern England. The main sarsen structure at Stonehenge is graded according to the same convention, with the tallest monoliths framing a view of the midwinter sunset (Pollard & Ruggles 2001). This comparison raises few chronological problems. The trilithons at Stonehenge were erected between 2620 and 2480 BC (Darvill *et al.* 2012). Excavations at Scottish recumbent stone circles have produced radiocarbon dates ranging from 2500 to 1900 BC. There are dates between 2500 and 1700 BC for Clava Cairns in a neighbouring region. It is likely that all the examples in northern Britain date from the later part of this range (Bradley 2016c).

Early studies of monuments in north-east Scotland commented on their resemblance to portals, closed by the introduction of a recumbent stone (Bradley 2005). Excavation at Hillhead supported this idea by finding an earlier enclosure whose entrance was blocked in this way (Bradley & Clarke 2016, 7–26). Fieldwork has established that the stone circles were erected when the sites were going out of use. The same applies to those surrounding Clava Cairns.

In contrast to earlier monuments, recumbent stone circles were directed towards the south and west. In some cases, they were positioned so that the area outside the entrance was concealed by the recumbent stone. This encouraged the idea that the structures were directed towards the sky. There have been claims that the views between the tallest stones focused on the setting sun, the position of the moon, or even a distant area of high ground (Welfare 2011, 191–255). This may be true in individual cases, but the dominant impression is of a doorway, closed on a massive scale when the site went out of use. Whatever the detailed arrangement at individual sites, these circles faced the dark side of the sky. There is little to show how they were employed. They produce few artefacts apart from broken quartz; nearly all the burials found there date from later periods; and the main activity for which there is evidence is simply the lighting of fires.

Wedge tombs in Ireland (Fig. 5.4)

It seems more than a coincidence that the last megalithic tombs in Ireland should date from the same period as Scottish Clava Cairns and recumbent stone circles. Although their ground plans are very different, Irish wedge tombs share important features with the last chambered tombs in northern Britain. Unlike earlier examples, most are orientated towards the SW or WSW, and again their components are graded by height (Walsh 1995). The monuments in both countries are associated with cup marks. They also feature deposits of quartz, although this material was already important during an earlier period at Newgrange (M. O'Kelly 1982). A feature that distinguishes wedge tombs from structures of similar age in Scotland is the presence of burnt bones in primary contexts. Because these burials can be dated directly it is possible to establish their chronology. These Irish tombs appeared between 2540 and 2300 BC (Brindley & Lanting 1992; O'Brien 1999; Schulting *et al.* 2008). Their main period of use was over by 1500 BC and probably well before that time. Like Scottish recumbent stone circles, they produce Beaker pottery.

The conventional description 'wedge tomb' refers to the ground plan of many – but not all – of these monuments, which are straight sided and wider towards the W: the position of the entrance. The profile of these buildings is especially informative. The largest building stones were towards the broader end, and the roofs of wedge tombs increased in height from the northeast, where human remains were most frequent, to an entrance facing W or SW. The rising profile of the covering slabs recalls the grading of the standing stones at Scottish sites of the same date. They increased in height so that, seen from the side, the entire structure was directed to the sky.

Wedge tombs are found mainly in the north and southwest of Ireland, but their architecture was by no means uniform. As Paul Walsh has observed, the basic concepts were the same, yet there were important regional distinctions in the ways in which they were organised. The south-western part of the tombs featured a 'portico':

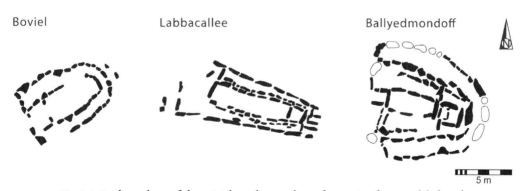

Fig. 5.4. *Outline plans of three Irish wedge tombs. Information from Walsh (1995).*

an impressive entrance that communicated between the living and the dead. He emphasised the distinction between monuments in which the mortuary deposits could be accessed and those where they remained out of reach. There were examples where the door could have been opened and closed at intervals (Walsh 1995).

Despite the broad similarities between Scottish and Irish sites, there are differences, too. The architecture of well-preserved wedge tombs makes it possible to determine their alignments more precisely than those of recumbent stone circles. Directions were important and wedge tombs placed more emphasis on the west than the south.

'False portals' in Scotland and Wales (Fig. 5.5)

The porticos of Irish wedge tombs recall an unusual component of a few sites in Britain. The terms 'blind entrance' or 'false portal' rarely appear in accounts of Bronze Age monuments as they usually describe features of megalithic tombs. Perhaps that is because the Neolithic structures were accessible and were equipped with passages and chambers. In later cairns, on the other hand, any human remains were sealed by an impermeable layer of rubble. When older graves were reopened, they were found by cutting into the mound (Petersen 1972).

The clearest account of a false portal is Derek Simpson's description of his excavation at Kintraw where he excavated a circular cairn on the west coast of Scotland. Once again, the kerbstones were larger towards the south and west. It was here that a remarkable feature was found:

> The two slabs projecting from the kerb and the slab which formed the back of this feature were the only stones which had been set into stone holes ... The area between

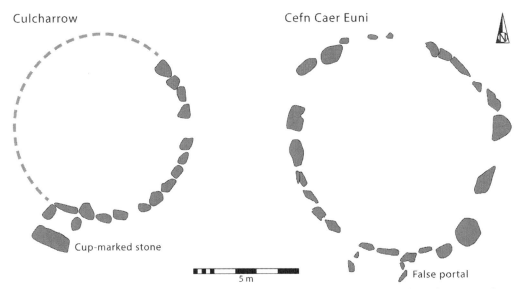

Fig. 5.5. Two Bronze Age round cairns with false portals on the south-west side. Information from RCAHMS (1974) and F. Lynch (1986).

the side slabs had been carefully blocked with small stones between which were layers of charcoal. The whole setting thus formed a false portal to the mound ... Running parallel with the kerb was a recumbent monolith ... covered by collapsed cairn material (Simpson 1967, 57).

There are five similar structures in the same part of Scotland, three of which have now been excavated. The example at Culcharron is particularly relevant as it featured a recumbent stone like that at Kintraw; it had cup marks on both faces (Peltenberg 1972). Similar features were associated with two small cairns inside the main stone circle at Temple Wood. They were modified more than once but were associated with cremated bone dated between 1450 and 1200 BC (J. Scott 1989). The other examples of false portals were recorded by field survey at Clachadow and Lochbuie (RCAHMS 1974, 49 & 1980, 58).

Similar features are recorded on three sites in Wales: the cairns at Cefn Caer Euni (F. Lynch 1986) and Aber Camddwr (Marshall & Murphy 1991), and a turf barrow at Mwdyl Eithin (Davies 1929, 13–18). Two of the monuments provided radiocarbon samples. A pit beneath the 'blind entrance' at Cefn Caer Euni was dated between 1800 BC and 1675 BC, and a similar feature at Aber Camddwr produced an estimate between 1690 and 1320 BC. Mwdyl Eithin is less accurately dated, but a secondary burial from the mound was associated with an Early Bronze Age Collared Urn. There was a standing stone just outside the cairn at Aber Camddwr, and at least three more formed a row aligned on the position of the portal.

Although they are not numerous, all the sites had features in common. The cairns or mounds were constructed on different scales – they ranged between 3 m and 15 m in diameter – but nearly all the portals were of similar dimensions; apart from those at Temple Wood, they can be compared with the entrances of Bronze Age roundhouses. The false portals contained charcoal, pieces of quartz, and small amounts of cremated bone. Two of the Welsh structures covered the positions of pits sealed by a level of slabs. All the examples in Scotland and Wales were on the same side of a mound or cairn. Again, they faced between SE and WSW (the commonest directions were SSW and SW).

The importance of midwinter

Although these sites have features in common, their orientations have been studied in different ways. The same applies to stone rows in Britain and Ireland, some of which are known to date from the same periods. It has always been tempting to connect the alignments of prehistoric structures with celestial events. Certain relationships are widely accepted, but others are more contentious.

Such studies conflated two approaches, each with its own validity. One was concerned with long distance alignments marked by accurately positioned files of standing stones. Fieldwork in the west of Scotland shows that they were orientated on the sun or moon at significant times of year (Ruggles 1984; Higginbottom 2020). The directions faced by other monuments were not – and could not be – equally precise. Recumbent stone circles and wedge tombs provide typical examples, but the case extends to Bronze Age cairns with false portals. They share an emphasis on the southwest but do not conform to an exact alignment. Nevertheless, it has always been tempting to look for the 'targets' associated with individual examples (MacKie 1974). Sometimes this has worked, but just as often it has failed.

A more general characteristic of these structures has been overlooked. Taken together, the directions faced by recumbent stone circles and mounds with 'false portals' cover the same range; that also applies to Clava Cairns. None falls outside a comparatively narrow band extending from SE to SW. Something similar applies to Irish wedge tombs, but they placed a greater emphasis on the western sky. Instead of considering the *alignment* of buildings on specific places or events, it is worth asking *which orientations were avoided*. Allowing for the difficulties of surveying some of the sites, the orientations of these buildings in Scotland and Wales were all between 135 degrees and 225 degrees. They correspond to the positions of the midwinter sunrise and the midwinter sunset respectively. This is the time of year when the sun travels the shortest distance across the sky. A few, like the passage graves at Balnuaran of Clava, were aligned on the sunset at the solstice, but it is even more striking that every one of these orientations is limited to the solar arc at a critical time of year. There is no reference to the position of the sun at any other point in its cycle. Of course, many monuments would have admitted sunlight during spring and summer, but that does not explain the strict emphasis on the southern and western sky. It must have been important at the time when they were built. By the late 3rd millennium BC midwinter had assumed a new significance.

On the sheer threshold of the night

This discussion has made several points. Between the Neolithic period and the Early Bronze Age the emphasis of many British and Irish monuments completely changed. It went from a concern with the rising sun to a new emphasis on the setting sun and possibly the night. There are few regions of Europe in which chambered tombs share the same emphasis on the southwest. The orientations of recumbent stone circles, Clava Cairns, wedge tombs and mounds with false portals suggest that they were associated with midwinter, and that may be when they were built.

There are two areas in which comparable patterns can be interpreted with the aid of literary evidence and folklore. One is south-west Ireland (Munster) during the Late Bronze Age. The other is part of Sweden during the Viking Age.

South-west Ireland

Similar phenomena are documented in Munster from the establishment of wedge tombs in the late 3rd millennium BC to Late Bronze Age developments more than a thousand years later. There are cairns, stone rows, and stone circles. They are smaller than many of the structures considered here but have the same association with cremation burials, cup marks, and quartz (O'Brien 2002 & 2012). Although they possess a distinctly local character, they show a continued emphasis on

the south-western sky. At times they seem to share characteristics with sites in
other regions, especially pairs of monoliths and longer alignments. There is also
a distinctive series of recumbent stone circles. They have been compared with
examples in north-east Scotland (Burl 2000, 264), but their chronology rules out any
connection between them. Those in northern Britain date between about 2500 and
1900 BC while their Irish equivalents were used during a much later period. The
similarities between them must be explained in other ways.

Recumbent stone circles provide the starting point for a different kind of analysis.
Rather than postulating direct links between distant regions, research has focused
on the associations of both groups of monuments. They were directed towards the
winter sky, and, like other structures, were characterised by the image of a closed
portal: an entrance between two tall uprights blocked by a massive stone. That is most
apparent at the Irish site of Drombeg where the circle was aligned on the midwinter
sunset (Fahy 1960). Other examples in Munster faced in the same direction, and the
same applies to the orientations of pairs of monoliths and those of longer stone rows.
They were like those of older wedge tombs.

They were directed towards the dark side of the sky, and in this case there is
good reason for supposing that their layout was directly related to the dead. In Irish
mythology Munster is where they travel to the afterlife (O'Brien 2002):

> [The] Otherworld was the realm of the death-god Donn ('the Dark One') ... He inhabited
> Tech Duinn ... identified by some as Bull Rock, a small islet [in County Cork] ... that
> is penetrated by a natural sea tunnel... The departure of the spirits of the dead was
> envisaged as following the course of the sun as it passed under the arch of Donn's
> dwelling into the sea and thence to the Otherworld ... The mythology of Donn survived
> in folk tradition to modern times (O' Brien 2012, 259).

This belief was of considerable antiquity and is documented in a poem that dates
from the 9th century AD. It is obvious that the sun setting in the southwest had a
significance that is overlooked in accounts of ancient timekeeping.

Middle Sweden

The only connection between stone settings in northern Scotland and south-west
Ireland was a link between the dead and the sunset. Similar structures were built in
another region, but it happened during a much later phase.

Some of the burial cairns erected during the Viking Age in Södermanland and
Uppland have a distinctive feature which is illustrated by the cemetery at Västerljung.
Here several circular monuments are supplemented by small rectangular structures
added to the exterior (Fig. 5.6; A-S. Gräslund 2001). In plan and dimensions, they
resemble the false portals associated with Bronze Age sites in western Britain. Again,
they have been considered as doorways communicating with the people buried inside
the tomb. Interpretations of this relationship vary between different authors. Drawing
on Arctic ethnography, Anne-Sofie Gräslund argues that they were associated with
offerings of food intended to sustain the dead. Birgit Arrhenius (1970), on the other

Västerljung

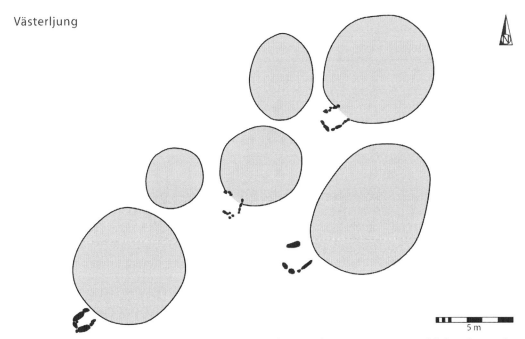

Fig. 5.6. Plan of the Viking cemetery at Västerljung, showing the stone structures added to the south-west side of the monuments. Information from A-S. Gräslund (2001).

hand, interpreted them as a 'dead man's doors' which would permit the deceased to leave the grave and communicate with the wider world. This practice is quoted in the Poetic Edda. Her approach is taken further in an article by Marianne Hem Eriksen (2013) entitled 'Doors to the dead'. She refers to medieval literary sources that tell how the deceased could communicate with the living. In some cases, people passed through these special portals to reach the realm of the dead. 'The door is not used for communication (creating connections) but as a boundary (creating oppositions) and as an architectural feature that the dead need to cross to get to the Otherworld' (M. H. Eriksen 2013, 193).

Her interpretation is like O'Brien's reading of the Irish evidence. In fact, the resemblance goes even further since the portals attached to Swedish cairns are on their south-west side. Eriksen's study shows that this association was more common than originally supposed, although it was just one regional tradition within Late Iron Age Scandinavia. She offers an explanation: '[It is possible that] the direction may be related to the passage of the sun ... Perhaps the ritualised doors of the Viking Age were aligned with the setting midwinter sun' (M. H. Eriksen 2013, 202).

Just as the movement of the sun may account for the similarities between practices in north-east Scotland and south-west Ireland, it could account for the startling resemblance between structures associated with mortuary monuments in Bronze Age Britain and the Viking Age in Scandinavia. They are worth considering, although they were geographically far apart.

Ancient skies

Did celestial events set a time scale for the creation and use of monuments? At one stage this was a popular interpretation among advocates of skyscape archaeology. Prehistoric people showed expert knowledge of the workings of the cosmos and applied it to practical effect in predicting the behaviour of the sun and moon. They determined the correct dates for important festivals and marked the key points in the agricultural cycle.

There is no doubt that a few constructions possessed accurate alignments, and that has been acknowledged by several generations of scholars, but these buildings were not necessarily orientated on celestial events. There was enormous variation. It applies to megalithic tombs from Menga in southern Spain where the 'target' is a mountain shaped like a human head (García Sanjuán & Lonzano Rodríguez 2016), to Maeshowe in northern Scotland which is directed towards the midwinter sunset (Downes 2020). The same point applies to settings of monoliths like Stonehenge (Pollard & Ruggles 2001). Others were not organised with the same precision. Either detailed orientations were never important or more general directions were what mattered in laying out these monuments. That is the implication of studies that identify a range of variation. Thus, long barrows may have been directed towards the eastern sky where the sun would rise throughout the year, while wedge tombs faced west and focused on the setting sun. Recumbent stone circles in north-east Scotland may have shared this feature, but their alignments (which were by no means accurate) were restricted to the arc that the sun travelled at midwinter. Obviously, there was a change of emphasis between the Neolithic period and the Bronze Age. More than that, the transformation affected communities in Britain and Ireland and had no equivalent on the near-Continent.

These developments were confined to a variety of specialised sites, many of which were associated with finds of human remains, cup marks, and quartz. For that reason, purely practical arguments fail. Nor were the orientations of many buildings exact enough to suggest much specialised knowledge in prehistoric societies. It is plausible to connect the main features of the solar year not only with the realities of food production but with attitudes to the dead. In Britain and Ireland those concepts changed during the later 3rd millennium BC, and it may be more productive to investigate them in their cultural setting than to place too much weight on exceptional cases. After all, there was only one Stonehenge, but there were many other settings of monoliths. Newgrange was designed so that the rising midwinter sun illuminated the central chamber, but the neighbouring monument at Knowth, which it resembles in many respects, was not associated with a similar phenomenon.

Rather than treating such structures as evidence of accurate time-reckoning, their symbolic and cultural associations ought to be the focus of research. They shed more light on ancient beliefs than they do on technical knowledge in the past. After many years of combining exact analysis with anachronistic reconstructions of past skills it is time to bring accounts of the ancient sky back to earth.

PART TWO

Pasts in retrospect

Chapter 6

Allusions and illusions

References to the past

Why were ancient monuments brought back into commission? Stonehenge provides the starting point for a broader discussion. How was it related to the burial mounds that cluster around it on Salisbury Plain, and how did these places develop over time? Both questions express the same concern. How were the construction and reconstruction of monuments related to the making of history? How were memories created and maintained, and when were their original connotations lost? They may have alluded to a past (or to several pasts), but at what point were those references based on an illusion?

Some illusions were shared by the scholars who studied these places. Like the cairn of Bredarör discussed in Chapter One, Stonehenge has been interpreted in relation to the archaeology of southern Europe. The great setting of sarsen uprights was supposedly designed by a foreign architect, and at one time the drawings of metalwork on the stones were identified with Aegean prototypes (Atkinson 1956, 92) – a classic instance of wishful thinking. The monument itself was dated to the Early Bronze Age. Discoveries of amber in nearby graves were drawn into the same equation. They became evidence of a far-reaching exchange system in which raw material obtained from the Baltic shoreline was represented in Wessex round barrows and in the shaft graves at Mycenae. That was the situation when Richard Atkinson wrote a general account of Stonehenge in 1956, but it changed during the decades in which his colleagues waited for the definitive account of his excavation (Barrett & Boyd 2019).

There were important developments during the intervening period. They were new approaches to social archaeology, and the impact of archaeological science. The first critiques built on well-established foundations. One of the most fundamental was an essay by Colin Renfrew (1968) which questioned the cultural and chronological connections between burials in Wessex and developments in Bronze Age Greece. In 1973 he followed it with another study which investigated the sequence of monuments leading to the building of Stonehenge. Its erection was the culmination of a lengthy process in which increasingly elaborate buildings were raised on the chalk. It began with the erection of causewayed enclosures in the Early Neolithic period and continued with massive henges before that structure was conceived. Stonehenge was a uniquely elaborate creation, but its architecture drew on local prototypes. The main difference is that they were built of wood.

New work in archaeological science has led to other insights. Radiocarbon dating established that the main setting of sarsens at Stonehenge was Late Neolithic, rather than Early Bronze Age as Atkinson and his contemporaries had supposed (Darvill *et al.* 2012). Although this method did a little to refine the chronology of barrow cemeteries in Wessex, they were confirmed as a feature of the Copper Age and Bronze Age. Thus, they could not be connected with the creation of the megalithic monument and had to be a subsequent development. Perhaps people chose to bury their dead around a structure that retained its significance long after it was built. At this point the mounds in the Stonehenge landscape seemed to be expressions of 'social memory'.

Research in archaeological science makes any notion of stable and prolonged traditions more difficult to sustain. Two new methods have changed the ways in which such relationships are viewed. The first is the study of isotopes preserved in samples of human bone. It sheds light on the region where a dead person had been brought up. It also identifies people who moved between one area and another during their lives (Parker Pearson *et al.* 2016). It became clear that almost half the individuals commemorated by Early Bronze Age barrows in Britain did not live near the places where they were buried (Parker Pearson *et al.* 2019). One way of explaining it is that the funerals of special people were conducted at important places. The surroundings of an impressive monument might have been among them. But there is little to show that its past could be remembered in detail.

In principle the dead buried around Stonehenge might have been the descendants of those who had built it. Still more unsettling are the results of studies of ancient DNA. Although this work is in its early stages, it shows that large parts of Europe were settled by immigrants during the 3rd millennium BC (Olalde *et al.* 2018). They were associated with new burial rites, new kinds of monument, and technological innovations including the use of metals. In southern England they are associated with Bell Beaker pottery with close parallels on the Continent. Radiocarbon dating shows that these processes took place after the period in which Stonehenge had first been built. At the same time the genetic evidence suggests that the settlers and their descendants dominated the insular gene pool for up to 16 generations before there was a significant contribution from the native inhabitants (Booth *et al.* 2021). It was during this interval that barrow cemeteries were established in great numbers around Late Neolithic (and earlier) constructions.

It is too soon to offer a dogmatic account of these findings, but one implication is clear. It seems less likely that the clusters of round barrows and graves around Stonehenge and similar buildings contained the burials of people whose ancestors had a direct connection with those monuments. Obviously, there was an awareness of the past significance of these places, and some of them remained in use. Equally clearly, there was a wish to associate later generations with powerful remains from antiquity, but this was a strategic decision. It was a conscious reconstruction and did not mean that these structures were built by the same population.

Stonehenge and its environs

The same issues can be studied on a local scale. Among the most distinctive features of the Stonehenge landscape are lines of burial mounds extending across the high ground around the site (Woodward *et al.* 2001; Leivers 2021). Although they were established after that monument was built, the barrows appear to be closely related. There is not enough information to consider this topic in much detail, as most of the mounds on Salisbury Plain were excavated many years ago. The records of this work leave problems, and the histories of individual cemeteries must be established – if at all – by studying the associated artefacts. At present there are too few radiocarbon dates to support a detailed analysis, but the forms of the earthworks in these cemeteries offer another source of information.

It is uncertain when some of these complexes were established and whether they were conceived as rows of mounds from the outset. Drawing on radiocarbon dates collected from a wider area, Paul Garwood (2007) has argued that linear cemeteries in southern England were a comparatively late development during the Early Bronze Age. They can include special kinds of barrows. Many were not far from older monuments, but this is not enough to show that the relationship between them was significant. Their orientations are more informative. Two complexes near Stonehenge refer to older structures.

At Winterbourne Stoke Crossroads there is a particularly close relationship between a Neolithic mound and a linear cemetery. The cemetery takes its axis from a long barrow of exceptional proportions whose alignment was extended when the later earthworks were built (Woodward *et al.* 2001). Although there is little dating evidence, their distinctive forms supply the missing information. The long mound is a classic example of its type and included a male burial dated between 3630 and 3360 BC (Parker Pearson *et al.* 2022, 28). The later cemetery includes several specialised monuments: bell barrows, disc barrows, a pond barrow, and monuments containing jewellery and diagnostic ceramics. The oldest deposits were associated with Beaker pottery, but the commonest finds from Sir Richard Colt-Hoare's excavation date to the Early Bronze Age.

Another row of mounds runs parallel to the Stonehenge Cursus (Fig. 6.1). That structure was already ancient when these barrows were built and is associated with a radiocarbon date of 3630–3370 BC (Parker Pearson *et al.* 2020, 66–88). One reason

Fig. 6.1. The Cursus Barrows near to Stonehenge. Photograph: Aaron Watson.

for supposing that it was commemorated a millennium later is that its ditch was recut as a series of pits, one of which is dated between 2910 and 2460 BC. A small henge was built on the same alignment, but its age is uncertain although it could be Neolithic (Parker Pearson *et al.* 2020, 39–40). There are indications that the row of barrows became longer over time. Towards one end there were Beaker graves, while the most elaborate mounds were constructed towards the opposite limit of the cemetery (Woodward 2000, fig. 68). It is likely that such monuments were used more than once, and they may have been enlarged during later phases. Again, the layout of a linear barrow cemetery was influenced by the presence of a Neolithic earthwork.

Barrow Hills

It is unfortunate that so little is known about the linear cemeteries near Stonehenge, but alignments of round barrows are not peculiar to the chalk. A similar group of monuments has been excavated in the upper Thames valley, 70 km to the northeast. Again, the later components referred to the presence of a major Neolithic earthwork, but in this case it was a causewayed enclosure. Unlike the sites just described, this complex is closely dated.

The sequence at Radley Barrow Hills began with the construction and use of the Abingdon causewayed enclosure which was bounded by a pair of parallel earthworks built and used during the 37th or 36th century BC (Fig. 6.2; Whittle *et al.* 2011, 407–21). Little is known about activity within its area, but outside the monument there were

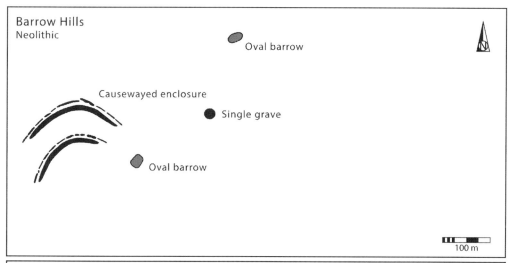

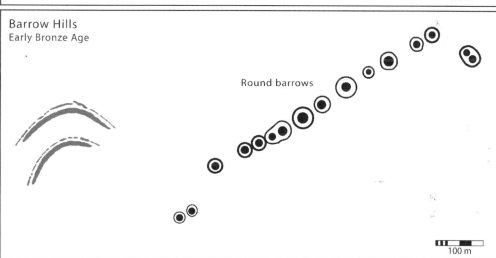

Fig. 6.2. Plans of the Neolithic and Early Bronze Age monuments at Barrow Hills. Information from A. Barclay and Halpin (1999).

three flat graves and a more complex mortuary structure not unlike those found beneath long barrows (A. Barclay & Halpin 1999, 19–34). Radiocarbon dating suggests that they were used three hundred years after the enclosure had been built and may have been contemporary with two oval mounds, one of them covering a pair of burials associated with grave goods (Bradley 1992).

There was only limited activity during the Late Neolithic period, although a small circular enclosure similar in form to a henge could date from this phase. Around 2400 BC, however, the cemetery was re-established, and a line of round barrows and flat graves was directed towards the position of the ancient remains. The authors of the definitive report conclude that the first burials were associated with early Beaker pottery. They were established close to the causewayed enclosure and the row of mounds gradually extended away from it (A. Barclay & Halpin 1999, fig. 9.8). The axis of the cemetery was eventually supplemented by a second row of monuments. Existing examples were enlarged, and some of the graves were reopened and reused throughout the later 3rd and earlier 2nd millennia BC. The process did not show any chronological gaps, but a significant interval separated a Neolithic oval barrow and flat graves from the causewayed enclosure, and a still longer interval divided these features from the initial development of the later cemetery. These intervals were about three hundred years and nine hundred years respectively.

The complex did not assume a special character until the first Beaker burials took place there. The lengthy rows of barrows developed later and, like those close to Stonehenge, contained an exceptional quantity and variety of artefacts. The first graves mark the inauguration of a cemetery that remained important for almost a millennium. This extended sequence may have run in parallel with developments on Salisbury Plain. In each case the cemetery did not reach its full extent until about 1850 BC, meaning that *in its later phases* it was most explicitly influenced by the presence of Neolithic monuments on the same sites. That is not consistent with an accurate recollection of the past.

Mounds and linear cemeteries in the southern Netherlands

The files of round barrows in Wessex and neighbouring regions are known in considerable detail, but in the absence of large-scale excavation it is hard to tell whether they typify a wider pattern. Fortunately, more impressive linear cemeteries are recorded on the Continent. Those in the Netherlands have been documented in detail and illustrate similar developments (Fig. 6.3).

Dutch cemeteries are considered in Quentin Bourgeois's monograph *Monuments on the Horizon* (2013). It draws on a wealth of excavated evidence and the results of radiocarbon dating. The overall sequence extends from about 3000 BC for nearly two millennia. During that time the mounds assumed remarkably similar forms. They were circular, and in certain phases their limits were emphasised by settings of posts. Some cemeteries were organised in straight lines extending across the landscape. They may have been constructed beside roads; others might have been orientated on the solstices. Their orderly layout seems to imply the existence of conventions that were respected over many years. Radiocarbon dates show that the alignments were established early in the local sequence and were extended during later phases. There were outliers, too.

But in this case the dating of these barrows does not support any model of continuous development. Bourgeois shows that there were two peaks in the construction of these monuments in the southern Netherlands, separated by an obvious gap between 2000 and 1800 BC. Earlier graves were reopened, and secondary burials were added. Barrows built between 3000 and 2000 BC were reused after an interval of about 750 years.

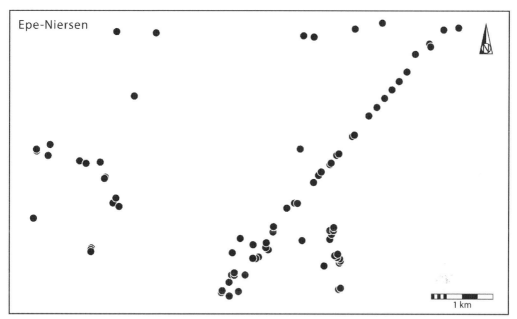

Fig. 6.3. The Dutch linear barrow cemetery at Epe Niersen. It was much more extended than its British counterparts. Information from Bourgeois (2013).

Distant and proximate relationships

These examples emphasise the importance of precise chronologies. It is possible to investigate the stages by which these groups of monuments came into being. Structures that seemed to have been used together can be placed in order, meaning that some connections prove to have been unexpectedly close, whilst others were more remote. It is necessary to distinguish between *proximate relationships* which might – but need not – have involved the same groups of people, and *distant relationships* where it is harder to establish any kind of continuity. The differences between them are important. This chapter considers proximate relationships between monuments during the Neolithic and the Bronze Age. More distant relationships between separate elements are discussed in Chapter Seven.

The pattern in the Low Countries resembled that in Britain, although the individual constructions were very different from one another, and the sequence was considerably longer. It is obvious that the development of barrows in the southern Netherlands did not proceed at an even pace. Individual monuments were related to one another according to different time scales. Proximate relationships are the easiest to identify and include those between primary and secondary deposits within the same grave, or those established between adjacent mounds as alignments of burial mounds first formed. On the other hand, there were lengthy gaps in which cemeteries apparently went out of use. During these phases few, if any, new barrows were built.

These intervals extended for at least ten generations, so that when activity resumed any relationship between the present and the past would have been a distant one. The point is even more obvious when ancient mounds were brought back into commission towards the end of the sequence, for now the interval was equivalent to almost 30 generations. Despite the orderly layout of the lines of barrows, they did not develop continuously. In that sense their final configuration is misleading. In no case is there much to suggest the workings of memory over an extended period.

Another approach draws on the new research in genetics mentioned earlier. The recovery of ancient human bone has important implications for sequences of these kinds. In the study area there appear to have been two main phases of migration. One was when large areas were colonised by farmers; this was discussed briefly in earlier chapters. The second was a period of settlement by new people (Olalde et al. 2018). The details of this process remain contentious and suitable samples are unevenly distributed, but for present purposes the basic outline seems clear. There is genetic evidence for sudden changes in northern, eastern, and western Europe. They were associated with two kinds of decorated pottery and their associations, although the exact relationship between them remains a matter for discussion. To the east and north they are represented by Corded Ware and / or Bell Beakers (Friss-Holm et al. 2021; Armit & Reich 2021). In the Low Countries these styles were used in sequence, but in Britain, Ireland, and north-west France only Beaker pottery is found. Both traditions have already featured in this account. Beakers played a part in the sequences illustrated by the Stonehenge landscape and that at Barrow Hills. Both Corded Ware and Bell Beakers were associated with the cemeteries investigated by Bourgeois (2013).

These changes cut across the orderly sequences of monuments on both sides of the North Sea and represent a fault line in the archaeology of prehistoric Europe. For instance, they distinguish the barrow cemeteries in the Netherlands from earlier megalithic tombs in the north of the country which were associated with farming communities (Bakker 1992). In the same way they separate the Neolithic components at Barrow Hills from the linear cemetery that succeeded them. It is improbable that new settlers would be able to account for the presence of older constructions if they were occupying unfamiliar landscapes. The survival of ancient earthworks and other features must have presented a challenge and their presence had to be explained (Bradley 2002). In order to do so, new memories were contrived.

Choosing a suitable past

Now a further question arises. If different communities took different approaches to the past, were certain kinds of monuments reused in preference to others? The information from Barrow Hills and the Stonehenge landscape suggests that local variations could have been important, yet the cemeteries of the southern Netherlands adhered to the same model over long periods of time.

Perhaps the best way of approaching these questions is to consider a period when different regions of Europe were affected by the same, or similar, processes. This was the settlement of people who used Bell Beakers. There were striking differences in the choices they made and their attitudes to what remained from the past (Sommer 2017). There is a further consideration. It is best to compare them when they apply to a single kind of structure. The obvious candidate is the megalithic tomb, as it might have been easier to recognise than an eroded earthwork and had more chance of remaining intact. The reception of these distinctive monuments is studied in four regions which have already figured in this book: Scotland, Ireland, the Netherlands, and north-west France (Fig. 6.4). The reason for choosing chambered tombs as an example is their obvious diversity. They did not conform to a single design and were built at different points during the Neolithic period. The one feature which does unite them is that almost all these conspicuous buildings had gone out of use by the time Bell Beakers appeared. That is why their existence might have posed a problem.

This discussion is organised around comparisons between different sequences.

The Netherlands

In three of these regions the distributions of chambered tombs overlapped with those of new styles of artefacts. A partial exception is in the Netherlands where the barrow cemeteries studied by Bourgeois (2013) have a separate distribution from earlier chambered tombs. The megaliths were further to the northeast where the Neolithic landscape contained the glacial erratics used to build *hunebedden* or 'giants' graves'. These structures were associated with the Funnel Beaker or TRB culture, and Jan Albert Bakker (1992) argued that they were erected between 3400 and 3000 BC. If so, their construction would have ended at about the time when the first round barrows associated with Corded Ware were being built further to the south. Bakker drew attention to a small number of cases in which hunebedden contained later material. The most striking was Bell Beaker pottery which was discovered in secondary contexts. Although he assumed that it must have accompanied unburnt burials, no human remains were found (in any case they would not have been preserved on such acid subsoils). He compared the forms of these vessels with those in settlements. As he said:

> The character of some of the pottery is quite different from that found in Bell Beaker single graves. Large amphorae and large storage pots seem to prevail; they are *almost never* found in single graves. Similarly, tall pot beakers are almost never found in Bell Beaker single graves, but do occur in settlements (Bakker 1992, 58; emphasis in the original).

In the circumstances it is uncertain whether these artefacts were associated with the treatment of the dead, or with other activities. The roles of places could have changed. It seems as if some of the tombs were reused after an interval, but it happened on a small scale, and they might have been treated in new ways.

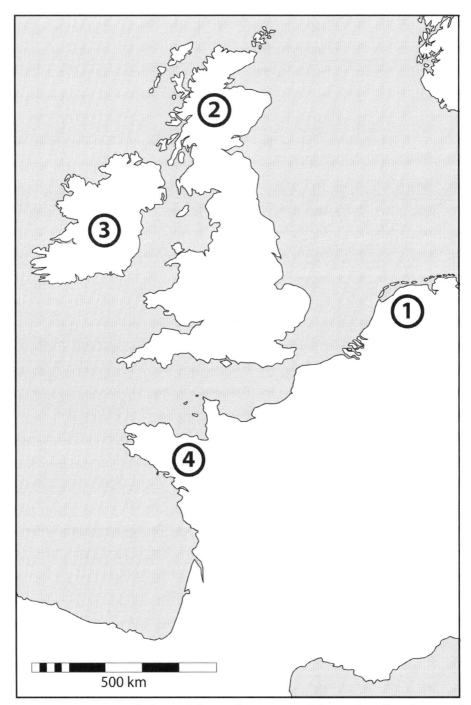

Fig. 6.4. Four regions in which megalithic tombs were reused during the Bell Beaker period.

Scotland

Bakker's account of the secondary deposits in hunebedden has points in common with Neil Wilkin's analysis of the Beaker pottery found in Scottish chambered tombs (Wilkin 2016). Here the relationship between megalithic cairns and wider developments may have been more complex, but one relationship is striking. The latest ceramics share features with those from similar contexts in northern Europe, yet the tombs themselves were of completely different kinds. Indeed, the practice of depositing artefacts in the remains of older structures took no account of the striking contrasts between local styles of architecture in northern Britain.

Wilkin discusses 24 megalithic tombs with sherds of Beaker pottery in the filling of their chambers, but human remains were found in only eight of them. Sherds in the same style were seldom associated with the closure of these cairns; that happened in just four instances. The artefacts themselves were distinctive. Rather than entire vessels, they were usually fragments which were worn, abraded, or even burnt, and again they resembled the finds from domestic sites. They belonged to vessels that had been a different size or shape from those in graves and were decorated in a simpler style.

In some ways these observations recall Bakker's account of the Bell Beaker pottery from hunebedden. Its closest parallels are with the artefacts found in settlements rather than graves. At the same time the Scottish evidence is rather different because a new kind of monument – the Clava Cairn – was constructed at this time; it featured briefly in Chapter Five. Sites of this kind were distributed across a region where chambered tombs built during the Neolithic period still remained accessible. Here there were also flat cemeteries and round barrows associated with Beaker burials. Clava Cairns feature both circular enclosures and passage graves. Their architecture combines the structural conventions of Late Neolithic stone settings with a recreation of the forms of more ancient megaliths (Bradley 2022). The past must have been an important resource.

Ireland

The significance of Beaker pottery and its associations has been studied in a recent monograph by Neil Carlin (2018). Despite the movement of copper across the Irish Sea, the funerary record is different from that in Scotland. Beaker graves like those in the north of Britain or the southern Netherlands were uncommon. Towards the east coast their place was taken by inhumation burials associated with a different style of decorated pottery – the Food Vessel (Waddell 1990; McSperron 2020) – but further to the north and west Beaker ceramics were associated with a new style of megalithic architecture: the wedge tomb. It has already featured in this account. Similar ceramics are found in secondary deposits at Neolithic monuments (Carlin 2018, 95–113).

Each of these elements needs to be considered separately. The graves with Food Vessels resemble those in Scotland; indeed, the linear cemetery near the coast in

Kilmartin Glen contains a concentration of artefacts and petroglyphs with parallels in Ireland (Watson & Bradley 2021). At the same time wedge tombs, which have Beaker associations, share one of their most distinctive features with Scottish Clava Cairns. As Chapter Five has shown, they are orientated towards the south and west.

Another feature raises more problems, as a significant number of megaliths in Ireland were reused during the Beaker phase. That should not be surprising as research in the Boyne Valley has shown that Neolithic passage graves retained their significance in the Late Neolithic period (Carlin 2017). What is remarkable is that Bell Beaker reuse of ancient tombs largely ignored the interiors of these monuments, even though their fabric might have remained in good condition. Instead, older styles of architecture were favoured during this phase, in particular, Early or Middle Neolithic portal dolmens and court tombs. This did not happen by chance, and it raises a problem. Whatever their ultimate origins, Chalcolithic settlers in Ireland could not have known the relative ages of those structures – they have been established only recently and some of the details remain controversial. On the other hand, strangers could distinguish between tombs that had been built or repaired in the recent past, and others that were obviously ruinous. Although the Scottish evidence is much more limited, there are hints of a similar distinction. Passage graves like Maeshowe show little sign of activity in the Beaker period, and older Clyde Cairns and Orkney Cromarty Cairns seem to have been preferred for reuse (Wilkin 2016). In Britain too little information exists to take the argument further, but there are indications that strangers to Ireland were assembling their own histories from the buildings they encountered there.

North-west France

This is another area in which megalithic tombs were reused during the Beaker period. In this case it conformed to practice over a larger area. Along the Atlantic coast from Brittany to Portugal collective burials are found as often as single burials, and in north-west France, Laure Salanova (2016) observes that they occur in different areas: multiple deposits follow the coastline, with others in river valleys. Individual Beaker graves, on the other hand, are a feature of more inland areas (Fig. 6.5; Salanova & Tchérémissinoff 2011; C. Gibson 2016; Favrél & Nicolas 2022).

The Breton examples play a prominent part in the discussion as they are frequently associated with megalithic tombs whose original roles had ended many years before. In Salanova's study it applied to 20% of the Neolithic examples in this region. An earlier account of Breton megaliths came to a similar conclusion (L'Helgouach 1965). These sites show a similar pattern to Irish and, possibly, Scottish monuments where older structures could be selected rather than those built more recently.

Salanova's results formed part of a broader analysis of this period in Atlantic Europe. Not only was the region associated with collective burials rather than single graves, it included a series of distinctive artefacts that were distributed from Portugal to western France. They included the copper arrowheads known as Palmela Points,

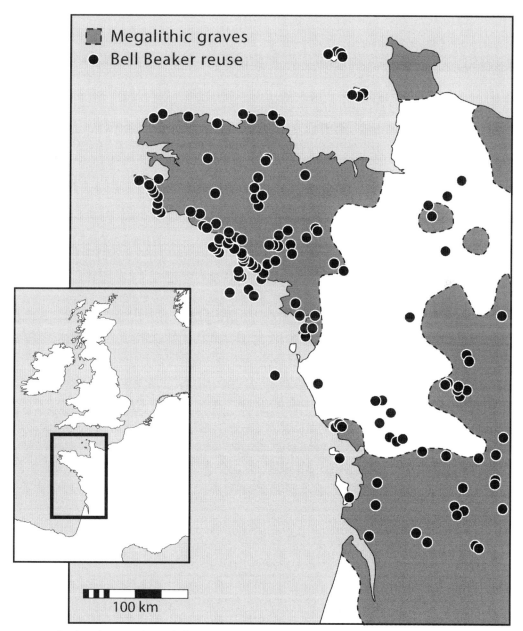

Fig. 6.5. The distribution of megalithic tombs in western and north-western France reused during the Bell Beaker period. Information from Favrél and Nicolas (2022).

and the finely decorated vessels called Maritime Beakers (Salanova 2016). Towards the south there were defended settlements with parallels in the west Mediterranean; Zambujal outside Lisbon provides the best-known example (Kunst 2017). There is no consensus on the original source(s) of Bell Beakers and their associations, but a strong case can be made for the Iberian Peninsula.

It is easy to treat the evidence in isolation, but it would be wrong to do so. Grand Pressigny flint from western France circulated over a wide area before the Bell Beaker period and an important connection was established with the Low Countries where artefacts made from this distinctive material were already deposited in Corded Ware graves (Mallet *et al.* 2012). Another connection was with Ireland as new research has shown that early axes, and ingots of the same metal, circulated in both countries (Gandois *et al.* 2019). That finding is particularly revealing as it reopens a long-standing discussion on the origins of wedge tombs.

Breton allées couvertes are relevant here. They featured briefly in Chapter Three which considered the links between their architecture and a series of timber buildings built during a subsequent phase. Radiocarbon dating combined with artefact analysis shows that mortuary structures of this type were reused on a significant scale long after they were first built. Not only would this bring them closer in time to the 'great houses' that share some of their features, it would also ally them with wedge tombs which have similar – but not identical – ground plans. This is not a new idea, but it would explain what otherwise seems a puzzling development (Schulting *et al.* 2008). Perhaps the forms of the Irish monuments did not refer to Neolithic origins but alluded to *the secondary reuse* of megalithic tombs in north-west France. If so, the link between these groups was strengthened by the presence of Beaker pottery. New settlers in Ireland, whose ancestry is indicated by DNA (Cassidy *et al.* 2016), made a direct reference to Continental practice, while their counterparts in Brittany related their activities to a more remote time in the past.

Summary: memory loss and founding fictions

This has not been a discussion of Bell Beakers or their relationship to Corded Ware. These are controversial issues that have yet to be resolved. Nor has it offered a detailed review of the genetic evidence provided by human remains. Again, they are important and controversial topics, but this period was chosen to shed light on another subject: the role of social memory in the development of earlier prehistoric monuments. This is a familiar theme and seems to have retained its influence in archaeology despite the dramatic results provided by archaeological science. The Bell Beaker horizon offered a convenient baseline for comparing similar phenomena between neighbouring parts of Europe. In fact, it revealed so much diversity that a significant question arose. Do the extended time scales of certain constructions raise a special problem? Given the lengths of time involved and the complexity of the field evidence, have archaeologists exaggerated the roles played by memory in the past? Is it the most appropriate term to use (Van Dyke & Alcock 2003; Jones 2007)? And have other important factors been underemphasised or overlooked?

The distinction between proximate and distant relationships is crucial and can apply at various scales. In some cases, close relations are easy to identify, especially in cemeteries. Some graves were reopened, and their contents were inspected (Petersen 1972). Fresh deposits were added, and relics were taken away. These contexts included objects that had been used over long periods, among them obvious heirlooms (Woodward & Hunter 2015). They could be represented in unfamiliar combinations of newer and older artefacts (Cooper *et al.* 2022). The positions of earlier burials were located accurately, and there were even cases in which the character of a later interment was influenced by that of its predecessors (Mizoguchi 1993). Graves might also be orientated on one another over a limited period (Last 1998), and when any covering mounds were reconstructed the positions of existing deposits seem to have been respected. The process probably extended to the first appearance of linear cemeteries In the Netherlands and Britain, although it will take detailed excavations like that at Over in eastern England to show this by radiocarbon dating (Garrow *et al.* 2014).

The use of scientific dating identified more distant relationships between monuments and associated deposits. The best example was the chronological disjunction between the age of the principal structure at Stonehenge and the origins of the barrow cemeteries in the surrounding area. Other Neolithic monuments showed the same relationship with later burial mounds. As this chapter has demonstrated, chronological separation was not the only problem. New studies of human bone have shown that some of the people who were buried nearby had never lived in the vicinity, and a surprisingly high proportion of the samples show that they, or their ancestors, were settlers from the Continent. Again, there was less sign of continuity than commonly supposed. The problem was not peculiar to southern England and applied to all four regions considered here.

If the connections between successive uses of the same monuments or groups of monuments were more remote than earlier researchers believed, it is obvious that some relationships were intentional and significant. The question is whether accurate memories were involved. Perhaps other relationships were contrived. The Bell Beaker period illustrated these points.

That process was obvious in the most enigmatic of the examples considered here. Beaker pottery was placed inside older megalithic tombs both in Scotland and the northern Netherlands, but in neither case was there much evidence that the new deposits were associated with the dead. Rather, they consisted of vessels, or parts of vessels, quite different from those in the single graves of the same period. Instead, they resembled the artefacts from settlements. This was not to say that specialised Neolithic tombs were reused as domestic sites, but it did raise the possibility that similar activities were carried out in both contexts. They may have included the preparation and consumption of food and drink. There were other links between these two regions. As Marc Vander Linden observed, they shared similar styles of ceramics and similar mortuary practices (2006, figs 114 & 116). Only the domestic buildings in these areas contrast with one another.

Another kind of connection was illustrated by the reuse of tombs in Ireland, Scotland, and France. Older monuments were chosen rather than those employed more recently. It was most obvious in Ireland, but the evidence was not peculiar to that country and also applied to Scottish sites, the latest of which played a more limited role. The same approach could account for the observation that Breton passage graves were selected more often than allées couvertes which were a later development. On the other hand, when those allées couvertes were reused for Beaker burials the close relationship between them was so important that it might have been copied in Ireland where it provided one source of inspiration for wedge tombs. In that case the most important issue may not have been the reference to an architectural tradition that developed during the Neolithic period. The connection was with the new roles of these structures on the Continent and could been an explicit statement of communal origins and identities.

Finally, the renewed construction of chambered tombs in northern Scotland suggested yet another relationship between the present and the past. It was the exact opposite of that inferred between Ireland and north-west France, and again it stretches any concept of social memory to its limits. In this case a traditional form of architecture – the passage grave – was revived at the time when the impact of new people and new beliefs was being felt. The Clava Cairns combined some of the features of stone circles with a recreation of megalithic tombs of a kind that could still be seen in the local landscape; in certain cases, the chambers of these early monuments remained accessible and might have offered a source of inspiration. One way of interpreting this development was as a restatement of traditional beliefs at a time when they were coming under pressure from outside (Bradley 2022).

These ideas have a wider application, and they are not restricted to the oldest constructions and their histories. Other approaches must be considered, too. The reuse of ancient monuments remained important during later phases, and Iron Age and early medieval examples can be equally informative. This discussion is continued in Chapter Seven.

Chapter 7

Associations and origins

Prehistoric Forteviot and Royal Forteviot

Forteviot is an attractive village, built in Arts and Crafts style, west of Perth in Scotland. The place has long been known as one of the centres of royal power in the early medieval period. It was where the king Cináed mac Alpin died in AD 858, but for many years the only physical evidence linked to its early history was a series of decorated stones, including a massive arch which must have formed part of a building. The site is in a fertile river valley with a variety of ancient structures, but the first indications of its field archaeology came when aerial photographs revealed a series of distinctive crop marks. While some of the levelled features did resemble Pictish examples, others had a very different character. In this case a Neolithic date seemed more likely.

Both ideas were confirmed by a campaign of fieldwork, the results of which were published together in 2020. The first volume, *Prehistoric Forteviot*, investigated a series of monuments first identified from the air (Fig. 7.1; Brophy & Noble 2020). The sequence began in the 30th century BC when part of the site was used as a Late Neolithic cremation cemetery. Then in the 28th century it was taken over as the position of an enormous timber enclosure and circular post settings were built there. Three hundred years later these features were supplemented or replaced by four small enclosures like the henges described in Chapter Four. Their ditches contained deposits of Beaker pottery. Access to these enclosures became more difficult once their entrances were closed, and finally, in the 21st century BC, the edge of one of these structures was buried beneath a cairn associated with an unusually rich inhumation burial. A second henge was completely covered by a mound: a development that has been recorded at other sites in Britain (A. Gibson 2010). The prehistoric monuments at Forteviot must have spanned at least eight hundred years. There were no obvious

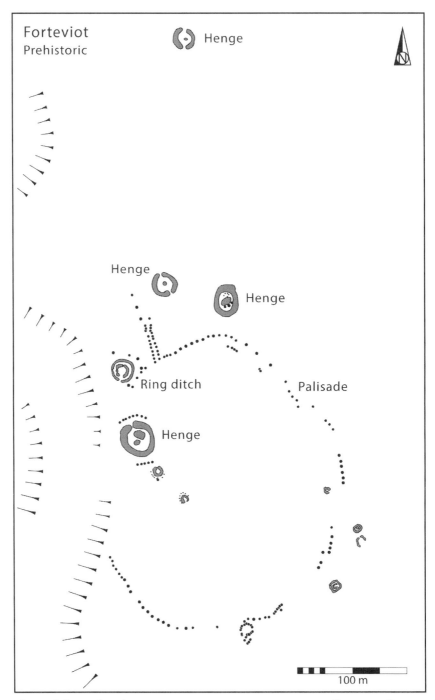

Fig. 7.1. The Neolithic and Early Bronze Age monuments at Forteviot. Information from Brophy and Noble (2020).

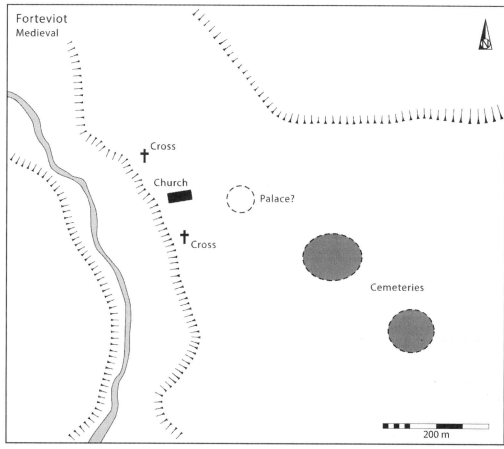

Fig. 7.2. The early medieval phase at Forteviot. Information from Campbell and Driscoll (2020).

breaks in the sequence, but the presence of a Beaker burial raises the problem considered in Chapter Six – it is not clear whether the local community had the same genetic makeup throughout this lengthy sequence. The chronological relationships between the prehistoric structures were both *proximate* and more *distant*.

The second volume, *Royal Forteviot*, introduces another chronological relationship between the monuments at this site (Campbell & Driscoll 2020). As well as further crop marks, the work was inspired by historical sources and by the presence of early medieval sculptures at Forteviot and in the surrounding landscape. The most readily identifiable elements were the ditches of square and circular burial mounds; flat graves also occurred close to the prehistoric earthworks (Fig. 7.2). Excavation showed that all these elements dated between the 4th and 9th centuries AD. From the outset the authors of both volumes were aware of the potential connections between structures built during separate phases, and these links were clearly evidenced in excavation. One of the prehistoric cists was reopened during the Pictish phase; and ancient artefacts could have been collected and deposited in later contexts. Although some details of the mortuary ritual are unfamiliar, the barrows have direct parallels at sites of similar date in Scotland (Mitchell & Noble 2017).

The coincidence of location with the earlier prehistoric complex is very striking indeed. Apart from a square enclosure dating from the late 1st century AD, there is little evidence of activity between the two main phases. That is not to say that the landscape was empty after the Bronze Age – there were two Roman camps in the vicinity, and fieldwork in the surrounding area has investigated important Iron Age sites (Brophy & Noble 2020, 295). Even so, the archaeology of Forteviot itself does not suggest any direct continuity between the monuments reported in these volumes.

One of the problems faced by the excavators was the extent to which those remains had been disturbed during the 1st millennium AD. Far from being an impediment to research, this was one of the most revealing elements in the archaeology of Forteviot. Not only were the visible signs of an ancient past supplemented by a new generation of graves and mounds, people dug into the remains of the prehistoric earthworks during the Pictish occupation of the site. For whatever reason, specific structures were targeted during this work, and it is worth considering why it happened and what, if anything, was taken from the ground. It seems as if the physical traces of the past were inspected in an antiquarian fashion. The modern excavators are surely right to interpret this activity as an attempt to form direct links between the early medieval use of this place and a more remote past whose elements could no longer be recalled. It added authority to what really were new developments. The authors concluded that:

> The reuse of an eminent prehistoric ceremonial centre [was] ... not incidental or accidental, but conceptually essential ... Forteviot is best understood as an ancient ritual complex of such spiritual and cosmological resonance that, by late Roman times, it had become a regional assembly place (Campbell & Driscoll 2020, 191).

That is a reasonable interpretation, but it leaves an interval of 2000 years between the prehistoric phase and developments in the 1st millennium AD.

All these features were obviously associated with the early medieval power centre known from historical sources. There is documentary evidence that Forteviot became a royal capital long after the older monuments had gone out of use. An early medieval 'palace' may underlie the modern houses, which were substantially rebuilt a century ago; despite small-scale reconnaissance, this has still to be proved. On the other hand, the decorated arch recovered from a riverbed on the edge of the village shows that it included at least one substantial building. Perhaps the early medieval burials identified by aerial photography were located outside the political and religious core.

There is one more element to consider. The early medieval complex may have begun as a secular centre, associated with assemblies and the inauguration of kings, but by the beginning of the 9th century AD it had assumed some of the attributes of ecclesiastical sites in northern Britain (Campbell & Driscoll 2020, 196–9). A formal layout of sculptures extended across the surrounding area. The designs on these stones referred to the Byzantine world.

These images were related to royal authority as well as Christian belief. Their siting introduces another consideration since they were addressed to people visiting this remarkable complex. Again, the link with Byzantium was important:

> At Forteviot we are seeing an attempt to introduce a new structure to the pattern of movement through the landscape which characterised the ceremonial processional tradition of Constantinople .... The ancient ceremonial centre [was] much more than a stage for royal inaugurations: the prehistoric monuments provided the platform for building an explicitly Christian kingdom (Campbell & Driscoll 2020, 211).

The authors of *Prehistoric Forteviot* discuss many of the issues that have already featured here. They include the interplay between accessible and inaccessible pre-Roman structures, and the relationship between open and closed monuments, yet the ideas considered in *Royal Forteviot* must be considered on their own terms. To some extent that is because they draw on other sources of information: historical accounts and the iconography of the sculptured stones. The discussion raises issues which should be considered now.

The approaches taken in these volumes recall the important distinction between *genealogical time* and *mythical time* discussed by Chris Gosden and Gary Lock in 1998. Influenced by ethnographic sources, they distinguished between two features that typify the renewed use of older structures:

> The first comes from the repeated reuse and maintenance of features with known antecedents to which the group (or part of it) returns on a regular basis to carry out activities of a prescribed type. The second aspect of reuse derives from activities at ancient features of the landscape, given new values within the contemporary setting (Gosden & Lock 1998, 4).

In the first case features may be associated with the work of named people and their activities in the past. Although accounts may change, they often draw on a notion of kinship which is 'not a static charter but a form of argument to be manipulated by those in the present' (Gosden & Lock 1998, 5). Relationships with the past depend on an idea of genealogy but do not rely on accurate recollection.

There are obvious limits to the extent to which past actions and relationships can be recalled. They vary between different societies according to their techniques for preserving information. Knowledge can be forgotten in as few as three generations (Henige 1974), but in other cases the process takes much longer. In one example quoted by Gosden and Lock (1998) genealogies remained intact for five hundred years.

At the same time histories may be revised until their original significance is forgotten. Physical remains surviving from a more distant past provide the material of myths that combine supernatural agencies with the actions of people in the past. Gosden and Lock consider the impact of these elements:

> Mythical history [derives] its contemporary force and power from its age, and, more particularly, from the fact that its obscure origins allow more latitude in evoking the past in the present (Gosden & Lock 1998, 6).

That is what allowed the prehistoric archaeology of Forteviot to be rewritten two millennia later.

Ales Stenar and Lejre

Not far from the cairn at Kivik discussed in Chapter One, another important monument is located by the sea. Although it has been much restored, the ship setting of Ales Stenar is one of the most visited archaeological sites in Scandinavia. In its surviving state it consists of 60 monoliths defining an enclosure 70 m long and up to 19 m wide (Fig. 7.3; Strömberg 2001). It extends from southeast to northwest and is aligned on the midsummer sunset.

There has been confusion over the antiquity of this structure, not least because a smaller ship setting near the cairn of Bredarör is dated to the Late Bronze Age (there are excavated monuments of the same date elsewhere in northern Europe). At one time the role of Ales Stenar was compared with that of Stonehenge, and an early origin was indicated by the presence of cup marks on the uprights. More recent research suggests it was used at the same time as the medieval occupation of Forteviot.

Although Ales Stenar had been disturbed, excavation by Marta Strömberg (2001) showed that the cup marks extended to the bottoms of the stones and would have

Fig. 7.3. The monumental ship setting of Ales Stenar. Photograph: David Castor (CCBY 4.0).

been concealed when they were erected. For that reason, she suggested that it was 'a monument of recycled boulders'. She obtained a series of radiocarbon samples from the site, and a new interpretation suggests that it was used between AD 690 and 1050 (Söderberg & Walleborn 2015). That is consistent with what is known about other elaborate ship settings, some of which are associated with runestones.

Until recently the original source of the monoliths remained unknown, but early accounts of Ales Stenar referred to smaller monuments in the vicinity. It took geophysical survey to identify the most likely candidate, which was only 20 m from the ship setting (Söderberg & Knarrström 2015). Excavation revealed a circular mound or cairn bounded by a ditch, with the remains of a 'long dolmen' in its centre. Perhaps it began as a Neolithic feature and was reconstructed during the Bronze Age. It was associated with a single radiocarbon date of 2580–2460 BC. If the ship setting was built of material taken from this structure, the cup marks could have been three thousand years old when the stones were reused.

That may not have happened by chance as ship symbolism played an important part in northern Europe during two separate periods. Early in the Bronze Age a few graves assumed the form of a small boat, but they were usually concealed beneath a mound or cairn. During the Late Bronze Age, however, the forms of larger vessels were displayed as arrangements of monoliths (Skoglund 2008; Wehlin 2022). Depictions of ships also featured on decorated metalwork (Kaul 1998), but it was not until the 1st millennium AD that stone settings of a similar kind were built again – there was a chronological gap of almost a thousand years. One explanation for the reappearance of ship settings is that the remains of older monuments could still be identified on the ground. Between AD 550 and 1000 they provided the prototypes for new constructions. But their forms evoked a distant past.

Writing in 2007, Felix Vestergard considered that relations with antiquity were especially important as communities in northern Europe encountered Christian beliefs. He dated the largest ship settings between AD 900 and 970 and interpreted them in this way:

> They should be understood as a means of securing and underlining a sense of heathen Norse identity at a time of political and religious change ... Some [examples] were physically linked to Bronze Age barrows. [It was] an attempt to stress links with the past ... before or during the process of conversion to Christianity (Vestergaard 2007, 190).

In the 1st millennium AD some of the great ship settings in northern Europe were associated with the sites of assemblies and royal centres (Sanmark 2019). This was true of Lejre in Denmark which is commonly identified as the setting of the epic poem *Beowulf* (Niles & Osborn 2007). Here excavation has documented a complex sequence (Christensen 2015). There were two successive foci, both of which featured exceptionally large timber halls. The first group is associated with radiocarbon dates between AD 450 and 600. One of the most massive buildings was beside a prominent Bronze Age barrow (Fig. 7.4); there were similar structures in the vicinity as well as

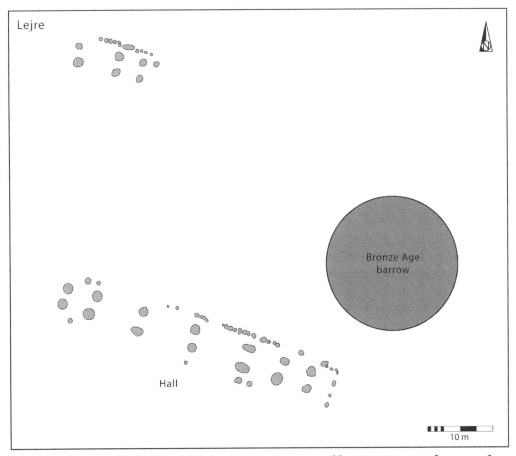

Fig. 7.4. Plans of two timber halls aligned on a Bronze Age round barrow at Lejre. Information from
Christensen (2015).

the remains of megalithic tombs. All these monuments were located on the same
side of a stream as the first wooden buildings. Later, another barrow, Grydehøj, was
constructed on its opposite bank. This mound was 5 m high and was the largest in
the area. Although its form resembled that of the Bronze Age earthworks, Grydehøj
was constructed as the first settlement was going out of use and covered a cremation
burial dated between AD 540 and 690. The dead person must have enjoyed a special
status and wore a costume decorated with gold.

A second group of halls was constructed on a new site 500 m away. These buildings
date between AD 700 and 1000. Now the stream separated the domains of the living and
the dead: a process that could have begun with the construction of Grydehøj. It was
during this phase that four ship settings were erected at Lejre. Only one is preserved
today, but they were apparently associated with a cemetery containing more than
fifty graves dating from the 9th and 10th centuries AD (S.W. Andersen 2007). Thus,
they would have been in use at the same time as the second settlement on the site.

The halls shared similar dimensions during both phases, although their plans show differences of detail. The main contrasts concern the relationships between them and the nearby monuments. In the earlier period people emphasised the *connection* between the newly built halls and a series of Neolithic and Bronze Age mounds in the vicinity, in particular a conspicuous round barrow. Grydehøj may have copied its distinctive form but was built on a significantly larger scale. Its construction helped to establish a *division* between the world of the living on one side of the stream and the domain of the dead which it faced across the water. That distinction became even more evident when the ship settings were built there.

Julie Lund and Elisabeth Arwill-Nordbladh (2016, 421) characterise the sequence in these terms:

> By locating the settlement only a few metres from ancient burial mounds, people in the settlement were connected to the long-term history of the place. This also contributed to strengthening social positions as it created an atmosphere of a deeply rooted connection to the distant ancestors of a mythical past. By establishing the Viking-Age cemetery specifically around Grydehøj a link was made to a more recent history.

Although the halls had features in common throughout the occupation of Lejre, the roles of other monuments were more diverse and owed their distinctive forms to structures built in the past, some of them in distant regions. That is obvious from the relationship between the Bronze Age mound incorporated in the earlier settlement and the later barrow which copied its appearance. It is still more evident with the ship settings whose forms may have referred to others built many years before. Such relationships are widely documented in northern Europe and illustrate Andrew Jones's concept of 'material citation' (2007).

In fact, they conformed to a wider pattern. Eva Thäte (2007) has shown that between 12% and 23% of all the Viking burials in regions of southern Scandinavia reused the remains of older monuments. In Denmark and Sweden people selected Bronze Age mounds rather than later constructions; the barrows that were chosen were among the larger examples. The relationship between these structures was so complex that it has caused confusion. At one time an enormous mound that covered the ship setting at the Danish royal centre of Jelling was interpreted as a rebuilt Bronze Age barrow, but this has been disproved (Holst *et al.* 2000). On the other hand, excavation showed that an equally massive construction in Sweden – King Bjorn's Tumulus which features in an early medieval saga – was actually of Late Bronze Age date (Kaliff & Oestergaard 2018; Ullén & Drenzel 2022). Their appearances are so similar that it is easy to appreciate the ambiguity.

Anglo-Saxon royal centres and the reuse of round barrows

When the early medieval royal site at Yeavering was excavated between 1953 and 1962 it seemed as if its only parallels would be found across the North Sea. The location was documented by the historian Bede who recorded the baptism of King Edwin and Queen Aethelburg by the missionary Paulinus, but wider interpretations were influenced by the description of Heorot in *Beowulf.* It is ironic that the epic described events taking place in Scandinavia although it was written down in England. Rosemary Cramp (1957) drew attention to possible links between the excavated buildings and those described in the poem.

Yeavering was excavated by Brian Hope-Taylor (1977). Understandably, his interpretation has dominated subsequent accounts of Anglo-Saxon royal centres in England. This had the result of making it into a type site and raises all the difficulties discussed in Chapter Two. Was it comparable with the other royal centres occupied during the 7th century AD? And, like Lejre, did they draw on the remains of ancient monuments? Yeavering has proved to be almost as exceptional in early medieval studies as Star Carr in the Mesolithic period.

The excavator's interpretation was straightforward, and so to some extent was a new version proposed by the writer more than three decades ago (Bradley 1987). Hope-Taylor saw Yeavering as a long-lived ceremonial centre with a history that extended without any significant break from the Neolithic period to the medieval phase. Alternatively, the sequence was discontinuous. The choice of this location as a centre of royal power was a political act that legitimised the authority of local rulers by referring to the past.

The new interpretation of Yeavering (*Gefrin* in Bede's account) can be amended in several ways. The sequence of excavated structures is not entirely clear (Scull 1991), nor is the detailed chronology of other Great Hall complexes in England (Scull & Thomas 2020), but a more important question is whether some features were peculiar to this site. One was a wooden 'grandstand': a kind of open-air theatre distantly related to Roman prototypes. Another was the siting of the principal buildings along an alignment marked by massive posts. The groups of human burials at Yeavering were unusual, too. Sarah Semple (2013) interprets these features as examples of 'royal theatre'.

At least sixteen Great Hall complexes have been recognised since *Gefrin* and its successor *Melmin* (Milfield) were identified from the air (McBride 2020). Some were discovered by the same method and others have been recorded by geophysical survey or excavation, but none of them has been investigated on such a large scale. Even so, they share many features, in particular the size and layout of the buildings. But do they provide evidence for consistent attitudes to recognisable features surviving from the past? Only half those studied in detail by Adam McBride (2020) are in places where prehistoric structures are documented. In most instances the earlier monuments can be identified as round barrows (there is one case – at Sutton Courtenay in the upper Thames valley – in which a cursus is also represented). At Yeavering, on the other hand, the earliest constructions were rather different (Hope-Taylor 1977). As well as a single round barrow, there was a stone circle. There was also a small henge; another has been excavated outside the royal centre at Milfield (Scull & A. Harding 1990).

Only two of the prehistoric features influenced the layout of the Anglo-Saxon complex (Fig. 7.5). One was a circular mound or ring ditch, and the other was

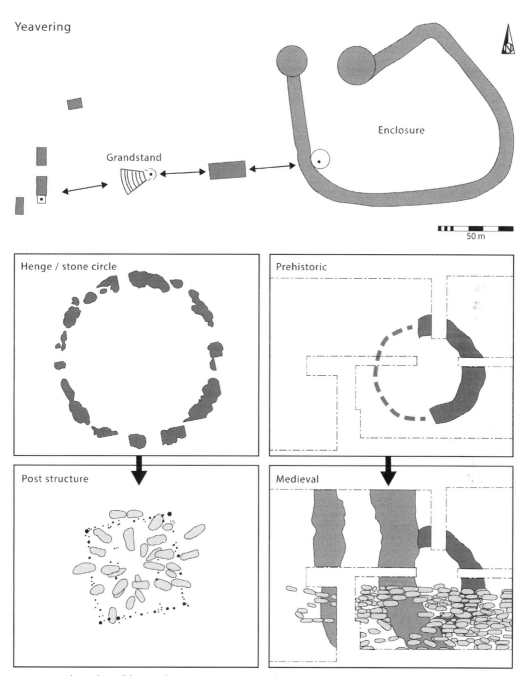

Fig. 7.5. Outline plan of the royal centre at Yeavering, showing how the alignment of medieval structures emphasised the positions of two prehistoric monuments. Information from Hope-Taylor (1977).

apparently the ring of monoliths. Its exact chronology is uncertain, but its plan recalls that of features at Forteviot and again it was associated with cremation burials. During the early medieval period the positions of both the structures at Yeavering were marked by large upright timbers, and other posts were erected in between them to establish the orientation of the royal centre. Then each of the prehistoric monuments was selected as the site of a cemetery. The putative stone circle was replaced by a square wooden building interpreted as a 'mortuary enclosure'. The sequence of events seems clear (Hope-Taylor 1977), yet the third prehistoric component at Yeavering – the only certain henge – played no part in the new layout. It seems to have been used for metal production and there is nothing to indicate that its earthwork was respected (Tinniswood & A. Harding 1991). By contrast, another example on the edge of the neighbouring complex at Milfield was reused as an inhumation cemetery during the 7th century AD (Scull & A. Harding 1990).

In some ways Yeavering was atypical, for the commonest connections were between Great Halls and the sites of Bronze Age round barrows: a pattern that recalls the situation at Lejre. Mounds were obviously important, but their remains did not always remain intact. Later buildings could be aligned on them or might cut across them. They could even be superimposed on these monuments. The important element was that their positions could still be identified, whether or not they were used. They provided physical evidence of connections with the past. In that respect the evidence has features in common with the archaeology of Forteviot. To quote Semple's book *Perceptions of the Prehistoric in Anglo-Saxon England* (2013, 226):

> The ancient monuments of the English landscape became mnemonic markers that assisted the new elite of the Anglo-Saxon Kingdoms in the curation and management of memory and legends ... The ancient in the landscape was pivotal to the shaping of early identities, the forging of intellectual narratives, and the emergence of a materiality linked to an aspirant elite that used the ancient to mould its power in the present.

The sites of other monuments became important during the same period. Howard Williams estimates that a quarter of all the Anglo-Saxon burials in England were in places with older earthworks or other features. Round barrows account for 61% of the total, compared with less than 10% for Neolithic long barrows, and just 7% for Iron Age hill forts. Roman remains were also significant, but only 18% of them were reused in the same way (Williams 1997). The clearest evidence spans the late 5th to the 7th centuries AD and includes isolated graves as well as cemeteries. After that time, groups of burials become less common at these sites.

Such cemeteries could be organised in various ways. Inhumation graves might cluster around older barrows or cut into the earthworks themselves. They could fan outwards from the centre of a mound or be arranged circumferentially around its perimeter. Others could be orientated on its remains. In the case of reused henges, they clustered inside the original enclosure, as happened at Milfield (Fig. 7.6; Scull & A. Harding 1990), but they could also be confined to the exterior; that was the case at

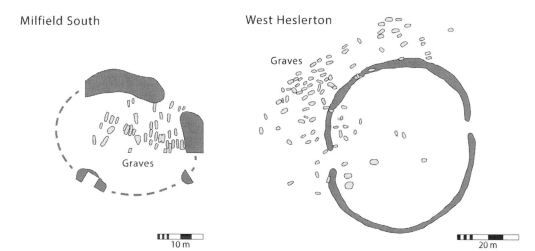

Fig. 7.6. Plans of the Anglo-Saxon cemeteries at Milfield and West Heslerton showing the positions of graves in relation to the earthworks of two henge monuments. Note that the monument at Milfield South was only partly excavated. Information from Scull and A. Harding (1990) and Haughton and Powelsland (1999).

West Heslerton (Haughton & Powelsland 1999). These relationships were not a matter of chance. In Howard Williams's terms they resulted from 'the ritual appropriation of the past' (Williams 2006).

Although insular kinds of monuments might be brought back into use, as certainly happened in other parts of Britain, Williams emphasises that in England these practices were associated with settlers from the Continent where similar conventions were already established:

> For immigrant Germanic groups as well as those indigenous groups that aspired to Germanic ideologies and status, the reuse of older monuments may have been used to portray themselves as the legitimate heirs of ancient peoples and supernatural beings that originally built those structures. Yet on another level, monument reuse could have evoked memories of imagined homelands across the North Sea. Rituals surrounding death at ancient monuments could have played out mythological narratives of gods and heroes and empowered genealogical links to the past (Williams 1998, 112).

The process was like that considered in Chapter Six where Neolithic sites were reused during the Chalcolithic period. Again the evidence of ancient DNA documents a period of settlement from other parts of Europe (Gretzinger *et al.* 2022). In both instances the sequence was interrupted, and such practices referred to distant places as well as distant times.

Christian attitudes to the past

Such relationships were never static and there is evidence that they changed during the later 1st millennium AD. The graves in the later cemeteries were not as richly furnished as their predecessors, but during the 7th century a few unusually lavish deposits were associated with single burials in conspicuous round barrows (Carver 2019, 394–410). These monuments are by no means common, and it is not known how often older structures were brought back into commission. Others were newly built, yet their appearance may still have evoked the forms of ancient mounds.

Like the Great Hall complexes, the richest single graves date from a period of political change when displays of extraordinary artefacts played a part in public events. They would have included assemblies taking place at special locations like the wooden theatre at Yeavering. One case in which both developments may have been linked is the cemetery of Sutton Hoo in eastern England where impressive and exotic grave goods were buried beneath a group of newly built round barrows. The famous ship burials covered by these mounds were inspired by those in Scandinavia (Carver 2005). A new programme of survey and excavation has identified what was probably a royal centre at Rendlesham, 6.5 km away (Scull *et al.* 2016; Minter & Scull 2022). Like Yeavering, its exceptional status was documented by the historian Bede who recorded that it was where the king of the East Saxons converted to Christianity.

Such developments had a wider significance for attitudes to the past. Burial rites seem to have changed. Fewer graves were associated with older round barrows, and those that have been found are not associated with the same quantity or variety of artefacts. The traditions of furnished burial that went back to the late 5th century AD lost much of their influence, although there were occasional exceptions (Carver 2019, 394–410). At the same time, royal sites at places like Lyminge in southern England and Forteviot in central Scotland were gifted to the church and became ecclesiastical centres (Blair 2018, 131–6). To some extent the structures associated with the new religion *confronted* those associated with pagan practices. Hope-Taylor (1977) argued that the site of one of the cemeteries at Yeavering was reused as a Christian church, but this was difficult to prove as his argument depended on historical evidence rather than the results of excavation. But this development was not peculiar to northeast England. The monumental sculptures erected around Forteviot document a similar process, and in this case their religious and political message is unambiguous. '[They were] used to repurpose (if not appropriate) the pagan ceremonial landscape' (Campbell & Driscoll 2020, 191).

The building of churches on other sites illustrates a similar process. It was consistent with the instructions of religious leaders to destroy pagan places of worship or to change their associations to conform with the new religion. Both processes are documented in Scandinavia (Andrén 2013). At Frösö in Sweden a church was built over the position of a tree associated with votive offerings. Others were constructed on top of existing mounds or beside older cemeteries. A more radical development occurred at Old Uppsala where a cathedral was built at a royal centre associated with a group of enormous barrows. The missionary Adam of Bremen records that the site had been used for sacrificing people and animals. Eventually this building was replaced by a similar structure in a new settlement not far away. Anders Andrén

(2013) records that the pillars of its chancel were supported by ancient runestones. In all these ways monuments associated with the new religion rejected the pagan past.

The same seems to have happened in Britain, although the evidence is not as decisive. The sites of Roman temples or mausolea could be appropriated by the followers of the new religion – this sequence is clearly documented at Wells Cathedral (Rodwell 2007) – but more often Christian churches were constructed in or beside prehistoric earthworks or stone circles. Some examples are well known and provide examples of what was evidently a wider phenomenon, although the dating evidence is seldom adequate. They can be associated with the remains of henges, as happened at Knowlton or Avebury, and with settings of monoliths, as at Stanton Drew. At Rudston in north-east England a church was built beside the tallest standing stone in Britain. It had been the pivotal point in a concentration of Neolithic monuments. The same seems to have happened in Scotland where the decorated arch at Forteviot could have come from an ecclesiastical building located on a prehistoric site.

If one approach was to assimilate powerful relics from the past, another was to treat them as threatening and alien to the new system of belief. This has not always been appreciated and helps to explain some extraordinary burials dating from the Middle and Late Saxon periods. They are particularly relevant as they come from celebrated sites.

The clearest evidence is from Sutton Hoo. Once the barrows had gone out of use the site assumed a very different character and between the 8th and 11th centuries AD it was where two groups of execution victims were buried. Thirty-nine graves have been found (Fig. 7.7; Carver 2005, 315–59). Careful investigation confirmed that

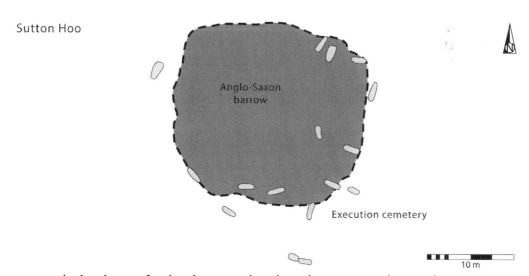

Fig. 7.7. The distribution of medieval execution burials in relation to an Anglo-Saxon barrow at Sutton Hoo. Information from Carver (2005).

the corpses were of people who had been violently killed. There was even a square setting of post holes with a radiocarbon date of AD 690–980 which might have marked the position of a gallows. Similar cemeteries were associated with other kinds of monuments. Although many of them were repurposed prehistoric mounds, they also included linear earthworks and Iron Age hillforts (Reynolds 2009).

The distribution of 'outcast burials' is mainly in southern and eastern England where a series of radiocarbon dates extends between AD 650 and 1200 (Reynolds 2009, table 23). These deposits share several characteristics. Bodies, usually those of men, could be deposited face down in the ground. There is evidence that their hands or legs were tied together. There are indications that certain people had been decapitated, and individual bodies were mutilated. Of course, they may have been killed in battle or random acts of violence, but the strongest arguments are that they were the victims of judicial executions. The locations of their graves provide another clue. Many were associated with older round barrows, but they could also be found at crossroads and beside highways, along territorial boundaries documented in Anglo-Saxon charters, or beside older land divisions. They were kept apart from the world of the living but occupied conspicuous positions in the landscape.

Individual burials may have had a similar significance but when they were first identified they were misunderstood. One was a skeleton found by Sir Mortimer Wheeler in the Neolithic bank barrow at Maiden Castle. The body was of an adult man who 'had been hacked with considerable force by a sharp instrument' (Wheeler 1943, 20–22). Wheeler considered that the grave was contemporary with the prehistoric mound, but a new analysis showed that the injuries were inflicted by a metal sword, meaning that the bones must have been of later date. This was confirmed by a radiocarbon determination in the 7th century AD (Brothwell 1971). This extraordinary burial was not related to the early history of this monument but to a period of reuse.

The same applies to a grave that was found at Stonehenge and initially attributed to the Roman period. The bones attracted the attention of a Welsh dentist Wystan Adams Peach (1961). He persuaded himself that they were those of King Arthur who had built the monument in 1800 BC. Peach even paid for a radiocarbon date, but when it indicated an early medieval context, he questioned the result. In 2002, a new study of the remains showed that the man had been buried between AD 600 and 690. He had been decapitated (Pitts *et al.* 2002). The mutilated corpse at Maiden Castle was of similar age and both may have been execution victims, buried in places with special histories and associations. In fact, the name Stonehenge refers to the massive lintels on the site and compares them with a gallows.

This interpretation is consistent with changing attitudes to ancient monuments remains expressed in Anglo-Saxon literature and iconography. After the adoption of the new religion the past seemed increasingly dangerous. Certain places were feared and could no longer be exploited as a source of social power. If the richest graves had provided a medium for display, now the victims of judicial executions had to be kept at a distance. The argument is summarised in Semple's monograph. By the Late Saxon period:

> The sources ... echo a clear archaeological signature and together they attest to the emergence of some types of ancient monuments, notably barrows, as places synonymous with fear, damnation, with monstrous inhabitants, and with hell (Semple 2013, 235).

Summary

This chapter has focused on the 1st millennium AD in parts of Britain and Scandinavia, for it was during this period that many earlier prehistoric monuments were brought back into commission, perhaps at times of political change. In many cases it is tempting to link these processes directly and to suggest that the new developments drew strength from their associations with the past. They added legitimacy to developments that were entirely new, and in most cases the references to the achievements of previous generations had little basis in reality. This has been a dominant strand in studies of how the past was treated in the past.

But the extended histories of monument reuse in England and southern Scandinavia also suggest a second approach. With the adoption of Christianity, attitudes to earlier structures began to change. People rejected the associations between ancient earthworks, stone settings, and pagan beliefs. New constructions such as churches, crosses, and sacred wells *confronted* the features connected with the past. Other places that had once been significant became increasingly marginal. Now they were avoided and were suitable locations in which to dispose of criminals.

Much of the current literature is concerned with the authority of the past. But it considers only one approach to monumental time. The rejection of history must have been equally significant, but it has still to receive its due from archaeologists. *Attitudes* and *associations* were just as important as *memories* – however those memories were understood – and they require more attention in the future.

Chapter 8

Oral literature and the histories of monuments

Time and oral literature

I must start with a word of explanation. The title of this chapter can be misunderstood. It refers to two subjects that have sometimes been considered together – the composition of oral literature and the development of monuments in the past – but it does not follow the most obvious line of enquiry and archaeological evidence is not used to date the texts. This has been a widespread practise, but it can lead to confusion. Thus, the Irish epic *The Táin* has been interpreted as an eyewitness account of society in the pre-Roman Iron Age, but, if so, the source material would have been a millennium old when it was written down. This approach can be either naïve or sophisticated and is not considered here. Instead, the present account suggests that in the past *both categories of evidence developed along similar lines.* Taken together, such processes shed light on ancient conceptions of the past.

Hengest, Horsa, and Woden
Anglo-Saxon royal genealogies provide an ideal point of departure (Sisam 1954). Although they are known from documentary sources, they could be composed in alliterative verse suitable for recitation on public occasions. Most of them begin with a simple premise. The ancestors of the royal lines were the brothers Hengest and Horsa, who supposedly invaded south-east England in the 5th century AD. They were direct descendants of the Norse god Odin (Woden). Between six and twelve generations had elapsed before the descent lines were written down.

Such genealogies were codified and performed in public as a way of strengthening royal authority. They referred to a distinguished past and to links with otherworldly powers. The same practice was followed in northern Europe where the process took a more extravagant form, so that here the royal ancestors included Classical gods and a participant in the Trojan War. Most of the dynasties in Anglo-Saxon England were content with only one divine ancestor. Even that was to change with the adoption of Christianity.

Noah and Adam

It is obvious that the past was important throughout the sequence. It provided a source of political authority but was entirely malleable and histories could be revised. The course of events could not be recalled with any accuracy – how far back memories remained intact is still a matter for debate – but their earlier stages were subject to manipulation. There is no reason to discount the documentary sources entirely, but the first sections of these genealogies must have been strategic fictions. With the adoption of the Christian religion descent from a pagan god was no longer appropriate, so elements associating later rulers with supernatural powers were dropped from these accounts. Instead, there were attempts to trace royal descent back to Old Testament sources. Now the biblical figures of Adam and Noah took the place of Woden.

Beowulf

Even the epic poem *Beowulf* begins by explaining the hero's descent. Before it was written down, the story would have been performed in front of an audience. The text was recited from memory and evoked a world of heroes, dramatic deeds, supernatural beings, and events taking place long ago. How would the listeners have understood them? When did those events happen – in a recent past, or in one that was beyond recall? And were the stories set in locations that could still be identified, or did they occur in an imaginary world? These questions have engaged scholars who consider the narrative in relation to the modern landscapes of Denmark and Sweden (Overing & Osborn 1994; Niles & Osborn 2007). Some authorities have claimed that the feasting hall of Heorot was situated at Lejre (Christensen 2015).

Even more pressing problems arise. Like other oral epics, *Beowulf* is known from a written text, although the age of the only manuscript is uncertain; in any case there are indications that it drew on an earlier copy that no longer survives (Lapidge 2000). How long was the interval (if any) between oral performances of the poem and the time when it was first written down? Why were its contents preserved so long after its composition, and how did that process colour its subsequent reception? These questions are not confined to the Anglo-Saxon poem and have also been asked by scholars studying the Ulster Cycle in Ireland (Mallory 2016) and the works of Homer in Greece (Sherratt & Bennet 2017b).

The past in performance

The composition of oral epics calls for special skills. They include impressive feats of memory and, in the case of those composed in verse, the ability to frame the contents according to a strict literary form. These effects must be a result of training and experience, and such skills are uncommon. Poets, bards, or storytellers enjoy a special status in ethnographic and historical accounts. That is only emphasised by the contexts in which they perform.

The texts indicate that in the past they were recited on particular occasions, such as royal inaugurations, funerals, assemblies, and feasts. They were addressed to distinguished audiences and the performances probably happened at special locations. Among the most plausible candidates are some of the monuments considered in earlier chapters – prehistoric henges, mounds, and the Great Halls of the early Middle Ages. The timber 'grandstand' at Yeavering may well have fulfilled this role, but so could a variety of ancient earthworks and stone settings which had suitable acoustic properties for use on public occasions. Their ability to project and amplify sound can be shown by experiment (Watson & Keating 1999).

Ethnographic accounts shed some light on the character of oral literature, especially in Africa and the Balkans. Two books, both published some time ago, have been particularly influential. It seems appropriate that they have such memorable titles. The first is Albert Lord's *The Singer of Tales* which appeared in 1960. It built on the pioneering work of Milman Parry who had died many years before; his collected papers appeared a decade later (Parry 1971). Together these scholars had recorded and studied traditional poetry in Bosnia and showed how its construction shared features with the work of Homer. Although their thesis was not accepted by every Classical scholar, most agreed that it shed new light on the relationship between oral poetry and written texts.

The other book is by the anthropologist Jack Goody who published *The Domestication of the Savage Mind* in 1977. He was also concerned with the nature of oral performances, and, like Parry and Lord, he recorded and compared their contents in the field. He also discussed the contrast with written texts. He drew on his observations in Ghana and argued that the adoption of writing has fundamental implications for the interpretation of traditional narratives and the understanding of past events.

These works provide insights into the ways in which oral literature is composed and performed. It can celebrate local origins or identities and narrate a distinguished past. Here the recitation of genealogies plays an important role. Both books emphasise some important distinctions between texts performed on public occasions and those which are subsequently written down. In oral sources the same events may feature in several versions, and elements from different stories or poems can be brought together and combined. There is less concern with an overarching structure. Inconsistencies or repetitions do not raise the problems that would affect a written account, and separate versions cannot be compared in any detail.

Those studies show that the contents of oral literature vary between different performances so that there is no definitive version of the text. Performers may add new material or omit passages that were included on other occasions. They can also modify the narrative according to their audience. The contents of epic literature are known to change over the generations even though the presenters try to maintain the traditional format. They mean to respect the all-important narrative, but this is difficult to achieve, and they may not be aware of the extent of variation from one occasion to another. It would be easy to explain these changes because the texts are committed to memory, but, as Goody observed, in some respects bards compose their material in the course of performance. Other factors may be equally significant. There are no written sources with which to compare the oral accounts and, unlike the actors in a theatre, these 'singers of tales' cannot learn their material from a script.

In the circumstances how are the contents recalled? A clue is provided by those texts that were eventually written down. There is a fundamental distinction between poetry and prose. Verse offers less scope for improvisation and is simpler to recall. Prose is much more flexible. An epic framed in verse form – for example *The Iliad* or *The Odyssey* – is composed according to a strict metrical pattern. In the same way, the text of *Beowulf* depends on the systematic use of alliteration: a fundamental characteristic of Anglo-Saxon poems. Both techniques make the material easier to remember, so that it becomes difficult to depart from the usual contents. There are repeated formulae that can act as mnemonics during an oral recitation. Descriptive devices that conform to the appropriate metre are repeated at various points, allowing the presenter to maintain a continuous flow. These elements persuaded scholars that Homeric epics codified stories that began as oral recitations.

False memories and unreliable narrators

Mythical time is important here. Should *The Iliad* and *The Odyssey* be treated simply as entertaining stories about the past? In 1935, the French author Jean Giraudoux wrote a play with the striking title *La guerre de Troie n'aura pas lieu* (*The Trojan War Will Not Take Place*). It raised a question that has preoccupied generations of scholars. Did such a conflict really happen? Can the poems of Homer be accepted as historic documents and, if so, how were the poems related to the events they described? Both were set in the Mycenaean Age – the period whose archaeology cast a spell over investigators of Stonehenge and Bredarör – but they were written down much later. That process may have taken place only gradually. Five hundred years or more passed since the time the poems described.

The texts of both epics create chronological problems, for they refer to artefacts and practices that are likely to date from different phases; they may also draw on sources assembled from separate regions. The argument certainly applies to the weapons and jewellery described in the texts. Most are not Mycenaean types, and others assumed forms that remained in use after that period. In the same way, the battle scenes described in *The Odyssey* feature modes of combat which are not likely to have been employed together. For the most part the material culture of *The Odyssey* and *The Iliad* resembles that of the 8th century BC rather than earlier periods. As Oliver Dickinson says, 'It is hard to see that any genuine memories lie behind the tale of the Trojan War' (2017, 14).

One of the best-known passages in *The Iliad* is *The Catalogue of Ships* which lists the Greek participants in the war. Dickinson criticises the ways in which this information has been used by scholars. Palaces documented by excavation are never mentioned in the poem, and the geography of the Catalogue raises serious difficulties. Only Mycenae, Pylos, and Troy play a significant role in both the text and the archaeological record:

> I would assert that in every major region of the Mycenaean mainland, the picture presented by the 'Catalogue' is more or less *wrong* ... I believe it symbolises the nature of the epic tradition as a whole. In its account of social conditions and material culture, the epic tradition simply cannot be made to fit a single period; rather, it is a poetically created amalgam of features of different periods (emphasis in the original; Dickinson 2017, 11).

The Irish sources raise a similar question. They are considered in Jim Mallory's book *In Search of the Irish Dreamtime* (Mallory 2016). His choice of title is revealing – again the ancient tales describe a version of history that was imaginary but of great significance. They record heroic stories set in a distant past and tell of events that were thought to have happened long before the texts were written down. Like the poems attributed to Homer, the Ulster Cycle contains some obvious anachronisms. Although the narrative refers to places which had been occupied in the Iron Age, the most distinctive artefacts, and the materials of which they were made, do not correspond to those recorded in the archaeology of that period. Instead, they resemble the equipment of the Viking Age. Like the distinctive objects described in *The Odyssey* and *The Iliad*, they must be related to the time when the stories were set down in their current forms. These chronological disparities would not have been apparent to the original audiences who were not archaeologists.

But there are certain contrasts between these sources. At least some of the locations that feature in the Ulster Cycle do provide archaeological evidence dating from the prehistoric period. In four cases a direct link connects them to the present day. The names of places seem to have been more resilient than the stories told about them (Waddell 2018). Thus, the Hill of Tara is called *Teamhair* in the text, Knockaullin is the current version of *Dún Ailinne*, and early medieval *Cruachain* is now Rathcroghan. Even Navan Fort echoes its Old Irish equivalent *Emain Macha*. The geography of ancient Ireland was recalled more accurately than that of ancient Greece.

The buildings described by Homer are not like Mycenaean architecture, but there is a controversial link between the Great Houses associated with Irish sites and the enormous timber buildings revealed by excavation and geophysical survey. They date from the late 1st millennium BC and the first two centuries AD (Mallory 2016, 146–56). This evidence requires careful handling. Roundhouses of smaller proportions were occupied in the early medieval period, and some were still inhabited not long before the tales were written down. The size of the largest structures could have been exaggerated in the written sources – like so many elements, everything was represented on a grand scale. Alternatively, buildings of these proportions really existed at the time. They were very rare, but Richard Warner (2018) argues that they are documented by archaeological evidence. What is apparent is that Iron Age earthworks survived in all these places, and their presence had to be explained.

Recording oral sources

Beowulf

Oral sources assumed a new importance when they were recorded in permanent form. In England that happened after the Conversion and probably was the work of monks. The final version of *Beowulf* attempted to equip the ancient narrative with a Christian moral. This has led to confusion because in some ways it represented a forced marriage between incompatible systems of belief. This development recalls the important changes in the use of monuments discussed in Chapter Seven – after the 8th century AD places associated with a pagan past were altered or even shunned. In time the poem may have been revised to accommodate the new religion, and its narrative was represented as a battle between good and evil. That could have been why for the first time the text of the poem was written down.

Irish sources

The Irish sources were also recorded by monks who were well read and familiar with Latin. The scribes made some attempt to recreate the past since they incorporated material taken from Classical authors and the Bible (Mallory 2016). This was not always recognised and led early scholars to accept the antiquity of the tales (Jackson 1964). In fact, the oral narratives were written down in the late 1st millennium AD. The 'royal centres' of the Iron Age – sites like Navan Fort and the Hill of Tara – had been impressive, and so had the great timber buildings associated with them. Their construction must have consumed a vast amount of raw material. The early post-Roman period saw increasing fragmentation as a series of small kingdoms formed in Ireland (Gleeson 2018). It was not until the early medieval period that there are new signs of political unity. It witnessed the rise of the Uí Néill as the dominant dynasty (Bhreathnach 1993 & 1999). Traditional accounts of such powerful places might have offered a precedent for this development, and it may be why they were recorded.

Homer

Finally, the significance of the Greek epics was considered in an influential paper by Ian Morris. There are differences of opinion on when they were written down and the stages by which the poems assumed their definitive forms, but there seems little doubt that significant changes were happening at that time (Morris 1986). The texts recalled an aristocratic lifestyle and a heroic past. They were recorded as part of a wider political process that saw the establishment of the Panhellenic games and the creation of the first state sanctuaries. The *polis* originated during the same period. These developments promoted a stronger sense of unity and helped to create new identities. Morris suggests that alphabetic writing first developed in Greece during the same period. One incentive was to preserve these poems.

In every case the past was open to revision. The same was true of monuments, and they are considered now.

Writing it down

Did the written sources promote a new stability? They must have changed the character of accounts that had been performed in public, and, as Jack Goody recognised, in time they would allow different versions of the same material to be compared and combined (Goody 1977). They also created the conditions for a new kind of scholarship and would eventually inform the distinction between history and prehistory. But there were many problems along the way, and these can best be illustrated by returning to the archaeology of Greece and Ireland. It was a literal reading of Homer that led Heinrich Schliemann to excavate at Mycenae and Troy, with results that appear credulous today (Haubold 2017). In the same way, the role of Irish hillforts was interpreted in terms of the ancient *Book of Invasions* (Champion 1982), and those on the Aran Islands were seen as the last refuge of an embattled population. A century ago, that view was widely shared (Waddell 2005, 195).

In some ways investigations of monuments follow a similar path to the analysis of ancient sources. Indeed, the findings of field archaeology are generally recorded in texts of other kinds: in articles, monographs, drawings, photographs, archives, and museum displays. Their contents can be reassessed and are sometimes checked on the ground, but the structures they describe are generally sorted into *types* according to a process very like the ordering of written information. At one time material culture was studied as a kind of text, to be investigated using similar principles to literary theory (Hodder 1989). This approach was weakened by its emphasis on portable objects. Architecture in its widest sense played a limited role in this discussion.

Monuments of any kind present a problem. They are considered according to specific types, but how are those categories established in the first place? They are a product of one kind of field archaeology – generally topographical survey – and need to be compatible with current methods of cataloguing information, such as computer databases, inventories, and Historic Environment Records. By their nature they must treat these classes as fixed. Yet excavation provides a very different perspective. Did these structures necessarily take set forms, and would they have adhered to them over long periods of time? Did they pass from one category to another in the orderly succession that modern textbooks imply? It seems unlikely. More important, were they 'completed' – did they ever assume a definitive form? The surface traces that provide the basis for categorising monuments may represent nothing more than the stage at which the process of revision was abandoned. All traces of earlier elements were concealed from view.

Different kinds of survey – from remote sensing to the mapping of earthworks – create the diagnostic types used in wider syntheses, but intrusive investigations frequently take them apart again. Structures erected at different stages in the history of a particular site can be hidden or obscured over the course of time. Chapter One provided several examples of this process; perhaps the most informative was the medieval transformation of the largest mound at Knowth. Perhaps the 'types' which define the archaeology of monuments were as fluid as the contents of oral literature and could have changed to the same extent. They are an artefact of modern fieldwork and the records that illustrate its findings. Those categories need not reflect a past reality. Perhaps these buildings were subject to comparable developments to the performance of epic poetry and their histories could shed light on similar attitudes to antiquity. Even when people believed that they were conforming to an established tradition, there was scope for improvisation and innovation.

It is worth enumerating some of the parallels between these media. Excavation shows that many monuments changed their forms almost imperceptibly. Without any radical change, they shifted from one 'type' to another. New elements were added to the design and other features were eliminated. There was an appearance of continuity even when the structures were rebuilt. Many of them conformed to the same archetypes. In some cases, they retained a circular ground plan when other components changed; elsewhere linear monuments were extended. Exotic elements could be introduced in physical guise like the monoliths transported to Stonehenge (Parker Pearson *et al.* 2015). An alternative is the citing of distant models. A good example is the sharing of ground plans between Late Iron Age ship settings across northern Europe (Vestergaard 2007).

Another comparison is especially relevant here. The performers of oral texts are prompted by literary conventions – the repetition of formulaic descriptions at intervals during the narration, or the rules of composition in metrical or alliterative verse. They do not have any counterparts in prehistoric architecture. On the other hand, their origins might have been prompted by features that were already present. They might include 'natural' elements such as mounds or springs, but there could also be older constructions of similar or different kinds. Thus Muiris O'Sullivan (2005) suggests that in Ireland the Hill of Tara was already sacred before the first structures were built there. Later monuments were arranged around the remains of the passage tomb on its summit.

The distinction between *distant* and *proximate* relationships is important here and qualifies any simple notion of reuse. *Proximate* relationships might be compared with the revisions of oral texts made during performance – obvious examples include the anachronistic descriptions of artefacts in the work of Homer. More *distant* relationships, on the other hand, can be compared with the borrowings in Irish literature, for example the use of Classical or Biblical sources to add authenticity to accounts of the past.

These relationships are even more confusing when such texts are combined with field evidence. A telling example is George Petrie's survey of the Hill of Tara published in 1839. He provided an accurate plan of the surviving earthworks on the site and identified them by name according to a literary description dating from the early Middle Ages. By that means they were related to the structures described in ancient sources. The original account belonged to the distinctive genre known as the *dinnshenchas* (the lore of places) and seems to have been intended to celebrate the association between this famous site and the Ui Néill (Bhreathnach 1999). Again, it is important to consider the contexts in which traditions were written down.

A Hebridean case study

So far, this account has suggested that prehistoric monuments and oral literature 'developed along similar lines'. Here the argument is illustrated by an example which draws on some of the features considered already.

The architectural sequence at Calanais

The main group of structures at Calanais (sometimes spelt Callanish) is near the west coast of Lewis and is connected to the open water by Loch Roagh and Loch Barraglom (Richards 2013, 254–80; Ashmore 2016). The complex extends along a prominent ridge, which slopes down from a rocky crag called Cnoc an Tursa (Fig. 8.1). Local sea

Fig. 8.1. (Upper) The stone settings at Calanais seen on the skyline from the east. The crag, Cnoc an Tursa, is to the left, the stone circle is in the centre, and the Northern Avenue is to the right. (Lower) The natural 'cave' below Cnoc an Tursa. Photographs: Richard Bradley.

levels have changed since the Neolithic period and when the first monuments were built, this area of higher ground was cut off from its surroundings, although it was not quite an island. The complex has been investigated more than once, but not all the results of the excavations are published. As a result, there is some uncertainty about the exact sequence.

The main component of this complex is not the famous stone circle of Calanais Site 1 but the crag whose Gaelic name means The Hill of Sorrow. Seen from a distance, it resembles a great mound or cairn similar to those considered in Chapter One, and at its northern limit there is a geological feature that looks very like a chamber or a cave. Its entrance is framed by massive boulders. On excavation it contained charcoal and traces of hearths. Other features were found outside it.

The opening into Cnoc an Tursa was not modified by human agency, but small cairns may have been built on other parts of the outcrop. The lower ground to its north was cultivated from the later 4th millennium BC and included a small enclosure whose date and purpose are unknown. It was disturbed during a second period of arable farming, but after that time the site assumed a specialised role and the first of the famous stone settings were established there. They changed their character over a lengthy period starting about 3000 BC.

Calanais combined architectural features of kinds that occur separately on other sites: several stone rows, a stone circle, and a small round cairn associated with a megalithic chamber (Fig. 8.2). Specialists do not agree on the order in which these

Fig. 8.2. The Northern Avenue at Calanais viewed from the stone circle. Photograph: Richard Bradley.

components were built, but a few relationships have been established by excavation. Two parallel rows of monoliths, which are usually together treated together as the 'Northern Avenue', followed the crest of the ridge as far as a ring of standing stones. Three shorter alignments extended out from that circle: two of them at right angles to the principal axis, and a third which was directed towards the cave opening beneath Cnoc an Tursa.

That stone circle dominates most accounts of Calanais, and less attention is paid to the other elements. But this overlooks an observation that has always raised some problems. An exceptionally tall monolith is present inside the stone circle itself. Practical considerations mean that it must have been in position before the other stones were erected and it might originally have stood on its own. In fact, it had an obvious orientation. To the south it was directed towards the natural 'chamber', and to the north it was in line with another unusually high standing stone at the end of the Avenue. Perhaps these features were part of the earliest layout on the site; there is nothing to show whether the smaller stones in the same row were erected at this stage.

Although it is accepted that the central pillar was older than the monoliths around it, the date of the remaining elements is uncertain. Most interpretations consider both lines of monoliths in the northern setting as a single structure, but this may not be right. The western axis was aligned on the upright inside the stone circle. It was also directed towards the opening beneath Cnoc an Tursa, but the opposite row 10 m to its east changed direction as it approached the stone circle. Anyone moving down the Avenue would have entered that monument at a slight angle. It seems possible that its eastern component *was offset from an older file of uprights*. This could have happened when the circular setting was built. The files of smaller slabs extending out from that ring might have been erected at the same time.

From about 3000 BC that circle became the second focus of the complex. At some stage a clay platform was built there and then a small timber building. Its plan was like that of the megalithic tomb that followed it in the same position during the mid- to late 3rd millennium BC (Fig. 8.3). It was significantly later in date than most passage graves in northern Britain and incorporated structural elements that might have been inspired by the forms of older monuments. Like the wooden structure, its entrance established a new orientation towards the east.

An interpretation

Over time the ceremonial centre at Calanais changed in a similar fashion to an oral narrative. Its layout may have been modified, yet there is no sign of any radical transformation. Although it is difficult to arrange the structures in order, nearly all the elements referred to those already present. There was an appearance of continuity despite the evidence for change.

Perhaps this complex initially celebrated the importance of the crag. It was treated like a passage grave and could even have been considered as an entrance to the

Fig. 8.3. The megalithic tomb within the stone circle at Calanais. Photograph: Richard Bradley.

underworld. Its striking topography is celebrated by its Gaelic name, and even now the rock emits a shaft of light around the middle of the day. Almost all the structures at Calanais guided people towards the cave mouth. In an early phase this might have been achieved by a single alignment of monoliths. Afterwards movement was controlled by erecting a formal avenue and a ring of enormous standing stones. Lines of upright slabs to its east and west restricted access along the ridge and ensured that visitors had to pass through the enclosure before they could reach Cnoc an Tursa.

Eventually the situation changed again. The layout of the circle had meant that people crossed its interior to the east of the great standing stone, but during the Late Neolithic period that space was occupied by a wooden building of some kind. Then a cairn and a chambered tomb occupied the same position. They blocked the route originally established by the Avenue. At the same time this arrangement drew on the special associations of Calanais and reinforced the significance of underground chambers in its layout. Perhaps the new construction *replaced* the cave beneath Cnoc an Tursa. The complex still dominated its surroundings around the head of the loch, and yet it was strangely isolated. It might have been where people believed that they could pass between different worlds.

Continuous recreation
This example illustrates the way in which a sequence of monument 'types' could come about through emphatic but diverse restatements of a single narrative. It was

concerned with an important and unusual location, and the beliefs associated with it. They were commemorated in various guises for more than five hundred years. Comparison with oral literature suggests that accounts of ancestral figures could be revised according to changing circumstances, and this may have been equally true of stone settings like those at Calanais. Similar developments happened in other places, some of which have already featured in this book. The exact details are different, but in many cases they show how histories could be refreshed and maintained over long periods of time.

Chapter 9

Monumental times: Avebury and the Upper Kennet Valley

Introduction

Previous chapters have reviewed various relationships between monuments and conceptions of time. Some were more securely documented than others, and it is clear that no one model accounts for all these observations. Different notions must have coexisted in the past, as they do in the ethnographic present (Robb 2023). There is the important contrast between measured time – the scale of radiocarbon dating or artefact chronology – and experienced time which might include the agricultural cycle, human generations, and the passage of the seasons. One describes a scheme devised by archaeologists for their purposes, and the other refers to the lives of the people whom they study. Even broader distinctions are possible, but they do not account for every variation. There is the distinction between *genealogical time* and *mythical time* which has been considered already. There are everyday processes that can be described as *habitual*, and the extended scale at which more lasting structures were made. It has been called *public time* (Gosden 1994) and describes the subject of this book.

Chapter One introduced many of the key elements and illustrated them with a short account of sites in the Boyne Valley. It made the point that they provide indications of various time scales and that monuments which were built in very different circumstances coexist in the archaeological record (as their visible remains do today). It introduced the importance of *multi-temporality*. This concept poses a problem for those who display ancient monuments to the public. How should the surviving fabric be presented when it mixes features of various dates? They might have fulfilled separate functions in the past and now they are juxtaposed in a way that can cause confusion. The same discussion considered the Swedish cairn of Bredarör where the problem was made more severe because the excavator rebuilt the cairn to illustrate a thesis concerning the relationship between Mycenae and Bronze Age Scandinavia.

Multi-temporality provides an important corrective to simple ideas of how monuments were reused, but the lesson is seldom taken to heart. Fieldworkers and heritage managers rarely pay enough attention to the problems raised by ancient architecture – the succession of structures built in the same small areas; the phases of intense activity and the mysterious discontinuities that punctuate the histories of these places. The task of establishing a sequence seems more urgent than studying perceptions of time. As Chapter One observed, some examples might have been intended to celebrate a past, while others were directed to an uncertain future.

Perhaps it is worth considering the areas of tension between the field archaeologist's quest for order – for a clearly defined succession of different types – and the ways in which they referred to one another over the course of time. Did the forms, locations, or contents of these buildings allude to physical features that were already present? Or did people reject connections of this kind? Did such long intervals pass between the erection of different monuments that their roles had to be reimagined? And, if so, did any elements retain their significance in the long term?

This account has features in common with that in Chapter One as it considers another series of monuments whose histories extend from the Neolithic phase to the early medieval period. Again, the sites are very well known. This chapter does not offer a new interpretation of the structures around Avebury. Instead, the emphasis is on how they illustrate the themes introduced in this book.

To keep the argument within bounds, the review is in three parts. The first is restricted to the Early and Middle Neolithic periods, and the second considers the Late Neolithic. A third examines the Iron Age and the Late Saxon phases. The longest sections study what may have been an unbroken sequence from the early 4th millennium to the mid-3rd millennium BC. In contrast, developments in the 1st millennium AD were discontinuous. This recalls the important distinction between proximate and distant relationships in the past.

The 'natural' background

The focal point of the entire complex was the River Kennet and its tributary, the Winterbourne. They were linked to two important earthworks. The Winterbourne passed the great henge of Avebury and joined the Kennet in the lee of Silbury Hill. In turn, the Kennet was the principal tributary of the River Thames which it joined 60 km to the east (Fig. 9.1; Pollard & Reynolds 2002; Gillings & Pollard 2004). There were more monuments downstream, including an enormous Neolithic mound at Marlborough (Leary *et al.* 2013). Even now water emerges seasonally from the chalk. The one spring that rarely dries up is overlooked by the largest prehistoric mound in Europe. It was a mysterious phenomenon that might have been regarded with awe.

The surrounding hills had other characteristics. Until they were cleared by farmers from the Bronze Age onwards, they were covered by a distinctive kind of sandstone known as sarsen. Not only did it offer potential building material, its strange forms

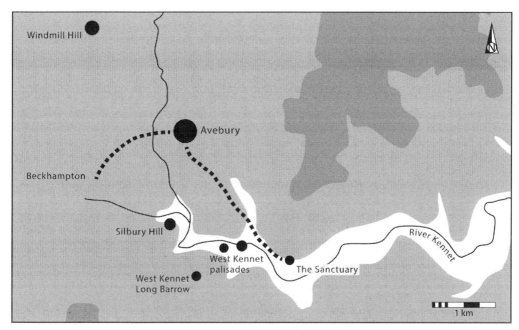

Fig. 9.1. Map showing the monuments discussed in Chapter Nine.

resembled those of petrified people or animals (Gillings *et al.* 2008; Gillings & Pollard 2016; Whitaker 2020 & 2022). The rock preserved the root structures of plants, giving it an organic appearance, which must have attracted attention because it could not be explained. Sarsen played a part in the histories of special artefacts. Several were used as polissoirs for working axes (Drisse 2017). Afterwards they were incorporated in the Neolithic monuments.

The sarsens around the Upper Kennet Valley commanded special attention because the tallest monoliths at Stonehenge were obtained from a source only 5 km from Avebury (Nash *et al.* 2020). It is no surprise that they were used in more local buildings. Other rocks were introduced from a distance and included pieces of oolite brought from an area 25 km to the west (I. Smith 1965, 33). They had special properties as they contained fossils that could be recognised as the remains of living creatures. They were employed as building material and used to temper pottery. Clay was another material that played a special role. It was collected from the river – surely an important association – and filled the sockets of several standing stones (Banfield 2016). A comparable phenomenon has been recognised at Stonehenge where non-local materials occur in equivalent contexts (Whitaker 2019).

In one sense these elements formed a 'natural' background to the Avebury complex, but, in another, they might have been among the features that gave this region its character. Perhaps they were treated as animate and the sarsens were living beings (cf. Jones *et al.* 2011).

The 'cultural' background

Early and Middle Neolithic
The earliest developments concern three kinds of structure, each of which has been considered already. They are long barrows (with or without internal chambers), a causewayed enclosure, and three wooden buildings which might have been the remains of houses. The features of the local landscape were important too, and that remained the case during later periods.

Long barrows
These monuments cluster around Avebury and have not been found in significant numbers down the Kennet valley further to the east. Those with radiocarbon dates were used between about 3700 and 3200 BC. Four have been excavated on a large scale but vary considerably in size. The best known, the West Kennet long barrow, was about twice the length of the smallest (Fig. 9.2; Pollard & Reynolds 2002, 58–70). The example at Horslip may have been built over an older mound or enclosure, and South Street long barrow overlay a group of sarsens (Ashbee *et al.* 1979). Not all of them were associated with human remains, but it did apply to the larger mounds, and to other examples recorded in the 19th century.

There are significant variations within this concentration of monuments. To the east there are mounds with stone chambers, while unchambered examples predominate towards the west (Piggott 1962). To a large extent the same division

Fig. 9.2. The façade of West Kennett long barrow. Photograph: Aaron Watson.

can be recognised among the excavated deposits (Gillings & Pollard 2004, 27–9). The megalithic mounds were associated with the disarticulated remains of many people, but the smaller 'unchambered' barrows were associated with a limited number of burials, and in some cases no human remains have been found there. It is likely that they date from separate phases. This interpretation depends on a few radiocarbon dates which suggest that the earthen long barrows were later than the megalithic examples and date from the second half of the 4th millennium BC (Whittle *et al.* 2011, 719–27). Perhaps researchers have conflated two phenomena. Less imposing mounds towards the west of the distribution 'closed' the use of places that *had been important in the past* (although they might be revisited during later periods). Further to the east, the mounds with stone chambers represented a different concept and were *directed towards a future* of uncertain duration.

Paradoxically, the excavated monument at West Kennet exemplifies both principles. It is a chambered tomb set in the eastern end of a long mound. One chamber was cleared during the 19th century, but four others remained intact until they were investigated in the 1950s (Piggott 1962). They contained at least 36 individuals whose bodies had been placed there over no more than fifty years. The primary deposits date from the 37th century BC. Certain details of the earthwork are particularly relevant to this account. It overlooked the source of the Kennet, and its axis was directed down the river. The entrance faced the morning sun. Its alignment must have been important because the earthwork seems to have been lengthened during a secondary phase.

The chambered tomb was used for half a century before it was closed, but it was brought back into use after a period of abandonment that could have lasted three hundred years (Bayliss *et al.* 2007, 85–101). At that stage it seems possible that part of the roof was removed, and the primary deposits were exposed. Then for almost a millennium the chambers were filled with additional material which included inhumation burials, disarticulated human bones, cremations, faunal remains, and a selection of artefacts. The excavators recognised 10 layers in the interior of the monument (Piggott 1962), and radiocarbon dating confirms that these were added in sequence (Bayliss *et al.* 2007). The process came to an end when decorated Beaker vessels were placed inside it during the late 3rd millennium BC.

The Windmill Hill causewayed enclosure
The sequence at West Kennet long barrow recalls the interplay between 'open' and 'closed' monuments, but the clearest example of an open-ended project is provided by the Windmill Hill enclosure (Fig. 9.3). It was used for up to four centuries from 3800 or 3700 BC (the available dates can be interpreted in more than one way). The site played an important part in the development of Neolithic studies in Britain because it was so prolific and was excavated on an ambitious scale (I. Smith 1965). The results of the original project have been reinterpreted in the light of further fieldwork (Whittle *et al.* 1999).

Windmill Hill

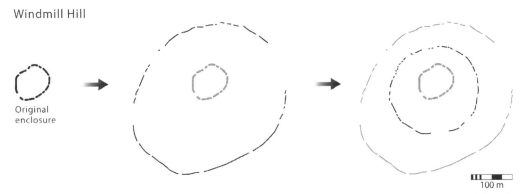

Original
enclosure

100 m

Fig. 9.3. The sequence of causewayed enclosures on Windmill Hill. Information from Whittle et al. (2011).

The earthworks on Windmill Hill consist of three circuits of banks and interrupted ditches. They are approximately concentric but the spaces in between them are greater towards the southwest. The ditches silted naturally, although certain deposits within their filling must have been deliberately covered over. In particular, that applies to articulated animal bones. The project identified important contrasts between the items found in each circuit and suggested the grading of space according to fairly strict conventions. The people who visited the monument – and anyone who lived there – must have accepted the correct forms of conduct and acknowledged them by leaving the right kinds of offerings in the appropriate places. These circuits had different emphases. Alasdair Whittle and his colleagues conclude that the outermost space related to 'more marginal or socially dangerous realms, whereas the interior perhaps had closer associations with more central aspects of life including consumption, sharing and the enactment of routine tasks' (Whittle *et al.* 1999, 371).

The inner earthwork contained animal bones associated with the processing and consumption of meat, together with large quantities of pottery and worked flint. They are like the finds from settlements. The outer ditch, on the other hand, contained articulated faunal remains, suggesting offerings of meat joints or the sacrifice of livestock. Excavation found human bones, especially those of children, and fragments of stone axes. The finds from the middle ditch shared elements with both collections. They included groups of cattle bones, and evidence for the working of sarsen, bone, and antler. Different kinds of pottery were associated with each of these earthworks.

Since that analysis was published, the Windmill Hill enclosure has been investigated by radiocarbon dating. Bayesian analysis shows the circuits were not built together, although their earthworks would have coexisted towards the end of the sequence (Whittle *et al.* 2011, 61–7). The inner enclosure was the earliest, followed by the large outer earthwork; the middle enclosure came last. The intervals between them were brief. How does this analysis affect interpretations of the monument?

There is no reason to question earlier accounts of the material placed in the ditches, but the radiocarbon dates mean that not all these deposits were contemporaneous, at least in their earlier stages: the character of the site must have varied over time. The simplest idea is that Windmill Hill began as a specialised settlement. Its primary role changed until it was more involved in the production of artefacts, feasting, sacrifices, and the commemoration of the dead. It may have retained a domestic core but developed into a public monument.

The new work has two implications. Archaeologists are used to dividing prehistoric structures into standard 'types'. Windmill Hill is no exception, and for many years it provided the model for causewayed enclosures in England. All three circuits took the same physical form and for that reason they were assigned to the same category. But the sequence identified by Bayesian analysis suggests that this site changed its nature although its configuration stayed the same. There is another way of understanding its development. The original enclosure was comparatively small, but during succeeding phases it was preserved inside two larger circuits which took more effort to build. The character of the monument was modified in ways that prehistorians find difficult to understand, but there is a possible explanation. Were the later earthworks intended to screen the original nucleus and to *commemorate, or even to protect,* its oldest component?

Houses?
The timber buildings in this complex are still more difficult to discuss. Little trace survives, but the sites of wooden structures have been recognised beneath the outer bank of the Windmill Hill enclosure (Whittle *et al.* 1999, fig. 220). Another was in the centre of the Southern Circle at Avebury (Gillings *et al.* 2019). The case depends on comparison with better-defined examples in other regions, yet the solitary example at Avebury seems to have been associated with a concentration of Neolithic artefacts. It is relevant to this account because its position was marked by a later setting of standing stones.

The Late Neolithic

The Avebury henge and stone circles
The layout of the main monument at Avebury seems easier to understand because of the way in which its parts have been restored and presented to the public (I. Smith 1965). Like the chambered tombs in the Boyne Valley, visitors encounter a mixture of prehistoric and 20th-century elements. During the 1930s, parts of the historic village of Avebury were cleared by Alexander Keiller to emphasise the remains of a more ancient past.

In its present form the monument combines several elements: a massive circular earthwork with four opposed entrances; a large stone circle which follows the inner edge of its ditch; and two smaller circles with settings of monoliths inside them (Fig. 9.4; Gillings & Pollard 2004). Avenues defined by pairs of standing stones lead from the south and west entrances; they will be considered later. Some of the sarsen uprights at Avebury remained in position, but others were re-erected when their locations were established by Keiller's excavation. Where individual monoliths

Avebury

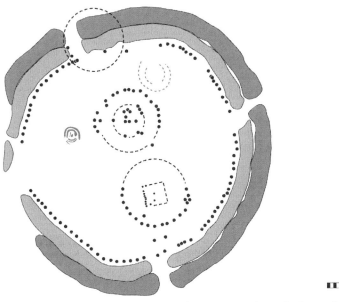

Fig. 9.4. Outline plan of the principal structures identified (or postulated) inside the Avebury henge monument. Information from Burl (1979), Gillings and Pollard (2004), and Gillings et al. *(2019).*

had been destroyed their positions were indicated by concrete markers. The entire layout gives the impression of a coherent design, but this is deceptive. In theory the complex brings together a number of distinct 'types' – a henge, three stone circles, two avenues, and a cove (a semicircular setting of uprights) – but the relationships between them are not straightforward.

Keiller's excavation of the monument was guided by his conception of how these elements were organised in the past. It influenced the placing of his trenches. He also drew on antiquarian sources that depicted the stone settings before they were disturbed or destroyed (I. Smith 1965). But the layout presented to visitors today is not as orderly as it seems to be (Gillings 2023). The great stone circle does follow the edge of the ditch and features unusually large monoliths at two of the entrances, but both the rings of uprights inside it are awkwardly located in relation to the plan of this earthwork. Its east and west entrances define an axis dividing the interior in two, but it cuts across the position of the Northern Circle. Similarly, an alignment between the other entrances is interrupted by this circle and its neighbour – the overall layout is asymmetrical. There have even been suggestions that a third ring of monoliths was projected in line with the other two. If so, the scheme was abandoned when only three of the stone sockets had been excavated. Such changes of plan become even more evident in the light of geophysical survey and aerial reconnaissance which have identified the sites of three additional structures (Pollard & Reynolds 2002, 37; Gillings *et al.* 2019). One was possibly an earthwork, while the others were timber circles or rings of pits. Their positions do not seem to be related to the remaining components of the henge, and they may have gone out of use at an early stage.

The order in which they were built has never been established. The Northern and Southern Circles enclosed other features: a sarsen cove, and the stone setting that might have marked the position of an earlier house. There is evidence that the monument changed its form. The earthwork that can be seen today replaced a smaller bank following the same course, but there is nothing to show which phase of the enclosure (if either) was associated with the great stone circle (Gillings & Pollard 2004, fig. 1). That setting of monoliths might even have existed as a freestanding element before the henge was built. It would explain why the standing stones in the south-west quadrant are bigger than those on the north-west side (Pollard & Reynolds 2002, 86); as Chapter Five has shown, this arrangement occurs at sites where they are not associated with an earthwork. If the outer circle was among the earliest elements, the layout of the bank and ditch could have changed the orientation of the enclosure – there are other places where a setting of standing stones was enclosed during a later phase. If the builders had intended a row of three stone circles – a view rejected in recent accounts – the abandoned structure at its northern limit must have been earlier than the earthwork which occupies the same position.

The purpose of this discussion is not to offer a new interpretation of Avebury but to draw attention to the problems of understanding its layout. There is not enough evidence to infer a coherent design, and more to suggest developments which were poorly integrated with one another. The avenues extending from the entrances give the same impression.

The Avebury avenues

Two avenues of paired stones led to (or from) the entrances of the earthwork. Both were related to the positions of other sites. The Beckhampton Avenue cut across an existing monument – an exceptionally late causewayed enclosure or a 'formative henge' – and made use of a wide gap in its circuit (Gillings *et al.* 2008, 7–57). Over a kilometre from Avebury a line of monoliths cut across its path and probably marked an original terminus. It was replaced by a 'cove' which was built on a smaller scale than its counterpart inside the Northern Circle. It is uncertain whether the avenue extended beyond this point, although an early account raises this possibility.

The West Kennet Avenue presents more difficulties. It is not known whether it ran continuously from Avebury to Overton Hill, and there have been suggestions that it was erected in segments or initiated as separate projects (Burl 1979, 188; Gillings *et al.* 2008, 141–2). Antiquarian sources suggest that it may have incorporated another cove (Burl 1979, 138–9), but this has not been confirmed. At its fullest extent it ran past a series of palisaded enclosures before ascending Overton Hill where it entered the Sanctuary.

The Beckhampton Avenue linked the henge at Avebury to a pair of outlying structures. But the layout of its counterpart raises problems. Its character changed where it was connected to other monuments. At Avebury this involved an abrupt change of direction. The same applies to its junction with the Sanctuary which was almost as awkwardly designed. Was this meant to screen the interior from view until people entered the enclosure, as Julian Thomas has suggested (1991, 214–16), or were these features built at different times? The junctions between them were executed so clumsily that they might have had separate origins; if so, they were connected in a later phase. It suggests a process of piecemeal development like the genesis of Avebury itself.

The West Kennet palisaded enclosures (Fig. 9.5)

During the Late Neolithic period a series of enclosures and timber settings was established on the lower ground overlooked by West Kennet long barrow (Whittle 1997). They were not far from the stone avenue leading up Overton Hill. One of the palisades spanned the river, and its neighbour may have done the same. They could have been built in succession, but together they took in a section of the river only 500 m from its modern source. They were supplemented by radial lines of posts which joined these separate elements or extended out from them. Other circular

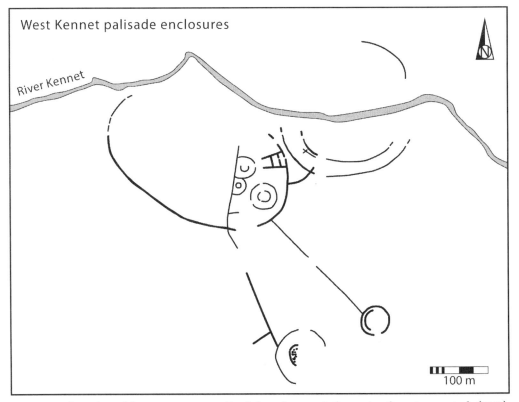

Fig. 9.5. Outline plan of the West Kennet palisaded enclosures. Information from Leary et al. *(2013).*

settings have been identified in the vicinity. Almost all the structures were conceived on an extravagant scale, but they were commonly replaced. They made lavish use of timber posts which were deeply bedded in the subsoil and held in place by enormous blocks of sarsen. The wood does not seem to have been recovered and there is evidence that it decayed *in situ*. The people who erected these monuments must have known that this would happen, and it may be why new ones were built nearby. Perhaps they were created at fixed intervals and some of them were created for particular events and then abandoned.

Enclosures of the same kind can be associated with large henges in Wessex but belong to a wider tradition shared between Britain and Ireland during the earlier 3rd millennium BC (Bradley 2019, 130–2). Those at West Kennet contained collections of animal bones which were probably the remains of feasts. They also featured a style of decorated pottery (Grooved Ware) associated with Late Neolithic monuments elsewhere in southern England. Similar material was placed inside the nearby chambered tomb at West Kennet which remained accessible and largely intact (Piggott 1962, 42–4).

The Sanctuary

The interplay between wood and stone was especially important at the Sanctuary which overlooked this complex from higher ground. Although it was linked to an avenue of paired monoliths, it was not far away from the palisaded enclosures. It is difficult to say how they were related to one another, or why they were built of different materials.

At one time there seemed to be a simple explanation for the contrast. There were important monuments in other places where timber structures were replaced in stone, but that does not account for the use of both wood and sarsen at the Sanctuary (Pollard 1992). The central building consisted of five concentric rings of posts of different proportions, as well as an outer circle of monoliths. The sequence of construction is not clear, but in one of the circuits standing stones were placed in between the wooden uprights with such precision that they must have been erected together – the overall design was a composite of different elements (Fig. 9.6). On its southwestern periphery an additional stone – it is not known whether it was upright or recumbent – provided a kind of threshold facing the direction of the midwinter sunset (the Stonehenge 'Altar Stone' shared the same characteristic; see Parker Pearson *et al.* 2022, 111–12). Whatever the merits of that comparison, the structure at the Sanctuary was at the centre of a large stone circle joined to the West Kennet Avenue. There were a few outlying monoliths that might have belonged to radial extensions to the monument similar to those identified among the enclosures on the valley floor.

Plans of the Sanctuary give the impression of an orderly design, but this could be entirely misleading. The first fieldwork at the site was published by Maud Cunnington in 1932, and it is obvious that the investigators expected to find a regular layout; any anomalies might have gone unnoticed. This was confirmed by a project sixty years later which showed that subsoil features had been overlooked (Pitts 2001). More important, it provided evidence that individual posts were replaced piecemeal; this

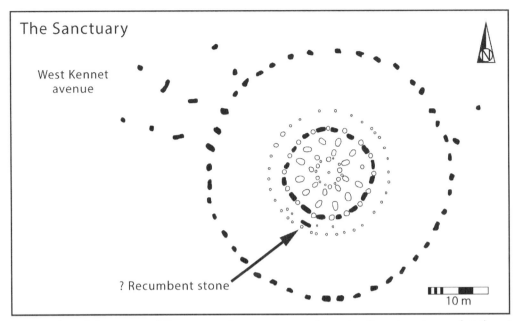

Fig. 9.6. Plan of the excavated features at The Sanctuary. Information from Cunnington (1932) and Pollard (1992).

was a regular occurrence. There were signs of alteration and improvisation that the original work had missed. Again, there was an obvious tension between the overall conception and its realisation on the ground. The same was true on a greater scale at Silbury Hill.

Silbury Hill
In its present form Silbury Hill is the largest prehistoric mound in Europe (Whittle 1997). It changed its character whilst it was being built, beginning as a circular enclosure bounded by a bank and ditch. At first there was a small central earthwork bounded by a circle of stakes, but it grew to enormous proportions over thirteen episodes of construction (Leary *et al.* 2013). There is little to suggest the execution of a single design. Despite all the changes of plan, the monument took a surprisingly short time to build. It was associated with few prehistoric artefacts, but its creation seems to have taken place between about 2500 and 2400 BC. The mound did not cover any burials – the first investigations of Silbury Hill were based on the false premise that this was an enormous Bronze Age round barrow. Its position overlooked the source of the River Kennet. More important, it was bounded by a ditch which still holds water today, and this feature was enlarged on one side to create an enormous pool. Anyone standing on the mound could have seen into the palisaded enclosures.

Like the other components of the Late Neolithic complex, its subsequent history is obscure.

From late prehistory to the early medieval period

The Roman phase

After the building of Silbury Hill, Early Bronze Age barrow cemeteries developed on the surrounding hills (Cleal 2005). Some people were buried in graves beside existing standing stones at the sites mentioned earlier. The henge at Avebury eventually went out of use, and fieldwork at West Kennet suggests that this place also lost its significance. It played little role until the Iron Age and Roman periods.

Then the earliest development may have been the construction of a wooden shrine at the foot of Silbury Hill. It has not been excavated but is documented by geophysical survey. Its plan resembles that of well-known structures on Iron Age sites (Leary *et al.* 2013, 260–1). It was located beside the confluence of two tributaries of the Kennet.

Activity resumed on a more impressive scale during the Roman phase (Fig. 9.7). The site was located at a river crossing on the way between Bath and Mildenhall – in fact the road was aligned on the mound. Between the 1st and 4th centuries AD (or even later) an extensive settlement developed around Silbury Hill. Part of it assumed a regular layout and may have been organised on a grid (Leary *et al.* 2013, fig. 9.7). Early excavations, combined with more recent surveys, identified the positions of masonry buildings and several wells. The nature of this activity remains in doubt. Its position on a major route encouraged the idea that this was a stopping point for travellers, a *mansio*, but the sheer size of the settlement revealed by remote sensing makes it more likely that it was a small unwalled town. The features encountered during early fieldwork have been difficult to explain, but Mark Corney (2001) has identified at least one of the stone buildings as the site of a temple. The mound, on the other hand, shows no sign of reuse. Few artefacts were found during excavation on its summit, but a significant collection of coins came from the top of the quarry ditch (Leary *et al.* 2013, 265–9). Otherwise, it seems as if the monument was respected but left unchanged.

Advocates of a practical interpretation of the site overlook its most obvious feature. The Roman settlement was built in a damp, inhospitable environment on two sides of the largest artificial mound in Europe. It also incorporated the spring at the head of one of the main watercourses in England. These features cannot be ignored in an attempt to find a tidy solution. It is likely that the source of the Kennet remained important during the Roman phase when the river gave its name to the nearby town of *Cunetio* (Rivet & C. Smith 1979). The significance of underground water may have been acknowledged by the presence of wells close to the base of the earthwork, and one account of the site considers the 'engaging possibility' that they originally surrounded the hill (Pollard & Reynolds 2002, 178). Nineteenth century excavations showed that they contained blocks of dressed stone, a stone column, metalwork, and coins. Were these deliberate deposits? The coins found in the ditch could have been placed in a pool when the valley flooded, as it does today. It was common for Roman sanctuaries to develop in such locations. In Gaul, the most famous example is at the source of the Seine (Detys 1994), and in south-east England a well-documented

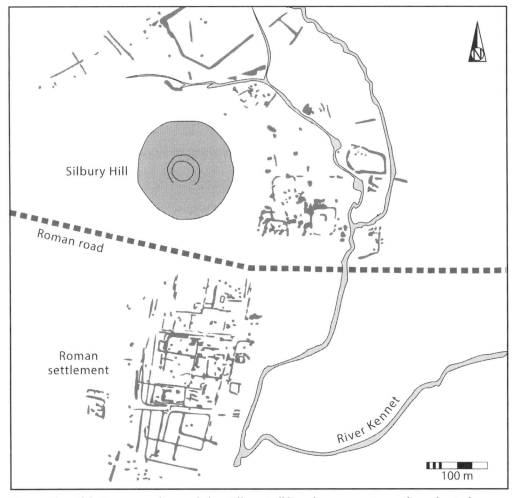

Fig. 9.7. Plan of the Roman settlement below Silbury Hill based on excavation and geophysical survey. Information from Leary et al. *(2013).*

parallel is the aptly named Springhead (Andrews 2011). For a second time Silbury Hill became a sacred place.

The early medieval phase
More confusion surrounds the early medieval use of Silbury (Fig. 9.8). The most dramatic discovery was the first to be made, and for that reason it is particularly difficult to discuss. Writing in 1743, William Stukeley recorded that:

> Workmen dug up the body of the great king there buried in the centre, very little below the surface ... Some weeks after I came luckily to rescue a great curiosity which they took up there: an iron chain ... It was a bridle (quoted by Leary *et al.* 2013, 6).

Fig. 9.8. Silbury Hill. Photograph: Aaron Watson.

He continued to document the find in later life and there seems no reason to doubt his account of the discovery. Although this artefact has been lost, his drawing of the bridle shows that it dated from the 11th century AD (Graham-Campbell 1992).

There have been other discoveries of early medieval weapons on Silbury Hill, although few are so precisely dated; there were four arrowheads, a spur, and a spearhead, as well as a stirrup mount found in the River Kennet (Leary *et al.* 2013, 289–91). They may have been associated with the final modification of the mound, for its upper levels were rebuilt during this period. The most recent excavation identified post holes cut into the top of the earthwork, one of which was associated with a radiocarbon date of 890–1030 AD (Leary *et al.* 2013, 284–7). It is difficult to interpret this evidence, but it seems more than a coincidence that Silbury Hill was used for the last time during a well-documented period of conflict between Viking raiders and the local population. The mound may have become a military stronghold (Pollard & Reynolds 2002, 26–7; Gillings & Pollard 2004, 110–12). At all events its history ended three and a half thousand years after it had been built.

That overlooks the unusual burial claimed by Stukeley. It has been described as a Viking grave, but the most recent account rejects that interpretation and argues that the bridle was simply one of the military artefacts associated with the defence of the hilltop. If, as Stukeley believed, this artefact was associated with human bones, the burial would be out of context so long after the Christian conversion in England. But it does make sense in a pagan setting, for inhumation burials with similar associations are common in Denmark, Sweden, and Norway. Anne Pedersen observes that 'equestrian burials' of this kind were often in reused barrows (2006 & 2014). This interpretation could shed new light on the final phase of activity at Silbury Hill. Perhaps the burial really was that of a Viking whose body was placed there according to a rite observed in Scandinavia. One of its features was the choice of an ancient mound. If the dead person was a Viking, commemorated according to the traditions of his own people, the placing of that grave evoked a past which the inhabitants of Wessex did not share.

Monumental times

Despite the impressive appearance of many monuments, some of their histories were remarkably unstable. The point was made in the poems quoted in Chapter One. The archaeology of Avebury and the Upper Kennet Valley provides an illustration. The final section summarises the outcome of this analysis.

It is best to abandon the distinction between nature and culture. Ancient structures frequently drew on processes and materials whose origins and character were a wonder to ancient people, who would have explained them in different terms from modern science. Such features were given particular emphasis and incorporated into new designs as if they stood for a mythical past. Newly built monuments might incorporate geological features, stones with unusual properties, watercourses, and springs. Views of the sky encouraged a 'circular' perspective on the world, and this was reflected in the plans of local constructions (Bradley 2012). At the same time there was a special emphasis on what lay underneath the earth. Avebury provides an excellent illustration of both principles, for the henge was constructed in a position where viewers would see the crest of the earthwork merging with a distant horizon (Watson 2001). The cove inside the Northern Circle faced the sun, and the enclosure ditch was exceptionally deep. If one feature played a more important part than any other, it might have been the River Kennet with its source below Silbury Hill. Fluctuations in the water table epitomised the cyclical processes evident in this landscape.

The choice of building materials is central to any account of the monuments. The Avebury complex illustrates a striking interplay between the deployment of timber and stone. It also saw the building of earthworks. Each would have lasted for a different length of time, and the people who built these structures must have known what would happen. It accounted for the use of stone in tombs, and a preference for timber in domestic contexts; that may explain the sequence within the Southern Circle. It was not only a question of survival or decay. Some buildings must have been designed for short periods of use, but others were meant to last a long time. There is a striking contrast between the extended lifespan of a mound like Silbury Hill and the replacement of short-lived features like the nearby palisades. But the best evidence of episodic activity comes from the Sanctuary on Overton Hill where excavation has shown that individual posts were replaced on a piecemeal basis. In fact, that complex sheds the clearest light on the properties of different materials. The sarsens employed in the avenue would last into a distant future – and so might Silbury Hill. But the timber enclosures had a very different character. They were left to decay and were replaced by similar structures in the vicinity. It is possible that some of them were built and used on one special occasion and abandoned straightaway. This raises a more general observation. The construction of some monuments ended activities in a particular place, but others provided only the starting point for entirely new developments. The West Kennet long barrow illustrates both models. Other Neolithic mounds at Avebury illustrate each of these options.

Such examples raise a further issue. To what extent did local monuments conform to the ideal types described in modern textbooks? Was there more fluidity, and did the people who built them necessarily have an ideal outcome in mind? They might have decided to pursue new options during the work, resulting in abrupt changes of plan. That could account for the awkward combination of different elements in the overall layout of Avebury, and the same approach describes the sequence of construction at Silbury. It is epitomised even more obviously by open-ended projects like the changing character of the enclosure on Windmill Hill. There were gradual variations as their meanings changed over the course of time.

Such changes resemble the gradual modifications that characterise the formation of oral literature, and the relationships between different structures on the ground might have resembled a kind of narrative. This has already been observed in the Avebury complex where Joshua Pollard and Andrew Reynolds comment that:

> Movement along the course of the avenues ... influenced what people could see in the landscape, and thus served as a mnemonic device, leading [them] to recall the presence and connections between places and natural features ... We see the avenues as creating *'narrative experiences'* by which myths and histories relating to particular places could be retold ... through the orchestrated movement of participants during ceremonies (2002, 105; my emphasis).

The same would apply to many other features. The case is not restricted to those connected with processions.

The relationships expressed by such narratives could have taken many forms. Although they might refer to other features in the vicinity, they could also draw on distant sources of inspiration. For instance, the form of Silbury Hill might have referred to the passage graves of the Boyne Valley which may still have remained in use (Carlin 2017). Similarly, the putative Viking grave on the summit of that mound could have cited current practice in Scandinavia. New developments might also refer to the visible remains of a much more ancient past, even though its actual significance was lost. On an extended time scale this would explain the relationship between the Silbury mound and the Roman complex that developed around its base. On a shorter scale, the same applies to the Beaker burials that cluster around the Neolithic monuments at Avebury, and especially those associated with older standing stones (Cleal 2005). The new evidence of stable isotopes and ancient DNA shows that a radical transformation was taking place.

Time which antiquates antiquities

It was difficult to decide how to end this book. I tried various possibilities, and then one morning I woke up with a half-remembered phrase in my mind. Eventually I tracked it down. It came from a passage in Sir Thomas Browne's *Urn Burial* which I decided to use as the epigraph.

He was one of the first authors to write about monuments and must have been the most eloquent. For Browne, they were memorials to the dead, and the burials he described were hidden underground. But in another passage, he discussed conspicuous forms of architecture. Whatever their builders intended, such structures did not provide lasting reminders of the past, nor were they able to impose themselves on the future: 'Pyramids, arches, obelisks were but the irregularities of vain-glory and wild enormities of ancient magnanimity'.

Archaeologists define monuments in a broader sense. These buildings can shed light on ancient conceptions of time, but they do so with one important difference. The first chapter stressed the significance of multi-temporality, and it is a theme that that has run throughout this book. That is why it is called *Monumental Times* (in the plural). Much confusion can be caused as treating every example in the same way. Some buildings were directed towards a future just as others commemorated a past, but they were employed for very different durations, from periods lasting for centuries down to one event. They could be reshaped and reimagined, either as a continuous process, or discontinuously and at wide intervals. Their functions and forms were unstable, and numerous variants coexisted. Their construction and deployment served many roles. People in the past may not have wanted to build ideal forms of monuments, nor need they have shared consistent systems of belief. All these elements changed as a result of human agency. It would be wrong to look for models that work in every case. Instead, this account has traced particular *themes*. And there could be others.

Time is the archaeologist's medium, but investigating past temporalities is challenging and has obvious limits. Despite the current emphasis on memory, much has been forgotten and too little has survived. As Thomas Browne observed: 'The iniquity of oblivion ... deals with the memory of man without distinction to merit of perpetuity. Who can but pity the founder of the Pyramids?'

Bibliography

Allen, M. and Gardiner, J. 2002. A sense of time: Cultural markers in the Mesolithic of southern England? In B. David and M. Wilson (eds), *Inscribed Landscapes: Making and marking place*, 139–53. Honolulu, HI, University of Hawai'i Press.

Andersen, N. 1997. *The Sarup Enclosures*, vol. 1. Aarhus, Jutland Archaeological Society.

Andersen, S.H. 1991. Bjørnsholm: A stratified *køkkenmødding* on the Central Limfjord, north Jutland. *Journal of Danish Archaeology* 10, 59–96.

Andersen, S.H. 2004. Danish shell middens reviewed. In A. Saville (ed.), *Mesolithic Scotland and its Neighbours*, 293–411. Edinburgh, Society of Antiquaries of Scotland.

Andersen, S.H. and Johansen, E. 1990. An early Neolithic grave at Bjørnsholm, north Jutland. *Journal of Danish Archaeology* 9, 38–58.

Andersen, S.W. 2007. Lejre: Ship settings, Viking graves, Grydehøj. In Niles and Osborn 2007, 144–50.

Andrén, A. 2013. Places, monuments and objects: The past in ancient Scandinavia. *Scandinavian Studies* 85, 267–81.

Andrews, P. 2011. Springhead religious complex. In P. Andrews, E. Biddulph, A. Hardy and R. Brown, *Settling the Ebbsfleet Valley*, 13–134. Oxford and Salisbury, Oxford Wessex Archaeology.

Aranda Jiménez, G., Diaz-Zorita Bonilla, M., Hamilton, D., Miles, L. and Sánchez Romero, M. 2020. The radiocarbon chronology and temporality of the megalithic cemetery of Los Millares (Almería, Spain). *Archaeological and Anthropological Sciences* 12, 104–21.

Armit, I. and Reich, D. 2021. The return of the Beaker Folk? Rethinking migration and population change in British prehistory. *Antiquity* 95, 1464–77.

Arrhenius, B. 1970. Tür der Toten. Sach- und Wortzeugnisse zu einer frühmittelalterlichen Gräbersitte in Schweden. *Frühmittelalterliche Studien* 4, 384–94.

Ashbee, P., Smith, I. and Evans, J. 1979. Excavations of three long barrows near Avebury. *Proceedings of the Prehistoric Society* 45, 207–300.

Ashmore, P. 2016. *Calanais: Survey and excavation 1979-88*. Edinburgh, Historic Scotland.

Astrup, P.M. 2018. *Sea Level Change in Mesolithic Southern Sweden*. Moesgaard, Jutland Archaeological Society.

Atkinson, R. 1956. *Stonehenge*. Harmondsworth, Penguin.

Bailey, G., Galanidou, N., Peeters, H., Jöns, H. and Mennenga, M. (eds). 2020. *The Archaeology of Europe's Drowned Landscapes*. Cham, Springer.

Bakker, J.A. 1992. *The Dutch Hunebedden: Megalithic tombs from the Funnel Beaker Culture*. Ann Arbor, MI, International Monographs in Prehistory.

Banfield, E. 2016. Sticky notes: Some thoughts on the use of clay in the Neolithic deposits within the Avebury megalithic complex. *Norwegian Archaeological Review* 49, 99–112.

Barclay, A., Field, D. and Leary, J. (eds). 2020. *Houses of the Dead?* Oxford, Oxbow Books.

Barclay, A. and Halpin, C. 1999. *Excavations at Barrow Hills, Radley, Oxfordshire. Oxford, Volume. 1*. Oxford, Oxford Archaeological Unit.

Barclay, G. and Maxwell, G. 1998. *The Cleaven Dyke and Littleour*. Edinburgh, Society of Antiquaries of Scotland.

Barrett, J. and Boyd, M. 2019. *From Stonehenge to Mycenae*. London, Bloomsbury.

Barrett, J., Bradley, R. and Green, M. 1991. *Landscape, Monuments and Society: The prehistory of Cranborne Chase*. Cambridge, Cambridge University Press.

Bayliss, A. 2015. Quality in Bayesian chronological models in archaeology. *World Archaeology* 47, 677–700.

Bayliss, A., Marshall, P., Richards, C. and Whittle, A. 2017. Islands of history: The Late Neolithic timescape of Orkney. *Antiquity* 91, 1171–89.

Bayliss, A. and Whittle, A. (eds). 2007. Histories of the dead: Building chronologies for five southern British long barrows. *Cambridge Archaeological Journal* 17 supplement.

Bernhardt, G. 1986. Die linearbandkeramischer Siedlung von Köln-Lindenthal. *Kölner Jahrbuch* 19, 7–165.

Bhreathnach, E. 1993. The topography of Tara: The documentary evidence. *Discovery Programme Reports* 2, 68–76.

Bhreathnach, E. 1999. Authority and supremacy in Tara and its hinterland. *Discovery Programme Reports* 5, 1–23.

Bintliff, J. (ed.) 1991. *The Annales School and Archaeology.* Leicester, Leicester University Press.

Bird-David, N. 1999. Animism revisited: Personhood, environment and relational epistemology. *Current Anthropology* 40, 567–91.

Blair, J. 2018. *Building Anglo-Saxon England.* Princeton, NJ, Princeton University Press.

Blanco-González, A. and Kienlin, T. (eds). 2020. *Current Approaches to Tells in the Prehistoric Old World.* Oxford, Oxbow Books.

Blank, M., Sjögren, K-J. and Storå, J. 2020. Old bones or early graves? Megalithic burial sequences in southern Sweden based on 14C datings. *Archaeological and Anthropological Science* 89, 12–89.

Boivin, N. and Owoc, M.A. (eds). 2004. *Soils, Stones and Symbols: Cultural perceptions of the mineral world.* London, UCL Press.

Booth, T., Brück, J., Brace, S. and Barnes, I. 2021. Tales from the supplementary information: Ancestry change in Chalcolithic – Early Bronze Age Britain was gradual with varied kinship organisation. *Cambridge Archaeological Journal* 31, 379–400.

Bourgeois, Q. 2013. *Monuments on the Horizon: The formation of the barrow landscape throughout the 3rd and 2nd millennium BC.* Leiden, Sidestone.

Brace, S. and Booth, T. 2023. The genetics of the inhabitants of Neolithic Britain: A review. In Whittle *et al.* 2023, 123–46.

Brace, S., Diekmann, Y., Booth, T., Falyskova, Z., *et al.* 2019. Ancient genomes indicate population replacement in early Neolithic Britain. *Nature: Ecology and Evolution* 3, 765–71.

Bradley, R. 1987. Time regained: The creation of continuity. *Journal of the British Archaeological Association* 140, 1–17.

Bradley, R. 1989. Darkness and light in the design of megalithic tombs. *Oxford Journal of Archaeology* 8, 351–9.

Bradley, R. 1992. The excavation of an oval barrow beside the Abingdon causewayed enclosure, Oxfordshire. *Proceedings of the Prehistoric Society* 58, 127–42.

Bradley, R. 1993. *Altering the Earth: The origins of monuments in Britain and continental Europe.* Edinburgh, Society of Antiquaries of Scotland.

Bradley, R. 1998. *The Significance of Monuments.* London, Routledge.

Bradley, R. 2000a. *The Good Stones: A new investigation of the Clava Cairns.* Edinburgh, Society of Antiquaries of Scotland.

Bradley, R. 2000b. *An Archaeology of Natural Places.* London, Routledge.

Bradley, R. 2002. *The Past in Prehistoric Societies.* London, Routledge.

Bradley, R. 2005. *The Moon and the Bonfire: An investigation of three stone circles in north-east Scotland.* Edinburgh, Society of Antiquaries of Scotland.

Bradley, R. 2011. *Stages and Screens: An investigation of four henge monuments in northern and north-eastern Scotland.* Edinburgh, Society of Antiquaries of Scotland.

Bradley, R. 2012. *The Idea of Order: The circular archetype in prehistoric Europe.* Oxford, Oxford University Press.

Bradley, R. 2016a. Croftmoraig stone circle: A reinterpretation in the light of fresh excavation. In Bradley and Nimura 2016, 56–73.

Bradley, R. 2016b. Croftmoraig: The anatomy of a stone circle. In Bradley and Nimura 2016, 141–51.

Bradley, R. 2016c. After the Great Stone Circles. In Bradley and Nimura 2016, 112–21.

Bradley, R. 2019. *The Prehistory of Britain and Ireland*. 2nd edition. Cambridge, Cambridge University Press.

Bradley, R. 2020a. Time signatures: The temporality of monuments in Early and Middle Neolithic Britain. *Proceedings of the Prehistoric Society* 86, 1–11.

Bradley, R. 2020b. Keeping order in the Stone Age. In D. Hofmann (ed.), *Magical, Mundane or Marginal? Deposition practices in the Early Neolithic Linearbandkeramik culture*, 227–37. Leiden, Sidestone.

Bradley, R. 2021. *Temporary Palaces: The great house in European prehistory*. Oxford, Oxbow Books.

Bradley, R. 2022. Beyond comparison: The diversity of megalithic architecture. In L. Laporte and J-M. Large (eds), *Megaliths of the World*, 633–45. Oxford, Archaeopress.

Bradley, R. and Clarke, A. 2016. Excavations at Hillhead, Tarland: A recumbent stone circle and its history. In Bradley and Nimura 2016, 7–26.

Bradley, R. and Nimura, C. (eds). 2016. *The Use and Reuse of Stone Circles*. Oxford, Oxbow Books.

Brami, M., Winkelbach, L., Schulz, I., Schreiber, M., *et al.* 2022. Was the fishing village of Lepenski Vir built by Europe's first farmers? *Journal of World Prehistory* 35, 109–33.

Brandt, G., Haak, W., Adler, C.J., Roth, C., *et al.* 2013. Ancient DNA reveals key stages in the formation of central European mitochondrial genetic diversity. *Science* 342, 257–61.

Braudel, F. 1969. *Écrits sur l'histoire*. Paris, Flammarion.

Brindley, A. and Lanting, J. 1992. Radiocarbon dates from wedge tombs. *Journal of Irish Archaeology* 6, 19–26.

Britnell, W. and Whittle, A. 2022. *The First Stones*. Oxford, Oxbow Books.

Brophy, K. 2016. *Reading between the Lines: The Neolithic cursus monuments of Scotland*. London, Routledge.

Brophy, K. and Millican, K. 2015. Wood and fire: Scotland's timber cursus monuments. *Archaeological Journal* 175, 297–324.

Brophy, K. and Noble, G. 2020. *Prehistoric Forteviot: Excavations of a ceremonial centre in Eastern Scotland*. York, Council for British Archaeology.

Brophy, K. and Wright, D. 2021. Possible Neolithic ard marks and field boundaries at Welhill and Cranberry, Perth and Kinross. *Proceedings of the Society of Antiquaries of Scotland* 150, 233–47.

Brothwell, D. 1971. Forensic aspects of the so-called Neolithic skeleton Q1 from Maiden Castle, Dorset. *World Archaeology* 3, 233–41.

Brown, F. 2021. Stainton West: A Late Mesolithic and Early Neolithic site on the banks of the River Eden. In G. Hey and P. Frodsham (eds), *New Light on the Neolithic of Northern England*, 17–30. Oxford, Oxbow Books.

Brown, J. and Price, T.D. (eds). 1985. *Prehistoric Hunter Gatherers: The emergence of cultural complexity*. London, Academic Press.

Bunting, J., Farrell, M., Dunbar, E., Reimer, P., *et al.* 2022. Landscapes for Neolithic people in mainland, Orkney. *Journal of World Prehistory* 35, 87–107.

Burl, A. 1979. *Prehistoric Avebury*. New Haven, CT, Yale University Press.

Burl, A. 1993. *From Carnac to Callanish*. New Haven, CT, Yale University Press.

Burl, A. 2000. *The Stone Circles of Britain, Ireland and Brittany*. New Haven, CT, Yale University Press.

Burrow, S. 2010. The formative henge: Speculations drawn from the circular tradition of Wales and adjacent countries. In J. Leary, T. Darvill and D. Field (eds), *Round Mounds and Monumentality in the British Neolithic and Beyond,* 182–96. Oxford, Oxbow Books.

Byrne, F., Jenkins, G. and Swift, C. 2008. *Historic Knowth and its Hinterland*. Dublin, Royal Irish Academy.

Campbell, E. and Driscoll, S. 2020. *Royal Forteviot: Excavations at a Pictish power centre in eastern Scotland*. York, Council for British Archaeology.

Carlin, N. 2017. Getting into the groove: Exploring the relationship between Grooved Ware and developed passage tombs in Ireland c. 3000–2700 cal BC. *Proceedings of the Prehistoric Society* 83, 155–88.

Carlin, N. 2018. *The Beaker Phenomenon? Understanding the Character and Context of Social Practices in Ireland 2500-2000 BC*. Leiden, Sidestone.

Carson, R. and O'Kelly, C. 1977. A catalogue of the Roman coins from Newgrange, Co. Meath, and notes on the coins and related finds. *Proceedings of the Royal Irish Academy* 77C, 35–55.

Carsten, J. and Hugh-Jones, S. 1995. Introduction. In J. Carsten and S. Hugh-Jones (eds), *About the House: Levi-Strauss and Beyond*, 1–46. Cambridge, Cambridge University Press.

Carver, M. 2005. *Sutton Hoo: A seventh-century princely burial ground and its context*. London, British Museum Press.

Carver, M. 2019. *Formative Britain: An archaeology of Britain, fifth to eleventh century AD*. London, Routledge.

Cassen, S. 2009. *Exercise de stèle*. Paris, Errance.

Cassen, S., Audren, C., Hinguant, G., Lannuzel, G. and Marchand, G. 1998. L'habitat Villeneuve-Saint-Germain du Haut-Mée. *Bulletin de la Société préhistorique franaise* 95, 41–76.

Cassidy, L., Mariano, R., Murphy, E., Teasdale, M., Mallory, J. and Hartwell, B. 2016. Neolithic and Bronze Age migration to Ireland and establishment of the insular genome. *Proceedings of the National Academy of Sciences* 113, 368–73.

Catherall, P. 1971. Henges in perspective. *Archaeological Journal* 128, 147–53.

Chambon, P. 2020. 'Ciréron c'est Poincaré'. Dealing with geometry, Neolithic house plans and the earliest monuments. In A. Barclay *et al.* 2020, 47–58.

Chambon, P. and Thomas, A. 2010. The first monumental cemeteries of western Europe: The 'Passy' type necropolis in the Paris Basin around 4500 BC. In M. Furholt (ed.), *Megaliths and Identities*, 249–59. Bonn, Habelt.

Champion, T. 1982. The myth of Iron Age invasions in Ireland. In B. Scott (ed.), *Studies in Early Ireland*, 39–44. Belfast, Association of Young Irish Archaeologists.

Chapman, J. 1999. Burning the ancestors: Deliberate house burning in Balkan prehistory. In A. Gustafsson and H. Karlsson (eds), *Glifer och arkeologiska rum*, 113–26. Gothenburg, Institute of Archaeology.

Chapman, J. and Gaydarska, B. 2006. Does enclosure make a difference? A view from the Balkans. In A. Harding, S. Sievers and N. Venclová (eds), *Enclosing the Past*, 20–43. Sheffield, J.R. Collis Publications.

Childe, V.G. 1949. The origin of Neolithic culture in Northern Europe. *Antiquity* 23, 129–35.

Christensen, T. 2015. *Lejre bag Myten*. Moesgård, Jysk Arkaeologisk Selskab.

Clark, J.D.G. 1954. *Excavations at Star Carr*. Cambridge, Cambridge University Press.

Clark, J.D.G. and Rankine, W. 1939. Excavations at Farnham, Surrey. *Proceedings of the Prehistoric Society* 5, 61–118.

Cleal, R. 2005. 'Within the small compass of a grave'. Early Bronze Age burials in and around Avebury and the Marlborough Downs. In G. Brown, D. Field and D. McOmish (eds), *The Avebury Landscape*, 115–32. Oxford, Oxbow Books.

Cleal, R., Walker, K., and Montague, R. 1995. *Stonehenge in its Landscape: Twentieth century excavations*. London, English Heritage.

Conneller, C. 2004. Becoming deer: Corporeal transformation at Star Carr. *Archaeological Dialogues* 11, 37–56.

Conneller, C. 2022. *The Mesolithic in Britain*. London, Routledge.

Cooney, G. 2006. Newgrange – a view from the platform. *Antiquity* 80, 697–710.

Cooper, A., Garrow, D., Gibson, C., Giles, M. and Wilkin, N. 2022. *Grave Goods: Objects and death in later prehistoric Britain*. Oxford, Oxbow Books.

Corney, M. 2001. The Romano-British nucleated settlements in Wiltshire. In P. Ellis (ed.), *Roman Wiltshire and After*, 5–38. Devizes, Wiltshire Archaeological Society.

Coudart, A. 1998. *Architecture et société néolithique: l'unité et la variance de la maison danubienne*. Paris, Maison des sciences de l'homme.

Craig, O., Shilito, L.M., Albarella, U., Viner-Daniels, S., *et al.* 2015. Feeding Stonehenge: Cuisine and consumption at the Late Neolithic site of Durrington Walls. *Antiquity* 89, 1096–1109.

Cramp, L., Jones, J., Sheridan, A., Smyth, J., *et al.* 2014. Immediate replacement of fishing with dairying by the first farmers of the northeast Atlantic archipelago. *Proceedings of the Royal Society B* 281.

Cramp, R. 1957. Beowulf and archaeology. *Medieval Archaeology* 1, 57–77.

Crellin, R., Cipolla, C., Montgomery, L., Harris, O., and Moore, S. 2020. *Archaeological Theory in Dialogue*. London, Routledge.

Cunnington, M. 1932. The Sanctuary on Overton Hill, near Avebury. *Wiltshire Archaeological Magazine* 45, 300–35.

Darvill, T. 1996. Neolithic buildings in England, Wales and the Isle of Man. In T. Darvill and J. Thomas (eds), *Neolithic Houses in Northwest Europe and Beyond*, 77–111. Oxford, Oxbow Books.

Darvill, T., Marshall, P., Parker Pearson, M. and Wainwright, G. 2012. Stonehenge remodelled. *Antiquity* 86, 1021–40.

Davies, E. 1929. *The Prehistoric and Roman Remains of Denbighshire*. Cardiff, William Lewis.

Davis, S. and Rassmann K. 2021. Beyond Newgrange: Brú na Bóinne in the later Neolithic. *Proceedings of the Prehistoric Society* 87, 189–218.

Detys, S. 1994. *Un people pélerins. Offrandes de pierre et de bronze des Sources de la Seine*. Dijon, Revue Archéologique de l'Est et du Centre-Est, supplément 30.

Dickinson, O. 2017. The will to believe: Why Homer cannot be 'true' in any meaningful sense. In Sherratt and Bennet 2017a, 10–19.

Dietrich, L. 2021. *Plant Food Processing Tools at Early Neolithic Göbekli Tepe*. Oxford, Archaeopress.

Dingwall, K., Ginnever, M., Tipping, R., Van Wessel, J. and Wilson, D. 2019. *'The Land was Forever': 15,000 years in north-east Scotland*. Oxford, Oxbow Books.

Downes, J. 2020. A cosmological interpretation of the Neolithic burial monuments in Orkney. In Doyle 2020, 36–53.

Doyle, P. (ed.) 2020. *Pathways to the Cosmos*. Dublin, Wordwell.

Drisse, M. 2017. Polissoirs: Social memory in the Avebury landscape. In R. Shaffrey (ed.), *Written in Stone*, 275–302. St Andrews, Highfield Press.

Edmonds, M. 2019. *Orcadia. Land, Sea and Stone in Neolithic Orkney*. London, Head of Zeus.

Edmonds, M., Evans, C. and Gibson, D. 1999. Assembly and collection: Lithic complexes in the Cambridgeshire Fenland. *Proceedings of the Prehistoric Society* 65, 47–82.

Eogan, G. 1984. *Excavations at Knowth, Volume 1*. Dublin, Royal Irish Academy.

Eogan, G. 1986. *Knowth and the Passage Tombs of Ireland*. London, Thames and Hudson.

Eogan, G. 2009. Dowth passage tomb: Notes on possible structural sequence. *Riocht na Midhe* 20, 1–4.

Eogan, G. 2012. *The Archaeology of Knowth in the First and Second Millennia AD*. Dublin, Royal Irish Academy.

Eogan, G. and Cleary, K. 2017. *The Passage Tomb Archaeology of the Great Mound at Knowth*. Dublin, Royal Irish Academy.

Eogan, G. and Roche, H. 1997. *Excavations at Knowth, Volume 2*. Dublin, Royal Irish Academy.

Eogan, G. and Shee Twohig, E. 2022. *The Megalithic Art of the Passage Tombs at Knowth, County Meath*. Dublin, Royal Irish Academy.

Eriksen, M.H. 2013. Doors to the dead: The power of doorways and thresholds in Viking Age Scandinavia. *Archaeological Dialogues* 20, 187–214.

Eriksen, P. and Andersen, N. 2016. Dolmens without mounds in Denmark. In L. Laporte and C. Scarre (eds), *The Megalithic Architectures of Europe*, 79–87. Oxford, Oxbow Books.

Evans, C., Edmonds, M. and Boreham, S. 2006. 'Total archaeology' and model landscapes: Excavation of the Great Wilbraham causewayed enclosure, Cambridgeshire, 1975–6. *Proceedings of the Prehistoric Society* 72, 113–62.

Evans, C. and Hodder, I. 2005. *A Woodland Archaeology: The Haddenham Project, Volume 1*. Cambridge, McDonald Institute for Archaeological Research.

Evans, C., Pollard, J. and Knight, M. 1999. Life in woods: Tree-throws, 'settlement' and forest cognition. *Oxford Journal of Archaeology* 18, 241–54.

Fahy, E. 1960. A recumbent stone circle at Drombeg, Co. Cork. *Journal of the Cork Historical and Archaeological Society* 64, 1–27.

Favrél, Q. and Nicolas, C. 2022. Bell Beaker burial customs in north-western France. *Proceedings of the Prehistoric Society* 88, 285–320.

FitzPatrick, E. 2004. *Royal Inauguration in Gaelic Ireland c. 1100–1600*. Woodbridge, Boydell Press.

Fowler, C. 2021. Ontology in Neolithic Britain and Ireland: Beyond animism. *Religions* 12(4), 249.

Friss-Holm Egfjord, A., Margaryan, A., Fischer, A., *et al.* 2021. Genomic steppe ancestry in skeletons from the Single Grave Culture in Denmark. *PloS One* 16(1): e0244872.

Fyfe, R., Twiddle, C., Sugita, S., Gaillard, M-J., *et al.* 2013. The Holocene vegetation cover of Britain and Ireland: Overcoming problems of scale and discovering patterns of openness. *Quaternary Science Reviews* 73, 132–48.

Gandois, H., Burlot, A., Mille, B. and Le Carlier de Veslud, C. 2019. Early Bronze Age axe-ingots from Brittany: Evidence for connections with south-west Ireland. *Proceedings of the Royal Irish Academy* 119C, 1–36.

García Sanjuán, L. and Lonzano Rodríguez, J. 2016. Menga (Antequera, Málaga, Spain): Biography of an exceptional megalithic monument. In C. Scarre and L. Laporte (eds), *The Megalithic Architectures of Europe*, 3–16. Oxford, Oxbow Books.

Garrow, D., Meadows, J., Evans, C. and Tabor, J. 2014. Dating the dead: A high-resolution radiocarbon chronology of burial within an Early Bronze Age barrow cemetery at Over, Cambridgeshire. *Proceedings of the Prehistoric Society* 80, 207–36.

Garwood, P. 2007. Before the hills in order stood: Chronology, time and history in the interpretation of early Bronze Age round barrows. In J. Last (ed.), *Beyond the Grave - New Perspectives on Barrows*, 30–52. Oxford, Oxbow Books.

Ghesquière, E., Chambon, P., Giazzon, D., Hachem, L., *et al.* 2019. Monumental cemeteries of the 5th millennium BC: The Fleury-sur-Orne contribution. In J. Müller, M. Hinz and M. Wunderlich (eds), *Megaliths, Societies, Landscapes*, 177–90. Bonn, Habelt.

Gibbons, M. and Gibbons, M. 2016. The Brú: A Hiberno-Roman cult site at Newgrange? *Emania* 23, 67–78.

Gibson, A. 2010. Excavation and survey at Dyffryn Lane henge complex, Powys, and a reconsideration of the dating of henges. *Proceedings of the Prehistoric Society* 76, 213–48.

Gibson, A. (ed.) 2019. *Bell Beaker Settlement of Europe*. Oxford, The Prehistoric Society.

Gibson, C. 2016. Closed for business or cultural changes? Tracing the reuse and final blocking of megalithic tombs during the Beaker period. In J. Koch and B.Cunliffe (eds), *Celtic from the West 3*, 83–110. Oxford, Oxbow Books.

Gillings, M. 2023. Alterity, otherness and nomad geometries: New trajectories for the interpretation of Late Neolithic monuments. *Cambridge Archaeological Journal* 33(2) 325–48.

Gillings, M. and Pollard, J. 2004. *Avebury*. London, Duckworth.

Gillings, M. and Pollard, J. 2016. Making megaliths: Shifting and unstable stones in the Neolithic of the Avebury landscape. *Cambridge Archaeological Journal* 26, 537–59.

Gillings, M., Pollard, J. and Strutt, K. 2019. The origins of Avebury. *Antiquity* 44, 480–99.

Gillings, M., Pollard, J., Wheatley, D. and Peterson, R. 2008. *Landscape of the Megaliths: Excavation and fieldwork on the Avebury monuments, 1997-2003*. Oxford, Oxbow Books.

Gleeson, P. 2018. Gathering communities: Locality, governance and rulership in early medieval Ireland. *World Archaeology* 50, 100–20.

Gleeson, P. 2020. Archaeology and myth: Making the gods in early medieval Europe. *Medieval Archaeology* 64, 65–93

González Garcia, A. and Costa Ferrer, L. 2006. Orientation of megalithic monuments in Germany and the Netherlands. *Mediterranean Archaeology and Archaeometry* 6, 201–8.

Goldhahn, J. 2013. *Bredarör på Kivik: en arkeologisk odysée*. Kalmar, Kalmar Studies in Archaeology.

Goody, J. 1977. *The Domestication of the Savage Mind*. Cambridge, Cambridge University Press.

Gosden, C. 1994. *Social Being and Time*. Oxford, Blackwell.

Gosden, C. and Lock, G. 1998. Prehistoric histories. *World Archaeology* 30, 2–12.

Gouletquer, P., Kayser, O., Le Goffic, M., Léopold, G., *et al.* 1996. Ou sont passés mésolithiques côtiers bretons? *Revue Archéologique de l'Ouest* 13, 5–30.

Graeber, D. and Wengrow, D. 2021. *The Dawn of Everything: A new history of humanity*. London, Allen Lane.

Graham-Campbell, J. 1992. Anglo-Scandinavian equestrian equipment in eleventh century England. *Anglo-Norman Studies* 14, 77–89.

Gräslund, A-S. 2001. Living with the dead: Reflections on food offerings in graves. In H. Beck, D. Geuenich and H. Steuer (eds), *Kontinuitäten und Brüche in Religionsgeschichte*, 22–35. Berlin, de Gruyter.

Gräslund, B. 1987. *The Birth of Prehistoric Chronology*. Cambridge, Cambridge University Press.

Greaney, S., Hazell, Z., Barclay, A., Bronk Ramsay, C., *et al.* 2020. Tempo of a mega-henge: A new chronology for Mount Pleasant, Dorchester, Dorset. *Proceedings of the Prehistoric Society* 86, 199–236.

Gretzinger, J., Sayer, D., Justeau, P., Altena, E., *et al.* 2022. The Anglo-Saxon migration and the foundations of the early English gene pool. *Nature* 610, 112–19.

Gron, K. and Sørensen, L. 2018. Cultural and economic negotiation: A new perspective on the Neolithic transition of southern Scandinavia. *Antiquity* 92, 958–74.

Grünberg, J.M., Gramsch, B., Laporte, L., Orscheidt, J. and Meller, H. (eds). 2016. *Mesolithic Burials: Rites, symbols and social organisation of early postglacial communities*. Halle, Landesmuseums für Vorgeschichte.

Haak, W., Lazaridis, I., Patterson, N., Rohland, N., *et al.* 2015. Massive migration from the steppe was a source for Indo-European languages in Europe. *Nature* 522, 207–11.

Harding, J. 2003. *Henge Monuments of the British Isles*. Stroud, Tempus.

Hargrave, M., Berle Clay, R., Dalton, R. and Greenlee, D. 2021. The complex construction history of Poverty Point's timber circles and concentric ridges. *Southeastern Archaeology* 40, 192–211.

Harmananşa, Ö. (ed.) 2014. *Of Rocks and Water: Towards an archaeology of place*. Oxford, Oxbow Books.

Harris, O. 2021. *Assembling Past Worlds*. London, Routledge.

Harris, O. and Cipolla, C. 2017. *Archaeological Theory in the New Millennium*. London, Routledge.

Haubold, J. 2017. Dream and reality in the work of Heinrich Schliemann and Manfred Korfmann. In Sherratt and Bennet 2017a, 20–34.

Haughton, C. and Powelsland, D. 1999. *West Heslerton: The Anglian cemetery*. Yedingham, Landscape Research Centre.

Hayden, B. 2014. *The Power of Feasts: From prehistory to the present*. Cambridge, Cambridge University Press.

Henige, D. 1974. *The Chronology of Oral Tradition: Quest for a Chimera*. Oxford, Clarendon Press.

Hensey, R. 2015. *First Light: The origins of Newgrange*. Oxford, Oxbow Books.

Hensey, R. and Shee Twohig, E. 2017. Facing the cairn at Newgrange, Co. Meath. *Journal of Irish Archaeology* 26, 57–76.

Herbaud, F. and Quarré, G. 2004. La parure néolithique en variscite dans le sud de l'Armorique. *Bulletin de la Société Préhistorique Française* 101, 497–520.

Herva, V.-O. and Lahelma, A. 2020. *Northern Archaeology and Cosmology: A relational view*. London, Routledge.

Higginbottom, G. 2020. The world begins here: Bronze Age megalithic monuments in western Scotland. *Journal of World Prehistory* 33, 25–134.

Higgs, E. (ed.). 1972. *Papers in Economic Prehistory*. Cambridge, Cambridge University Press.

Higgs, E. (ed.). 1975. *Palaeoeconomy*. Cambridge, Cambridge University Press.

Hodder, I. 1989. This is not an article about material culture as text. *Journal of Anthropological Archaeology* 8, 250–69.

Hodder, I. 2012. History-making in prehistory: Examples from Çatalhöyük and the Middle East. In A.M. Jones, J. Pollard, M. Allen and J. Gardiner (eds), *Image, Memory and Monumentality*, 184–93. Oxford, The Prehistoric Society.

Hofmann, D. 2013. Narrating the house: The transformation of longhouses in early Neolithic Europe. In A. Chadwick and C. Gibson (eds), *Memory, Myth and Long-term Inhabitation*, 32–54. Oxford, Oxbow Books.

Holst, M.K., Jessen, M., Andersen, S. and Pedersen, A. 2000. The late Viking-Age royal construction at Jelling, central Jutland, Denmark. *Praehistorische Zeitschrift* 87, 474–504.

Hope-Taylor, B. 1977. *Yeavering: An Anglo-British centre of early Northumbria*. London, HMSO.

Hoskin, M. 2001. *Tombs, Temples and their Orientations: A new perspective on Mediterranean prehistory*. Bognor Regis, Ocinara Books.

Ingold, T. 1980. *Hunters, Pastoralists and Ranchers*. Cambridge, Cambridge University Press.

Jackson, K. 1964. *The Oldest Irish Tradition: A window on the Iron Age*. Cambridge, Cambridge University Press.

Jeunesse, C. 2021. Societies without ancestors? Why are so few graves found in the European Upper Palaeolithic and Mesolithic? *Archäologisches Korrespondenzblatt* 51, 309–27.

Jones, A.M. 2007. *Memory and Material Culture*. Cambridge, Cambridge University Press.

Jones, A.M., Freedman, D., O'Connor, B. and Lamdin-Whymark, H. 2011. *An Animate Landscape: Rock art and the prehistory of Kilmartin, Argyll, Scotland*. Oxford, Oxbow Books.

Jordan, P. (ed.) 2011. *Landscape and Culture in North Eurasia*. Walnut Creek, CA, Left Coast Press.

Joseph, F., Julien, M., Leroy-Langelin, E., Lorin, Y. and Praud, I. 2011. L'architecture domestique des sites du IIIe millénaire avant notre ère dans le nord de la France. *Révue Archéologique de Picardie numéro special* 28, 249–73.

Joussaume, R. 2012. *L'enceinte Néolithique de Champ-Durand à Nieul-sur-L'Autise (Vendée)*. Chauvigny, Association des publications Chauvignoises.

Kaliff, A. and Oestergaard, T. 2018. *Bronze Age Håga and the Viking King Björn*. Uppsala, Uppsala University.

Kaul, F. 1998. *Ships on Bronzes: A study in Bronze Age religion and iconography*. Copenhagen, National Museum.

Kaul, F. 2017. Bronze Age archaeology and cosmology: Dialogues at the crossroads. *Acta Archaeologica* 88, 35–56.

Kenney, J. 2021. *A Welsh Landscape Through Time*. Oxford, Oxbow Books.

Kinnes, I. 1982. Les Fouillages and megalithic origins. *Antiquity* 56, 24–30.

Kinnes, I. 1992. *Non-megalithic Long Barrows and Allied Structures in the British Isles*. London, British Museum.

Kolb, M. 2005. The genesis of monuments among the Mediterranean islands. In E. Blake and A.B. Knapp (eds), *The Archaeology of Mediterranean Prehistory*, 156–78. Oxford, Blackwell.

Kolb, M. 2021. *Making Sense of Monuments*. London, Routledge.

Kunst, M. 2017. Zambujal 2013: Ein kuperzeitliche befistigte Gross-Siedlung? *Madrider Mitteilungen* 58, 1–30.

Lamdin-Whymark, H. 2008. *The Residue of Ritualised Action: Neolithic depositional practices in the middle Thames Valley*. Oxford, British Archaeological Reports British Series 466.

Lapidge, M. 2000. The archetype of Beowulf. *Anglo-Saxon England* 29, 5–41.

Laporte, L., Bizien-Jacklin, C., Wattez, J., Barreau, J-B., *et al.* 2015. Another brick in the wall: Fifth millennium BC earthen-walled architecture on the Channel shores. *Antiquity* 89, 800–17.

Laporte, L. and Bueno Ramírez, P. 2022. On Atlantic shores. The origins of megaliths in Europe? In Laporte and Large 2022, 1173–92.

Laporte, L. and Large, J-M. (eds). 2022. *Megaliths of the World*. Oxford, Archaeopress.

Laporte, L. and Tinévez, J.Y. 2004. Neolithic houses and chambered tombs of Western France. *Cambridge Archaeological Journal* 14, 217–34.

Large, J.M. and Mens, E. 2008. L'alignment du Douet à Hoëdic (Morbihan, France). *L'anthropologie* 112, 544–71.

Larsson, L. 1993. Relationer till ett röse – några aspekter på Kiviksgraven. In L. Larsson (ed.), *Bronsålderens Gravhöger*, 135–50. Lund, University of Lund Institute of Archaeology.

Last, J. 1998. Books of Life: Biography and memory in a Bronze Age barrow. *Oxford Journal of Archaeology* 17, 43–53.

Layton, R. 1986. Political and territorial structures among hunter gatherers. *Man* 21, 18–33.

Leary, J., Canti, M., Field, D., Fowler, P., *et al.* 2013. The Marlborough Mound, Wiltshire. A further Neolithic monumental mound by the River Kennet. *Proceedings of the Prehistoric Society* 79, 137–63.

Leary, J., Field, D. and Campbell, G. (eds). 2013. *Silbury Hill*. Swindon, English Heritage.

Leivers, M. 2021. The Army Basing Programme: Stonehenge and the emergence of the sacred landscape of Wessex. *Internet Archaeology* 56.

Lemercier, O. and Strahm, C. 2018. Nids de couscous et grandes maisons: l'habitat campaniforme et épicampaniforme en France dans son context Européen. In O. Lemercier, I. Sénépart, M. Besse and

C. Mordant (eds), *Habitations et l'habitat du néolithique à l'âge du bronze en France et ses marges*, 459–78. Toulouse, Archives d'écologie préhistorique.

L'Helgouach, J. 1965. *Les sépultures mégalithiques en Armorique*. Rennes, Travaux du Laboratoire d'Anthropologie Préhistorique de la Faculté des Sciences.

Lilios, K. 2020. *The Archaeology of the Iberian Peninsula: From the Palaeolithic to the Bronze Age*. Cambridge, Cambridge University Press.

Lord, A. 1960. *The Singer of Tales*. Cambridge, MA, Harvard University Press.

Loveday, R. 2006. *Inscribed across the Landscape: The cursus enigma*. Stroud, Tempus.

Lovis, W. and Whallon, R. (eds). 2016. *Marking the Land: Hunter gatherer creation of meaning in their environment*. London, Routledge.

Lucas, G. 2001. *Critical Approaches to Fieldwork: Contemporary and historical practice*. London, Routledge.

Lucas, G. 2021. *Making Time: The archaeology of time revisited*. London, Routledge.

Lucas, G. and Olivier, L. 2022. *Conversations about Time*. London, Routledge.

Lund, J. and Arwill-Nordbladh, E. 2016. Divergent ways of relating to the past in the Viking Age. *European Journal of Archaeology* 19, 415–38.

Lynch, A., McCormick, F., Shee Twohig, E., McClatchie, M., *et al.* 2014. Newgrange revisited: New insights from excavations at the back of the mound in 1984-8. *Journal of Irish Archaeology* 23, 13–82.

Lynch, F. 1986. Excavation of a kerb circle and ring cairn at Cefn Caer Euni, Merioneth. *Archaeologia Cambrensis* 135, 81–120.

MacKie, E. 1974. Archaeological tests on supposed prehistoric astronomical sites in Scotland. *Philosophical Transactions of the Royal Society* A 276, 169–94.

MacKie, E. 1977. *Science and Society in Prehistoric Britain*. London, Elek.

MacKie, E. 2022. *Professor Challenger and the Lost Neolithic World*. Oxford, Archaeopress.

Madsen, T. 1979. Earthen long barrows and timber structures: Aspects of early Neolithic mortuary practices in Denmark. *Proceedings of the Prehistoric Society* 45, 156–78.

Madgwick, R., Lamb, A., Sloane, H., Nederbragt, A., *et al.* 2019. Multi-isotope analysis reveals that feasts in the Stonehenge environs and across Wessex drew people and animals throughout Britain. *Science Advances* 5(3).

Mallet, N., Ihuel, F. and Verjux, C. 2012. Le diffusion des silex du Grand-Pressigny au néolithique. *Révue archéologique du Cenre de la France* Supplément 38, 131–47.

Mallory, J. 2016. *In Search of the Irish Dreamtime: Archaeology and early Irish literature*. London, Thames and Hudson.

Marshall, E. and Murphy, K. 1991. The excavation of two cairns with associated standing stones in Dyfed. *Archaeologia Cambrensis* 140, 28–76.

Masset, C. and Soulier, P. 1995. *Allées couvertes et autres monuments funéraires dans la France du Nord-Ouest: allées sans retour*. Paris, Errance.

McBride, A. 2020. *The Role of Anglo-Saxon Great Hall Complexes in Kingdom Formation, in Comparison and in Context AD 500-750*. Oxford, Archaeopress.

McClatchie, M., Bogaard, A., Colledge, S., Whitehouse, N., *et al.* 2016. Farming and foraging in Neolithic Ireland: An archaeobotanical perspective. *Antiquity* 90, 302–18.

McFadyen, L. 2007. Neolithic architecture and participation: Practices of making in early Neolithic Britain. In J. Last (ed.), *Beyond the Grave*, 22–9. Oxford, Oxbow Books.

McHugh, R. and Scott, B. 2014. The prehistoric archaeology of County Fermanagh. In C. Foley and R. McHugh (eds), *An Archaeological Survey of County Fermanagh*, 55–164. Belfast, Northern Ireland Environment and Heritage Service.

McSperron, C. 2020. *Burials and Society in Late Chalcolithic and Early Bronze Age Ireland*. Oxford, Archaeopress.

Meillassoux, C. 1972. From reproduction to production. *Economy and Society* 1, 93–105.

Mens, E. 2008. Refitting megaliths in western France. *Antiquity* 82, 25–36.

Mercer, R. and Healy, F. 2008. *Hambledon Hill, Dorset: Excavation and survey of a Neolithic monument complex and its surrounding landscape.* Swindon, English Heritage.

Meyer, C., Kürbis, O., Dresely, V. and Alt, K. 2018. Patterns of collective violence in the Early Neolithic of Central Europe. In A. Dolfini, R. Crellin and M. Uckelmann (eds), *Prehistoric Warfare and Violence,* 21–38. Cham, Springer.

Midgley, M. 2005. *The Monumental Cemeteries of Prehistoric Europe.* Stroud, Tempus.

Midgley, M. 2008. *The Megaliths of Northern Europe.* London, Routledge.

Millican, K. 2016. *The Timber Monuments of Neolithic Scotland.* Oxford, British Archaeological Reports British Series 623.

Milner, N., Conneller, C. and Taylor, B. 2018. *Star Carr 1: A persistent place in a changing world.* York, White Rose University Press.

Minter, F. and Scull, C. 2022. Revealing royal Rendlesham. *Current Archaeology* 393, 14–15.

Mischka, D. 2011. The Neolithic burial sequence at Flintbek LA 3, North Germany, and the cart tracks: A precise chronology. *Antiquity* 85, 742–58.

Mitchell, F. 1992. Notes on some non-local cobbles at the entrances to the passage graves at Newgrange and Knowth, County Meath. *Journal of the Royal Society of Antiquaries of Ireland* 122, 128–45.

Mitchell, J. and Noble, G. 2017. The monumental cemeteries of Northern Pictland. *Medieval Archaeology* 61, 1–40.

Mithen, S. 2022. How long was the Mesolithic-Neolithic overlap in western Scotland? Evidence from the 4th millennium BC on the Isle of Islay and the evaluation of three scenarios for Mesolithic-Neolithic interaction. *Proceedings of the Prehistoric Society* 88, 53–77.

Mithen, S. and Wicks, K. 2018. The interpretation of Mesolithic structures in Britain. *Proceedings of the Prehistoric Society* 84, 77–110.

Mizoguchi, K. 1993. Time in the reproduction of mortuary practices. *World Archaeology* 25, 223–35.

Mizoguchi, K. 2013. *The Archaeology of Japan.* Cambridge, Cambridge University Press.

Morris, I. 1986. The use and abuse of Homer. *Classical Antiquity* 5, 81–138.

Müller, J. 2011. *Megaliths and Funnel Beaker Societies in Change 4100–2700 BC.* Amsterdam, Kroon-Voordecht 13.

Müller, J. 2017. *Grossteingräber, Grabenwerke, Langhügel.* Darmstadt, Theiss.

Murray, H., Murray, C. and Fraser, S. 2009. *A Tale of Unknown Unknowns: A Mesolithic pit alignment and a Neolithic timber hall at Warren Field, Crathes, Aberdeenshire.* Oxford, Oxbow Books.

Nash, D., Ciborowski, J., Ullyott, S., Parker Pearson, M., *et al.* 2020. Origins of the sarsen megaliths at Stonehenge. *Science Advances* 6.

Nicolas, C., Favrel, Q., Rousseau, L., Ard, V., Blanchet, S., *et al.* 2019. The introduction of the Bell Beaker Culture in Atlantic France: An overview of settlements. In A. Gibson 2019, 329–52.

Niles, J. and Osborn, M. (eds). 2007. *Beowulf and Lejre.* Tempe, AZ, Medieval and Renaissance Texts and Studies 223.

Noble, G. 2006. *Neolithic Scotland: Timber, stone, earth and fire.* Edinburgh, Edinburgh University Press.

Noble, G. 2017. *Woodland in the Neolithic of Northern Europe: The forest as ancestor.* Cambridge, Cambridge University Press.

O'Brien, W. 1999. *Sacred Ground: Megalithic tombs in coastal south-west Ireland.* Galway, National University of Ireland.

O'Brien, W. 2002. Megaliths in a mythologised landscape: South-west Ireland in the Iron Age. In C. Scarre (ed.), *Monuments and Landscape in Atlantic Europe,* 152–76. London, Routledge.

O'Brien, W. 2012. *Iverni: A prehistory of Cork.* Cork, Collins Press.

O'Kelly, M. 1982. *Newgrange: Archaeology, art and legend.* London, Thames and Hudson.

O'Kelly, M., Cleary, R. and Lehane, D. 1983. *Newgrange, Co. Meath: The Late Neolithic/ Beaker Period Settlement.* Oxford: British Archaeological Reports International Series 190.

O'Kelly, M. and O'Kelly, C. 1982. The tumulus of Dowth, Co. Meath. *Proceedings of the Royal Irish Academy* 83C, 135–90.

Olalde, I., Brace, S., Morten, E., Allentoft, M.E., *et al.* 2018. The Beaker phenomenon and the genomic transformation of northwest Europe. *Nature* 555, 190–6.

Ó Néill, J. 2013. Being prehistoric in the Iron Age. In M. O' Sullivan, C. Scarre and M. Doyle (eds), *Tara from the Past to the Future*, 249–55. Dublin, Wordwell.

O'Nualláin, S. 1972. A Neolithic house at Ballyglass near Ballycastle, Co. Mayo. *Journal of the Royal Society of Antiquaries of Ireland* 102, 49–57.

O'Nualláin, S. 1998. Excavation of the small court cairn and associated hut sites at Ballyglass, near Ballycastle, Co. Mayo. *Proceedings of the Royal Irish Academy* 98C, 125–75.

O'Sullivan, M. 2005. *Duma na nGiall, Tara: The Mound of the Hostages.* Bray, Wordwell.

Olivier, L. 2011. *The Dark Abyss of Time.* Lanham, Alta Mira Press.

Outram, A. and Bogaard, A. 2019. *Subsistence and Society in Prehistory: New directions in economic archaeology.* Cambridge, Cambridge University Press.

Overing, G. and Osborn, M. 1994. *Landscapes of Desire: Partial stories of the medieval Scandinavian world.* Minneapolis, MN, University of Minnesota Press.

Parker Pearson, M., Bevins, R., Ixer, R., Pollard, J., *et al.* 2015. Craig Rhos-y-felin: A Welsh bluestone quarry for Stonehenge. *Antiquity* 89, 1131–52.

Parker Pearson, M., Chamberlain, A., Jay, M., Richards, M., *et al.* 2016. Beaker people in Britain: Migration, mobility and diet. *Antiquity* 90, 620–37.

Parker Pearson, M., Pollard, J., Richards, C., Thomas, J., Tilley, C. and Welham, K. 2020. *Stonehenge for the Ancestors. Part 1: Landscape and monuments.* Leiden, Sidestone.

Parker Pearson, M., Pollard J., Richards, C., Thomas, J., Tilley, C. and Welham, K. 2022. *Stonehenge for the Ancestors. Part 2: Synthesis.* Leiden, Sidestone.

Parker Pearson, M., Pollard J., Richards, C., Thomas, J., Tilley, C. and Welham, K. 2023. *Durrington Walls and Woodhenge: A place for the living.* Leiden, Sidestone.

Parker Pearson, M., Sheridan, A., Jay, M., Chamberlain, A., Richards, M. and Evans, J. (eds). 2019. *The Beaker People: Isotopes, mobility and diet in prehistoric Britain.* Oxford, The Prehistoric Society.

Parry, M. 1971. *The Making of Homeric Verse: The collected papers of Milman Parry.* Oxford, Clarendon Press.

Peach, W.A. 1961. *Stonehenge: A new theory.* Cardiff, privately published.

Pedersen, A. 2006. Ancient mounds for new graves – an aspect of Viking-age burial customs in southern Scandinavia. In A. Andrén, K. Jennbert and C. Raudvere (eds), *Old Norse Religion in Long-term Perspective*, 346–53. Lund, Nordic Academic Press.

Pedersen, A. 2014. *Dead Warriors in Living Memory: A study of weapon and equestrian burials in Viking-age Denmark, AD 800–1000.* Copenhagen, National Museum.

Peltenberg, E. 1972. Excavation of Culcharron cairn, Benderloch. *Proceedings of the Society of Antiquaries of Scotland* 104, 63–70.

Petersen, F. 1972. Traditions of multiple burial in Later Neolithic and Early Bronze Age England. *Archaeological Journal* 129, 22–55.

Pétrequin, P., Cassen, S., Errera, M., Klassen, L., Sheridan, A. and Pétrequin, A-M. (eds). 2012. *Jade: Grandes haches alpines du Néolithique européen.* Besançon, Presses Universitaires de Franche-Comté.

Petrie, G. 1839. On the history and antiquities of Tara Hill. *Transactions of the Royal Irish Academy* 18, 25–232.

Piggott, S. 1962. *The West Kennet Long Barrow Excavations 1955-56.* London, HMSO.

Pitts, M. 2001. Excavating the Sanctuary: New investigations on Overton Hill, Avebury. *Wiltshire Archaeological Magazine* 94, 1–23.

Pitts, M., Bayliss, A., McKinley, J., Boylston, A., *et al.* 2002. An Anglo-Saxon decapitation and burial at Stonehenge. *Wiltshire Archaeological and Natural History Magazine* 95, 131–46.

Pollard, J. 1992. The Sanctuary, Overton Hill: A re-examination. *Proceedings of the Prehistoric Society* 58, 213–36.

Pollard, J. and Reynolds, A. 2002. *Avebury: The biography of a landscape.* Stroud, Tempus.

Pollard, J. and Ruggles, C. 2001. Shifting perspectives: Cosmology and patterns of deposition at Stonehenge. *Cambridge Archaeological Journal* 11, 69–90.

Prendergast, F. 2020. Skyscape, culture and the Irish passage grave tradition. In Doyle 2020, 72–89. Dublin, Wordwell.

Prendergast, F., O'Sullivan, M., Williams, K. and Cooney, G. 2017. Facing the sun. *Archaeology Ireland* 31(4), 10–17.

Pryor, F. 1998. *Etton*. London, English Heritage.

Pyzel, J. 2020. Houses of the living, houses of the dead: A view from the Polish lowlands. In A. Barclay *et al.* 2020, 39–46.

Racky, P. and Anders, A. 2008. Late Neolithic spatial differentiation at Polgá-Csöszhalom, eastern Hungary. In D. Bailey, A. Whittle and D. Hofmann (eds), *Living Well Together?*, 35–53. Oxford, Oxbow Books.

Randsborg, K. 1993. Kivik: Archaeology and ideology. *Acta Archaeologica* 64, 1–147.

Randsborg, K. and Merkyte, I. 2011. Bronze Age Universitas: Kivig / Kivik revisited. *Acta Archaeologica* 82, 163–80.

Rassmann, C. 2011. Identities overseas? The long barrows in Britain and Denmark. In M. Furholt, F. Lüth and J. Müller (eds), *Megaliths and Identities*, 167–76. Bonn, Habelt.

RCAHMS. 1974. *Argyll, vol. 2*. Edinburgh, HMSO.

RCAHMS. 1980. *Argyll, vol. 5*. Edinburgh, HMSO.

Reich, D. 2018. *Who We Are and How We Got Here: Ancient DNA and the new science of the human past*. Oxford, Oxford University Press.

Renfrew, C. 1968. Wessex without Mycenae. *Annual of the British School at Athens* 63, 277–85.

Renfrew, C. 1973. Monuments, mobilisation and social organisation in Neolithic Wessex. In C. Renfrew (ed.), *The Explanation of Culture Change*, 539–58. London, Duckworth.

Reynolds, A. 2009. *Anglo-Saxon Deviant Burials*. Oxford, Oxford University Press.

Richards, C. 2013. *Building the Great Stone Circles of the North*. Oxford, Windgather.

Richards, C. and Jones, R. 2016. *The Development of Neolithic House Societies in Orkney*. Oxford, Windgather.

Risch, R., Friederich, S., Küssner, M. and Meller, H. 2022. Architecture and settlement dynamics in Central Europe from the Late Neolithic to the Early Bronze Age. *Proceedings of the Prehistoric Society* 88, 123–54.

Rivet, A.L.F. and Smith, C. 1979. *The Place-names of Roman Britain*. London, Batsford.

Robb, J. 2009. People of stone: Personhood and society in prehistoric Europe. *Journal of Archaeological Method and Theory* 16, 162–83.

Robb, J. 2023. On ontological impurity: Conceptualising time in archaeology. In C. Nimura, R. O'Sullivan and R. Bradley (eds), *Sentient Archaeologies*, 183–9. Oxford, Oxbow Books.

Robin, G. 2009. *L'architecture des signes*. Rennes, Presses Universitaires de Rennes.

Rodwell, W. 2007. *Wells Cathedral: Excavations and structural studies, 1978–93*. London, English Heritage.

Ross, A., Ulm, S. and Tobane, B. 2013. Gumminggurru: A community archaeology journey. *Australian Archaeology* 76, 62–8.

Ruggles, C. 1984. *Megalithic Astronomy: A new archaeological and statistical study of 300 western Scottish sites*. Oxford, British Archaeological Reports British Series 123.

Ruggles, C. 1999. *Astronomy in Prehistoric Britain and Ireland*. New Haven, CT, Yale University Press.

Salanova, L. 2016. Behind the warriors: Bell Beakers and identities in Atlantic Europe. In J. Koch and B. Cunliffe (eds), *Celtic from the West 3*, 13–40. Oxford, Oxbow Books.

Salanova, L. and Tchérémissinoff, Y. (eds). 2011. *Les sépultures individuelles campaniformes en France*. Paris, CNRS Éditions.

Sanmark, A. 2019. *Viking Law and Order: Places and rituals of assembly in the medieval north*. Edinburgh, Edinburgh University Press.

Scarre, C. 2010. Rock of ages: Tempo and time in megalithic monuments. *European Journal of Archaeology* 13, 175–93.

Scarre, C. 2011. *Landscapes of Neolithic Brittany*. Oxford, Oxford University Press.

Scarre, C. 2020. Sunrise orientations and the European megalithic phenomenon. In Doyle 2020, 8–23. Dublin, Wordwell.

Schuldt, E. and Gehl, O. 1972. *Die mecklenburgischen Megalithgräber*. Berlin, Deutscher Verlag der Wissenschaften.

Schulting, R. and Richards, M. 2001. Dating women and becoming farmers: New palaeodietary and AMS dating evidence from the Breton cemeteries of Téviec and Hoëdic. *Journal of Anthropological Archaeology* 20, 314–46.

Schulting, R., Sheridan, A., Clarke, S. and Bronk Ramsay, C. 2008. Largantea and the dating of Irish wedge tombs. *Journal of Irish Archaeology* 17, 1–17.

Schulz Paulsson, B. 2017. *Time and Stone: The emergence and development of megaliths and megalithic societies in Europe*. Oxford, Archaeopress.

Scott, D. 2016. The solar lunar alignments of the Orkney-Cromarty and Clava Cairns. *Journal of Skyscape Archaeology* 2, 45–66.

Scott, D. and McHardy, S. 2020. *The Stones of the Ancestors*. Edinburgh, Luath Press.

Scott, J. 1969. The Clyde Cairns of Scotland. In T.G.E. Powell (ed.), *Megalithic Enquiries*, 175–222. Liverpool, Liverpool University Press.

Scott, J. 1989. The stone circle at Temple Wood, Kilmartin, Argyll. *Glasgow Archaeological Journal* 15, 53–125.

Scull, C. 1991. Post-Roman phase 1 at Yeavering: A reconsideration. *Medieval Archaeology* 35, 50–67.

Scull, C. and Harding, A. 1990. Two early medieval cemeteries at Milfield, Northumberland. *Durham Archaeological Journal* 6, 1–29.

Scull, C., Minter, F., and Plouviez, J. 2016. Social and economic complexity in early medieval England: A central place complex on the East Anglian kingdom at Rendlesham, Sufffolk. *Antiquity* 90, 1594–612.

Scull, C. and Thomas, G. 2020. Early medieval Great Hall complexes in England: Temporality and site biographies. *Anglo-Saxon Studies in Archaeology and History* 22, 50–67.

Semple, S. 2013. *Perceptions of the Prehistoric in Anglo-Saxon England*. Oxford, Oxford University Press.

Sheridan, A. 2010. The Neolithicisation of Britain and Ireland: The 'big picture'. In B. Finlayson and G. Warren (eds), *Landscapes in Transition*, 89–105. Oxford, Oxbow Books.

Sheridan, A. and Whittle, A. 2023. Ancient DNA and modelling the Neolithic-Mesolithic transition in Britain and Ireland. The genetics of the inhabitants of Neolithic Britain: A review. In Whittle *et al.* 2023, 169–81.

Sherratt, S. and Bennet, J. (eds). 2017a. *Archaeology and Homeric Epic*. Oxford, Oxbow Books.

Sherratt, S. and Bennet, J. 2017b. Introduction. In Sherratt and Bennet 2017a, ix-xvi.

Simpson, D. 1967. Excavations at Kintraw, Argyll. *Proceedings of the Society of Antiquaries of Scotland* 99, 54–9.

Sims, L. 2006. The 'solarisation' of the moon: Manipulated knowledge at Stonehenge. *Cambridge Archaeological Journal* 16, 191–207.

Sisam, K. 1954. Anglo-Saxon royal genealogies. *Proceedings of the British Academy* 39, 287–48.

Skoglund, P. 2008. Stone ships: Continuity and change in Scandinavian prehistory. *World Archaeology* 40, 390–406.

Smith, C. and Lynch, F. 1987. *Trefignath and Din Drifol: The excavation of two megalithic tombs in Anglesey*. Cardiff, Cambrian Archaeological Association.

Smith, I. 1965. *Windmill Hill and Avebury*. Oxford, Oxford University Press.

Smyth, J. 2014. *Settlement in the Irish Neolithic: New discoveries at the edge of Europe*. Oxford, Oxbow Books.

Smyth, J. 2020. Houses of the living, houses of the dead: An open and shut case from Ballyglass Co. Mayo. In A. Barclay *et al.* 2020, 145–58.

Söderberg, B. and Knarrström, A. 2015. New light on Ale's Stones. *Lund Archaeological Review* 21, 87–106.

Söderberg, B. and Walleborn, B. 2015. Monumental makeover? Remains of a long dolmen close to the ship-setting Ale's Stones. In L. Larsson, F. Ekingren and B. Söderberg (eds), *Small Things, Wide Horizons: Studies in honour of Birgitte Hårdh*, 281–8. Oxford, Archaeopress.

Sommer, U. 2017. The appropriation or the destruction of memory? Bell-Beaker 're-use' of older sites. In K. Hoffmann, R. Bernbeck & U. Sommer (eds), *Between Memory Sites and Memory Networks*, 33–70. Berlin, Edition Topoi.

Sørensen, L. and Karg, S. 2014. The expansion of agrarian societies towards the north: New evidence for agriculture during the Mesolithic / Neolithic transition in Southern Scandinavia. *Journal of Archaeological Science* 51, 256–62.

Startin, B. 1978. Linear Pottery Culture houses: Reconstruction and manpower. *Proceedings of the Prehistoric Society* 44, 143–59.

Startin, B. and Bradley, R. 1981. Some notes on work organisation and society in prehistoric Wessex. In C. Ruggles and A. Whittle (eds), *Astronomy and Society in Britain during the Period 4000-1500 BC*, 289–96. Oxford: British Archaeological Reports British Series 88.

Steffens, J. 2009. *Die Neolithischen Fundplätze von Rastof, Kreis Plön*. Bonn, Habelt.

Stevens, C. and Fuller, D. 2012. Did Neolithic farming fail? The case for a Bronze Age agricultural revolution in the British Isles. *Antiquity* 86, 707–22.

Stout, G. and Stout, M. 2008. *Newgrange*. Cork, Cork University Press.

Strömberg, M. 2001. Ale's Stones: A monument of recycled boulders? *Lund Archaeological Review* 7, 77–87.

Sweetman, D. 1985. A Late Neolithic / Early Bronze Age pit circle at Newgrange, Co. Meath. *Proceedings of the Royal Irish Academy* 85C, 195–221.

Thäte, E. 2007. *Monuments and Minds: Monument re-use in Scandinavia in the second half of the first millennium AD*. Lund, Acta Archaeologica Lundensia.

Thom, A. 1967. *Megalithic Sites in Britain*. Oxford, Clarendon Press.

Thomas, J. 1988. Neolithic explanations revisited: The Mesolithic–Neolithic transition in Britain and South Scandinavia. *Proceedings of the Prehistoric Society* 54, 59–66.

Thomas, J. 1991. *Understanding the Neolithic*. London, Routledge.

Thomas, J. 2006. On the origin and development of cursus monuments in Britain. *Proceedings of the Prehistoric Society* 72, 229–41.

Tilley, C. 2004. *The Materiality of Stone*. Oxford, Berg.

Tinniswood, A. and Harding, A. 1991. Anglo-Saxon occupation and industrial features in the henge monument at Yeavering, Northumberland. *Durham Archaeological Journal* 7, 93–108.

Ullén, I. and Drenzel, L. 2022. Håga revisited: New analysis from the Bronze Age megabarrow (Uppsala län) in Sweden. *Archäologisches Korrespondenzblatt* 52, 157–80.

Vander Linden, M. 2006. *Le phénomène campaniforme dans l'Europe de 3ème millénaire avant notre ère; synthèse et nouvelles perspectives*. Oxford, Archaeopress.

Van Dyke, R. and Alcock, S. (eds). 2003. *Archaeologies of Memory*. Oxford, Blackwell.

Vestergaard, F. 2007. Monumentale skibssætninger i Danmark og Skåne. *Kuml* 2007, 145–90.

Wace, A.B. 1940. The treasury of Atreus. *Antiquity* 14, 233–49.

Waddell, J. 1990. *The Bronze Age Burials of Ireland*. Galway, Galway University Press.

Waddell, J. 2005. *Foundation Myths: The beginnings of Irish archaeology*. Bray, Wordwell.

Waddell, J. 2018. *Myth and Materiality*. Oxford, Oxbow Books.

Waddington, C. 2007. Rethinking Mesolithic settlement, and a case study from Howick. In C. Waddington and K. Pedersen (eds), *Mesolithic Studies in the North Sea Basin and Beyond*, 101–13. Oxford, Oxbow Books.

Walsh, P. 1995. Structure and deposition in Irish wedge tombs: An open and shut case? In J. Waddell and E. Shee Twohig (eds), *Ireland in the Bronze Age*, 113–27. Dublin, Stationery Office.

Warner, R. 2018. The early medieval feasting-house and its Iron Age origin. *Ulster Journal of Archaeology* 74, 33–47.

Warren, G. 2022. *Hunter Gatherer Ireland: Making connections in an island world*. Oxford, Oxbow Books.

Watson, A. 2001. Composing Avebury. *World Archaeology* 33, 296–314.

Watson, A. and Bradley, R. 2021. A new study of the decorated cists in Kilmartin Glen, Argyll, Scotland. *Proceedings of the Prehistoric Society* 87, 219–30.

Watson, A. and Keating, D. 1999. Architecture and sound: An acoustical analysis of megalithic monuments in Britain. *Antiquity* 73, 325–36.

Wehlin, J. 2022. Baltic stone ships: Monuments of a 'maritory' in Late Bronze Age northern Europe. In D. Hofmann, F. Nikulka and R. Schumann (eds), *The Baltic in the Bronze Age*, 373–86. Leiden, Sidestone.

Welfare, A. 2011. *Great Crowns of Stone: The recumbent stone circles of Scotland*. Edinburgh, Royal Commission on the Ancient and Historical Monuments of Scotland.

Wheeler, R.E.M. 1943. *Maiden Castle, Dorset*. London, Society of Antiquaries.

Whitaker, K. 2019. What if none of the building stones at Stonehenge came from Wiltshire? *Oxford Journal of Archaeology* 38, 148–63.

Whitaker, K. 2020. 'Sarsen stones in Wessex': A Society of Antiquaries project contextualised and renewed. *Antiquaries Journal* 100, 432–56.

Whitaker, K. 2022. 'Connoisseurs of stone' everyday sarsen stone in Britain. *Proceedings of the Prehistoric Society* 88, 97–122.

Whitehouse, N. 2006. The Holocene British and Irish woodland fossil beetle fauna: Implications for forest history, biodiversity and faunal colonisation. *Quaternary Science Reviews* 25, 1755–89.

Whitehouse, N., Schulting, R., McClatchie, M., Barratt, P., *et al.* 2014. Neolithic agriculture on the European western frontier: The boom and bust of early farming in Ireland. *Journal of Archaeological Science* 51, 181–205.

Whittle, A. 1997. *Sacred Mound, Holy Rings: Silbury Hill and the West Kennet palisade enclosures*. Oxford, Oxbow Books.

Whittle, A. 2018. *The Times of their Lives*. Oxford, Oxbow Books.

Whittle, A., Bayliss, A. and Healy 2022. A decade on: Revised timings for causewayed enclosures in southern Britain. In J. Last (ed.), *Marking Place: New perspectives on Early Neolithic enclosures*, 203–22. Oxford, Oxbow Books.

Whittle, A., Healy, F. and Bayliss, A. 2011. *Gathering Time: Dating the Early Neolithic enclosures of southern Britain and Ireland*. Oxford, Oxbow Books.

Whittle, A., Pollard, J., and Greaney, S. (eds). 2023. *Ancient DNA and the European Neolithic*. Oxford, Oxbow Books.

Whittle, A., Pollard, J., and Grigson, C. 1999. *The Harmony of Symbols: The Windmill Hill Causewayed Enclosure, Wiltshire*. Oxford, Oxbow Books.

Wilkin, N. 2016. Pursuing the penumbral: The deposition of Beaker pottery at Neolithic ceremonial monuments in Chalcolithic and Early Bronze Age Scotland. In K. Brophy, G. McGregor and I. Ralston (eds), *The Neolithic of Mainland Scotland*, 261–318. Edinburgh, Edinburgh University Press.

Williams, H. 1997. Ancient landscapes and the dead: The reuse of prehistoric and Roman monuments as early Anglo-Saxon burial sites. *Medieval Archaeology* 41, 1–32.

Williams, H. 1998. Monuments and the past in Anglo-Saxon England. *World Archaeology* 30, 90–108.

Williams, H. 2006. *Death and Memory in Early Medieval Britain*. Cambridge, Cambridge University Press.

Woodbridge, J., Fyfe, R., Roberts, N., Downey, S., *et al.* 2014. The impact of the Neolithic agricultural transition in Britain: A comparison of pollen-based land-cover and archaeological C 14 date-inferred population change. *Journal of Archaeological Science* 51, 2216–24.

Woodward, A. 2000. *British Barrows: A matter of life and death*. Stroud, Tempus.

Woodward, A., Exon, S., Gaffney, V. and Yorston, R. 2001. *Stonehenge Landscapes: Journeys through real and imagined worlds*. Oxford, Archaeopress.

Woodward, A. and Hunter, J. 2015. *Ritual in Early Bronze Age Grave Goods*. Oxford, Oxbow Books.